Desert Island Discs

Roy Plomley was a BBC freelance when, in 1941, he devised the famous radio series *Desert Island Discs*. He was born in Kingston-upon-Thames and educated at King's College School. Although for over two hundred years all the male members of his family had been in various branches of medicine, his ambitions were theatrical and, after a spell as an advertising copywriter, he became an actor. After working in every kind of production from opera to pantomime, he began to specialize in radio, working on the French commercial stations, Radio Normandy and Poste Parisien, and the wartime Radio International. In 1949, he produced the first film to be made in this country especially for television. He still works in the theatre, as a playwright, and has had sixteen plays professionally produced. In 1975, he was made an OBE.

DESERT ISLAND DISCS

Roy Plomley

Fontana/Collins

First published in Great Britain by William Kimber & Co. Ltd 1975
First issued in Fontana 1977
Copyright © Roy Plomley 1975
Revisions and additional material copyright © Roy Plomley 1977

Made and printed in Great Britain by
William Collins Sons & Co. Ltd, Glasgow

To the late Henry Cecil
Kindest of Men

Contents

		Page
	Overture	11
1.	How it Started	13
2.	How it's Done	25
3.	Luxuries and Books and Desert Island Lore	38
4.	Writers	46
5.	Musicians	60
6.	Artists and Designers	74
7.	The Stage	86
8.	Singers	99
9.	Dancers	110
10.	Films	121
11.	Radio and Television	133
12.	Sport	151
13.	Politicians and Leaders	164
14.	Scientists and Divines	177
15.	A Castaway I Didn't Meet – the One Who Didn't Exist – the One Who Wasn't the Right One	189
16.	Answering the Mail	200
	The List	207

List of Illustrations

between pages 64 and 65

The author, cast away on the Thames foreshore. Courtesy of the *Daily Mirror*

With Jean Kent

With 'Sinbad' and producer Frederic Piffard. Courtesy of the BBC

With Dame Gladys Cooper. Courtesy of the BBC

With Beverley Nichols. Courtesy of Syndication International

Harold Pinter. Courtesy of the BBC

Sir Noël Coward. Courtesy of the BBC

between page 160 and 161

With five castaways in a BBC studio. Courtesy of Sport and General

Artur Rubinstein. Courtesy of the BBC

Pietro Annigoni. Courtesy of the BBC

Beverly Sills. Courtesy of the Royal Opera House, Covent Garden

With Dame Margot Fonteyn, the 750th castaway. Courtesy of the BBC

With Eileen Fowler. Courtesy of the BBC

With the Rt Hon. Jeremy Thorpe, MP. Courtesy of the BBC

With John Conteh. Courtesy of the BBC

With Dr Bronowski. Courtesy of the BBC

Overture

One day, perhaps, a grandchild will approach the old man in the chimney corner and ask: 'Grandfather, what work used you to do?' – and I shall turn my rheumy eyes to the upturned little face, and reply: 'I was principally known for asking celebrated people which eight records they would take to a desert island.'

Of course, *Desert Island Discs* takes only a day or two of my working week, and I do many other things as well, but when one has invented a popular radio programme and broadcast it for thirty-five years, it is inevitable that it should become a label attached to one's name.

Assuming that the grandchild goes off, with a puzzled expression, to think things out, and doesn't bother me with any supplementary questions, I shall then fall into a reverie, as old men in chimney corners do, and look back on all the distinguished, witty, brilliant and charming people with whom the programme has brought me into contact. I may also give a passing thought to the very small number whose wit, brilliance and charm, to me, appeared to be illusory – but only a passing thought because, out of over one thousand three hundred and seventy broadcasts, I can think of only three or four which I didn't enjoy.

All those celebrities have been my guests. I have laughed with them, lunched with them, listened to their troubles and their choice of music, calmed them into the relaxed state of mind in which broadcasts are best made (sometimes without achieving that state myself) and then shaken hands and said goodbye. Some of them, from different spheres of life, I have never seen again; some were already acquaintances and colleagues; some, whom I met for the first time in the programme, have become friends.

There are figures which, for various reasons, stand out in my memory, like the tallest peaks in a mountain range, and this book is about them. I apologize to the hundreds who have been left out – there just isn't room for everyone – and I express my grateful thanks to those who have been kind enough to jog my memory, especially Leslie Perowne, Winifred Timmins, Derek Lewis, Monica Chapman, Ronald Cook and Christine Skelton. Messrs. George G. Harrap & Co. Ltd have kindly permitted me to quote from James Agate's *Ego 5*.

I

How it Started

As a freelance broadcaster, I was devising record programmes for the BBC, and each programme meant finding a new idea. What I needed was an idea strong enough to last for six programmes.

I was just going to bed on the night of Monday, November 3rd, 1941, when I had the inspiration. I was living in digs in a Hertfordshire village, my coal fire had gone out, and I was already in my pyjamas: nevertheless, I sat down at my typewriter and wrote to Leslie Perowne, who was in charge of the lighter kinds of record programmes.

Dear Leslie,
Here is another idea for a series. DESERT ISLAND DISCS. If you were wrecked on a desert island, which ten gramophone records would you like to have with you? – providing, of course, that you have a gramophone and needles as well!

I heard nothing for sixteen days, then Leslie replied that he thought it an excellent idea, that he had discussed it with the people at the top, and would I now please give him a list of about a dozen people I would suggest to take part? The list I sent him has an evocative air of the period. It consisted of James Agate, Commander Campbell, Frances Day, Jack Payne, Christopher Stone, Pat Kirkwood, Dr C. E. M. Joad, Vic Oliver, Sandy MacPherson, Anna Neagle, Noël Coward, J. B. Priestley, Roy Rich, Arthur Askey, Robert Montgomery, Fred Gaisberg, Kay Cavendish and Harry Parry. 'Of course,' I added, 'a percentage of these would not play.' In fact, they all played except, for various reasons, J. B. Priestley, Roy Rich, Robert Montgomery and Fred Gaisberg.

Some days later I saw Leslie in his office and we arranged details. The programme was to be in the form of an interview, the ten records would be reduced to eight, to fit more easily into half an hour, and Frederic Piffard was to be the producer. To my delight, the series had been booked not just for six programmes but for eight.

My original idea for the opening and closing of each programme was to use the sounds of surf breaking on a shore and the cries of sea birds, but Leslie was concerned that there might be a lack of definition and insisted that we used music as well. I suggested three pieces: 'By the Sleepy Lagoon', by Eric Coates, 'Summer Afternoon Idyll', by the same composer, and Norman O'Neill's incidental music to James Barrie's play, *Mary Rose*. Freddy Piffard and I played through records of the three of them in his flat one evening, and we agreed that 'By the Sleepy Lagoon' was the obvious choice.

We had planned that my first guest would be Dr Joad, Head of the Department of Philosophy at Birkbeck College, in the University of London, whose contributions to the radio Brains Trust had revealed him as an admirable popularizer of difficult subjects and a tremendous 'character'. However, he was not available at the time we wanted him, so we changed our line of thinking and invited Vic Oliver.

That elegant Viennese comedian, who had fought in the Austrian army in the First World War, was at the peak of his career, and especially popular for his fast-paced broadcasts in *Hi, Gang!* with Bebe Daniels and Ben Lyon. I went to see him at the London Hippodrome, where he was starring in a musical called *Get a Load of This*. He gave me a list of records and his reasons for choosing them, and I went away and wrote a script. In those days, all programmes were scripted and, as the war was on, scripts were submitted for censorship. I thought a little comedy should be included, so I put in a few gags, such as:

Vic: I want you to know that I come from a long line of comedians.
Roy: I know. I've seen them queuing up.

Vic's manners were perfect, and when I gave him the script for his approval, he didn't even wince.

We recorded the programme in a bomb-damaged Maida Vale studio on the morning of January 27th, and it went on the air in the Forces Programme two evenings later at eight o'clock. Vic was a well-organized and efficient man, and the recording was over very quickly. Freddy had forgotten to bring the discs to Maida Vale, and we were both impressed when Vic sat down at a piano and demonstrated expertly the section of a Chopin Prelude which he wished to be played. At that time, he was known only as a comedian, and had not yet revealed his talents as a musician.

Frances Day, with her mop of blonde hair and her generous figure, was the most glamorous girl in wartime London, and I was looking forward to working with her. She invited me to call at the Victoria Palace, where she was playing in a revue called *Black Vanities*. Her dressing-room was a great social centre and, after the show, I squeezed my way into the jammed mass of service and civilian males who were paying court, and hung about until the crowd had cleared.

Eventually, we were left more or less alone to discuss our business, at which time Frankie was in her bra and knickers, in which she looked most delectable and I found it hard to concentrate on broadcasting. She tried to persuade me that she and Dr Joad should share the desert island, and that would have been an encounter to conjure with, but it was no good breaking the rules of the programme right at the start. We fixed the details of a recording, but then her agent and the BBC couldn't agree on a fee and it was cancelled. She appeared in the series eventually, but it was about fifteen years later.

So James Agate was our second castaway. I had read his brilliant, if subjective, drama criticism in *The Sunday Times* since I was a boy, and the first volumes of his autobiography, *Ego*, were on my bedside table. He invited me to lunch with him at the Savage Club, the first time I visited that fraternity of talent. A Manchester man of sturdy build, he looked like a bookmaker or a corn chandler. He had almost total recall, and his monologue – you couldn't call it conversation – was entertaining and outrageous. His manner was aggressive, and some of his mannerisms self-consciously Johnsonian. In fact, he struck me as a Johnson who was a little sad not to have a Boswell.

He asked that a number of records should be sent to his flat so that he could play them at his leisure and, by mistake, a disc of the signature tune, 'By the Sleepy Lagoon', was included in the box. That was new to him, and its soothing strains pleased him very much, so he included the disc as one of his chosen eight.

Shortly before we were to go on the air, there was a complication. He had chosen a record of Yvonne Printemps singing

'Je t'aime', from Oscar Straus's *Les Trois Valses*, and we received unexpected news from the Copyright Department that they had been unsuccessful in getting permission to play it. As the BBC's library of records was kept in the presumed safety of a hut in the garden of a Worcestershire mansion, all we could offer as alternatives were the few discs kept in London for emergency use. I'll let Mr Agate describe the incident in his own words, as he did in *Ego 5*.

At the last minute I am told that somebody somewhere won't release the copyright, even for cash. Will I take Madame Lily Pons to my island, and spend my sojourn there listening to the Waltz song from *Romeo et Juliette*? No, I will not. Will I have somebody else *Connais-tu-le pays*-ing?) No. Finally, with five minutes to go, I get desperate, and seeing the Maggie Teyte album lying about give the Forces Duparc's *Phydile*, the least suitable song in the world. Revise my script but no time to change running order, so that I have to follow this with 'I Hear You Calling Me'!! Now McCormack may very well come after Printemps, but *not* Marshall after Duparc. But by this time I don't care, and chuck it all at 'em – Handel, Rachmaninov, Duparc, Marshall, Johann Strauss, Walton, Eric Coates, and Tchaikovsky, and hear afterwards that the Duparc was the best liked of the lot!

It is surprising that the memory of this ebullient man should have been eclipsed almost completely. Stories of past Brother Savages are often to be heard in the club, but I seldom hear Agate's name mentioned there. I believe his nine volumes of *Ego* ('Will the ninth be choral, dear James?' asked one of his cronies) have real value, and will one day be read, as is the Goncourt *Journal*, as a study of the literary and artistic life of an era.

Third, came Commander Campbell, a talkative retired sea-dog who had made a reputation on the Brains Trust, spinning travel yarns with such opening lines as : When I was in Patagonia . . .' As he was living far out of London, I had no opportunity to meet him before our broadcast, and I wrote the script from notes which he sent me. He was an affable, easy-going man, with a large pink face from which blue eyes twinkled through gold-rimmed spectacles.

As one comes to expect the memory of that first series, broadcast so long ago, is more vivid in my mind than recollections of many more recent programmes. If you have no objection, I'll continue to list them one by one.

To meet Charles B. Cochran, the most gifted theatrical impresario of this century, I visited his Old Bond Street office. All his plays, revues and musical comedies were immaculately presented; his Young Ladies were enchanting, the costumes gorgeous, the settings magnificent, the lighting exciting. He travelled the world in search of ideas and talent. The trouble was that he spent so much on achieving perfection that, no matter how busy the box office became, he seldom made money for his backers: however, it was an honour to lose money in a Cochran production – it was lost in the cause of art.

He presented me with a list of records which was complete nostalgia, recalling his associations with Noël Coward, Chaliapin, Yvonne Printemps (no copyright difficulties this time) and Jeritza. He was not yet seventy, but gave the impression of being older, moving slowly and heavily and leaning on a stick. I was to meet him again, six or seven years later, on a transatlantic liner, still travelling in search of new attractions. Very frail, he stayed in his state-room throughout the voyage, appearing only once, to watch a film which was so bad that he must have regretted the effort it cost him.

My fifth castaway was Pat Kirkwood, then starring at His Majesty's Theatre in a musical called *Lady Behave*, Pat was only just twenty-one – she doesn't look all that much older today – and had been a star for three and a half years, since making a sensational impact on the West End in the unpromising role of Dandini in a Princes Theatre pantomime. It was a meeting I should have enjoyed enormously, but I had tonsillitis and could only croak miserably and feverishly.

The following week, I interviewed her boss, Jack Hylton, the bandleader turned impresario, who was presenting *Lady Behave*. Jack was another nostalgic castaway, and he chose several records by his recently dispersed orchestra. He was greatly excited to hear them again and conducted each one as it was played, subsiding into his chair with a crash as it finished, and then having difficulty in finding the place in his script.

For our next castaway, we found a man with actual desert island experience, Captain A. E. Dingle, who wrote sea stories under the pen-name, 'Sinbad'. Years before, he had set off with a companion to try to locate the wreck of the *Strathmore*, which had gone down off one of the Crozet Islands, in the Indian Ocean, with a very large sum of money in the skipper's strong-box. It was a shoestring expedition, equipped with a second-hand diving-suit and a small sailing sloop, which they navigated by an alarm clock. Driven off their moorings during a storm, they struck hard by night on a desert island called St Paul, their craft being completely destroyed. St Paul is a bleak, volcanic island, with no vegetation except patches of coarse grass; they kept themselves alive during their eleven weeks' ordeal by eating raw penguin and goat meat and drinking warm rainwater. Incredibly, they found treasure there. They came across a broken old hulk half buried in the sand. Thinking it would provide firewood, and metal for making fish hooks, they began digging it out with their hands. Among the wreckage was an iron strong-box containing two thousand Australian gold sovereigns which, when the two castaways were eventually rescued by a barque that came in response to their distress signals, they concealed in goatskins which they tied to their bodies.

Just before we went on the air, as he was leaning forward across the table, I noticed a deep scar running from his wrist towards his elbow.

'That looks a nasty wound,' I remarked.

He pulled up his sleeve, revealing the length of the scar. 'A Chinese cook ran amok,' he said casually. 'He came at me with a knife, but I had one too, and I pinned him to the mast through the throat.' A colourful character, Dingle!

For a change of pace, Freddy Piffard and I decided for one programme to ignore the celebrated, and pay tribute to the lower ranks of the entertainment business. The only London theatre to have stayed open throughout the Blitz was the Windmill, which then ran a non-stop revue dedicated to the bare charms of young womanhood. It was also a nursery for tyro comedians, who accepted the challenge of trying to capture the attention of a male audience waiting doggedly for the next unveiling. We invited Joan Jay, a Windmill girl, to be our guest.

Pretty, wide-eyed and dark-haired, Joan had to fit the live broadcast between her stage appearances, and she arrived at Broadcasting House in a taxi, wearing a blue coat thrown over a scanty Cuban costume.

Starting on the stage as a member of a juvenile troupe in a Blackpool summer show, she had been at the Windmill for four years, first in the chorus and then as *soubrette*. They performed a gruelling five shows a day, but there were two companies, and while one was playing the other was rehearsing the next edition.

When the Blitz had started, the management decided that the show would go on, come what may, and they asked for volunteers. The whole company volunteered. Sometimes there had been only a handful of people in the auditorium, and the building had rocked from near misses, but, while London burned, the show went on. At midnight, unable to reach their homes, the company bedded down in their dressing-rooms.

The theatre was never hit but, nevertheless, there were casualties. One night Joan and one of the electricians ran across the road from the stage door to fetch tea and sandwiches. A bomb fell. The electrician was killed, and Joan was pulled out of the rubble of glass and masonry by the juvenile lead, Nugent Marshall, who carried her back to the theatre. After three months in hospital, she returned to the show, and wore costumes specially designed to hide the scars on her body.

The records she chose were mainly light and cheerful, and they included 'Taboo', by the Lecuona Cuban Boys. It was a record they had played over and over again in the dressing-room to drown out the sounds of the Blitz – and she chose it to remind her of 'those very strange days, which were somehow rather marvellous'.

When our broadcast ended, she had nine minutes in which to get back to the theatre for her Cuban number. A taxi was waiting.

Now, the initial eight programmes had been broadcast, and the results had been gratifying. Good listening figures had been reported, and the series was receiving friendly attention in the press, particularly at the hands of gossip writers and the pur-veyors of light relief. It was, of course, a gift to the cartoonists, who like nothing better than a desert island joke. I was happy to hear that the series had been extended to fifteen. On the strength of it, I ordered myself a badly-needed new suit. In June 1940, I had escaped from France, where I had been working on a radio station run by the French government, and had left behind everything except the clothes I was wearing. Since my return, my financial status had not been firm enough to justify a visit to my tailor.

Looking back at the scripts of those early programmes, I find that I used to start by giving a lengthy biographical note. It was not until quite a long time later that I realized it was far better to ask my guests to supply such information themselves.

Now came our first clerical castaway, the Reverend Canon W. H. Elliott, Precentor of His Majesty's Chapels Royal, Vicar of St Michael's, Chester Square, and a popular broadcaster. He said he would appear only if he were allowed to write the script himself, and I was inexperienced enough to agree. What he produced was a sermon. It was a good sermon, but it was out of place in a programme designed as entertainment. At the end of the broadcast, he leaned back and said, 'I think I've put one over on you.' He had, and I didn't warm to him for it.

The following week, Arthur Askey was in the show. Always a joy to work with, he is one of the few comedians who are instinctively funny. He needs no props, no written script, no funny hat – he has a gift of being able to prattle away with such infectious cheerfulness that everyone chuckles with him. He is one of the only five people to have appeared three times in the series (the others are Robertson Hare, Celia Johnson, Emlyn Williams and Stanley Holloway) and I look forward to his fourth appearance.

He was followed by Eva Turner, at that time the only English prima donna of real international status. As Leslie Perowne had worshipped her from afar for many years, he elected to produce that programme himself.

Now Miss Turner (or Dame Eva, as she is now) is from Oldham and there is no nonsense about her; she is the last person in the world to put on an act. So why she decided to put on one for us, I shall never know.

After the broadcast, which had gone very well, the three of us dined at a restaurant in Brompton Road. As we came out into the blackout, we decided it was too early to go home, and Leslie suggested that we went into a pub on the corner. 'Oh, what fun!' carolled Miss Turner. 'Yes, let's do that. I've never been in a pub.' Leslie and I looked at each other, a little puzzled, but it was possible, we supposed, to have had a long and most successful career in opera, starting in the chorus of the Carl Rosa Company on tour, and yet, although fond of an occasional drink, never to have entered a saloon bar.

She professed herself delighted with the pub. She loved the engraved glass, the shining mahogany, the hunting pictures on the walls. We sat down at a table, and Leslie fetched the first round of drinks. Miss Turner, in her warmhearted way, insisted on buying the second round. 'Please let me,' she pleaded. 'But you must tell me what I have to do. Do I ask for the drinks at that counter?'

We explained the system, and she sailed over to the bar and ordered two half-pints of bitter and a glass of tawny port in the tones in which the Princess Turandot ordered the execution of a luckless suitor; and as she brought the glasses back in triumph to our table the only possible musical accompaniment would have been the Grand March from *Aida*, which was one of the pieces she had chosen for her desert island.

Some years later I was talking to Sir Bernard Miles, whom I knew to be an opera enthusiast and an old friend of Eva Turner's. 'Leslie Perowne and I took her on her first visit to a pub,' I boasted. Bernard's jaw dropped in amazement. 'You did what!' I gathered we had been deceived.

My following guest was from the jazz world: Harry Parry, a clarinettist who led the BBC's Radio Rhythm Club Sextet. A softly-spoken Welshman with a ready smile, he died in his thirties.

As a first representation of the graphic arts, we approached the sporting cartoonist, Tom Webster. A small man with an unassuming manner, he appeared to be going through an unfortunate phase in his personal life for he was drinking heavily. 'Come and talk to me,' he said, when I telephoned. For three evenings we talked as we lurched from bar to bar. He seemed quite incapable of making up his mind about his records, and made list after list, tearing each one up as useless. He was a pleasant and a talented person, but I gave a sigh of relief when the broadcast was over and he was released from his indecision. On the back of my script, he drew his famous racehorse character, Tishy.

I had never met Ivor Novello, who was to be our next castaway. I heard that he was charm itself, but I wasn't prepared for anyone quite so unaffected. As I was shown into his dressing-room at the Adelphi Theatre, where he was starring in a revival of his own musical play. *The Dancing Years* (which was unkindly known in theatrical circles as 'The Prancing Queers') he threw his arms in the air and shouted, cheerfully, 'You fool!' This was mildly disconcerting, especially as he happened to be stark naked at the time, but it appeared that he had heard a comedy programme of mine on the air a few evenings before, and it had made him laugh.

If ever there was a man to be truly miserable on a desert island it would have been Ivor Novello, because he rejoiced at being in a crowd of friends, and the procession in and out of his dressing-room was second only to that in Piccadilly Tube Station. A sensitive musician who never bothered to turn his composing talent to greater uses than sentimental operetta, he chose a programme of Bach, Brahms, two compositions by Delius and a song by the much-in-demand Yvonne Printemps. He also included a song by Debussy, 'Fleur', sung by Maggie Teyte, and he confessed to me that it was an ambition of his to have Maggie Teyte record one of his own songs. Alas, it was an ambition which was never realized. He was a great gramophile, and had a collection of eight thousand discs.

We now had only one programme left, and it was suggested that I should round off the series by being the castaway myself. I was to be interviewed by Leslie Perowne.

If anyone was to take the programme really seriously, it had to be me. I made a list of sixty titles, and then found it impossible to cross any off. Collecting records had been a hobby since I was eleven or twelve years old and, as announcer on commercial radio stations in France – Radio Normandy and Poste Parisien – I had introduced on the air thousands of hours of recorded music. I certainly knew a lot of records (I know even more now!) and how was I to select eight which might have to last the rest of my life? It made me realize what an impossible task I had been giving others every week. How could I know what sort of music I should enjoy next year? – or even next month? Every twenty-four hours, our brains are re-programmed by the day's happenings : each night we die, and a slightly different person is born the next morning. Our enthusiasms and interests change constantly – but in which direction it is impossible to forecast.

Eventually, I succeeded in eliminating all but eight records from my list, but looking at it afresh I can see only the Polovtsian Dances, from Borodin's *Prince Igor*, and a French cabaret song by Jean Sablon, that I would care to live with now.

As Leslie Perowne and Frederic Piffard and I left the studio after that broadcast, we congratulated ourselves on a successful series of fifteen programmes. Next morning, we'd get on with something else: for the moment, we'd go and have a drink. None of us had any expectation of *Desert Island Discs* coming back on the air. However, a few days later, a further series was commissioned and, with one long break of five years during which I was concentrating on acting, another of one year, and some short ones of a few months, it has continued ever since.

We did not realize, in those early days, that the permutations within the simple framework of the programme are infinite; I certainly did not realize that I was embarking on what was to be, to some extent, a life work.

Is it the oldest programme on the air? No, that honour belongs to *The Week's Good Cause*, which dates back to 1926. The *Scrapbook* programmes started in 1932, but they are broadcast only at rare intervals and they are mostly re-workings of about fifty basic editions. *Any Questions* began in 1941 – but *Desert Island Discs* is the oldest record programme, and certainly the oldest programme of any kind still presented by its creator.

What put the idea into my head? It is, of course, a variation of a very old game: which books would you choose to have on a desert island? When I submitted my idea, I believed it to be absolutely new and original, but, through the years, evidence has turned up to show once again that there's nothing new under the sun. A listener in Cambridge sent me a cutting from the June 1921 issue of a magazine called *The Music Teacher*, in which the results are given of a competition, set the previous month, in which readers were asked to imagine that they were 'about to retire into exile on a desert isle, with a gramophone and ten records', and to send in their selection.

The editor confessed that he was in trouble.

This has been an exceedingly popular competition [he wrote] but if we ever set another like it, we hope, as Mark Twain says, we may get what we deserve. It was so easy to set; but how on earth is one to judge it? . . . The cards have, almost without exception, contained the names of fine pieces; but just how is one to distinguish between the merits of the widely differing choices?

Then follows an analysis of the entries. 'Beethoven, of course, comes out on top, with a seventh of the entire total. Bach follows with an eleventh, and then there is a gap, the next in favour being Wagner and Chopin, who each get a twentieth of the votes.' The list is continued at some length, and there are some surprises: for instance, who would have thought that Mozart would get fewer votes than Vaughan Williams and Holst? And poor Verdi is near the bottom.

In the following year, 1922, in a book called *A Dominie Abroad**, A. S. Neill wrote:

It is a pastime of mine to ask people the following question: You have to spend five years on a desert island. You are allowed to take five books with you. Which? . . . I ask the same question with gramophone records in the place of books . . . Personally, I cannot make a selection, I only know that after three trials I should dismantle the gramophone and use the spring for an alarm clock or a rabbit trap.

Coming down to more recent times, in 1937 in a monthly pop music magazine called *Rhythm* my friend Spike Hughes also hit on the desert island idea, using it in his column over several months, analysing his own choice and then throwing the debate open to his readers, who sent in their lists of six jazz records. When I submitted my idea to the BBC I had no conscious memory of having read Spike's pieces, but there is no doubt that I had done so because, in my Radio Normandy days, I had been a regular reader of *Rhythm*.

Nevertheless, whatever may have planted the seed at the back of my mind, I was the first to apply the idea to a radio programme, and the world copyright of the series is my property. Not only has it been broadcast for more than thirty-five years on the domestic services of the BBC but it has been beamed to all corners of the globe on its World network; it has even been broadcast, with due acknowledgements, in Russian.

* Published by Herbert Jenkins, London.

2

How it's Done

'Desert Island Discs is the only programme the BBC puts out which completely ignores the musical likes and dislikes of listeners,' I tell my prospective castaway during an initial telephone call. 'I'm not asking you to choose your eight favourite records, nor the best ones, but those you'd choose to have with you if you were going to be completely isolated from civilization, possibly for the rest of your life. It must be a completely personal choice, and you mustn't allow yourself to be influenced by anyone at all.'

In choosing, he has first to consider what he would want the music to do for him on a desert island. Would he want it to evoke the past? There are those who say they would resolutely banish the past from their minds, because remembrance would be unbearably poignant. Others, feeling that the present would be miserable and the future most uncertain, decide to risk the pangs of nostalgia, and produce a list of discs that were once danced to or romanced to, or which formed a background to happy family occasions.

Then there are those who take music to perform the same function as crossword puzzles, choosing a fugue, for example, knowing there would be hundreds of hours of study in tracing its convolutions, or asking for difficult atonal or electronic music, hoping that time would bring understanding and enjoyment – but suppose it didn't!

Some, with one-track enthusiasm, choose mainly the work of an especially favoured composer; others give themselves an abbreviated history of music by choosing chronologically from Palestrina to Stockhausen. There are those, too, who choose pop, although one can imagine the despair of a castaway who is isolated for years with nothing but the bashing of electric guitars and the frenzied shouting of tin-eared vocalists who, by the time he is rescued, are probably out of the music business and back on their milk rounds. Pop music as a cheerful noise is fine, but for a lifetime's listening – no!

In due course I receive, by post or telephone, the list of records my castaway has chosen. In the case of an experienced broadcaster, this list may be meticulously detailed, with the catalogue numbers of the discs, and notes of the exact sections to be played: at the other extreme, I receive a list of eighteen discs, instead of the required eight, couched in the vaguest terms: Something by Bach . . . A Haydn quartet . . . Has Sinatra recorded anything by Gershwin?

I pass on the list to the producer in charge of the series, who orders the required records from the BBC's Gramophone Library, and I call in at the News Information office. In this busy and efficient department, approximating to a newspaper's 'morgue', are stored millions of press cuttings on all sorts of subjects and all sorts of people. By wading through cuttings, looking up reference books and occasionally making telephone calls to mutual acquaintances. I get to know quite a lot about my future guest.

I believe this preliminary research is the essential ingredient of a good interview. It has a disarming effect on a new acquaintance to find that you have primed yourself to talk about his interests, and it also enables one to guide an interview back on to course if it should start to ramble. I now have the facility to document myself in a single evening on astrophysics, clay-pigeon shooting or the repertoire of the oboe, but, unfortunately, as soon as the interview is over, the information vanishes from my mind, and I have to do my homework all over again next time I arrange to interview an astrophysicist, a clay-pigeon shooter or an oboist.

To prepare and record the programme is usually half a day's work. If my guest is someone I have not met before, I have a preference for the latter half of the day, so that I can invite him to lunch first and we can get to know each other over the meal.

Before all this happens, the BBC Bookings Department has contacted him and negotiated a fee. I make it a point not to know how much a castaway is being paid; it has nothing to do with me and I want to keep out of all monetary arguments. It is inevitable, however, that occasionally I get involved. One day I called on Anton Dolin at a Soho rehearsal room to have a preliminary chat, and found him none too happy. He was insulted, he said, by the fee he had been offered, and he began to attack me about it. I did my best to calm him down, and told him he was perfectly free not to accept the engagement if he didn't want to. After blowing off steam a little longer he decided to accept the cash insult, and all was sweetness and light.

Another advantage in working during the afternoon is that, if my guest should happen to be late for our appointment it merely means that we have a little less time for lunch, whereas, if he is late for a morning session, when I have planned a tight schedule leading up to a fixed-time recording, it can be harassing.

I happen to be one of those anxiety-ridden people who are seldom late for appointments, but I still have sympathy for the man who has a hangover or who has been stuck in a traffic jam. However there are limits. One morning I was in Broadcasting House awaiting the arrival of a young pop star. After cooling my heels for half an hour I was summoned to the telephone. It was the young idol in person – calling from Liverpool. He was sorry he was going to be a little late, but he'd got as far as Speke Airport and would be with me in a couple of hours!

After lunching with my guest, we take a taxi to Broadcasting House – or rather to Egton House, which stands next to it. It is a modern office building faced with a dark, shiny stone, so that it looks like the Number Two tour of the *Daily Express* building in Fleet Street. Most of its five floors are devoted to the planning, compilation and recording of disc programmes, ranging from pop requests to Radio Three concerts of contemporary music. The lower floors house the Gramophone Library.

If my guest has not visited the building before, I usually take him to see the library index, which is an impressive sight. A million discs are catalogued on cards in smoothly-running steel drawers. Not only is each item listed by title, but also by composer and by artist, so it adds up to three million entries.

I took the operatic tenor, Nicolai Gedda, to see the index. He had made his first record within a fortnight of his début, at Stockholm Opera House, and he was delighted to see how thick was the batch of index cards bearing his name. He then ran to the drawer containing the cards of his great rival, the Italian Franco Corelli, and measured his cards against Corelli's.

'I'm thicker than Franco!' he shouted happily.

The library was started in 1933, and since then the BBC has bought three copies of practically every disc issued in

Great Britain, plus as many foreign issues as a restricted allowance of overseas currencies will permit. Continual negotiations are carried out with dealers and collectors to buy pre-1933 issues, and some of the acquisitions are very valuable indeed. The oldest discs in the library date back to 1895, and some of the early vocal recordings have a market value of several hundred pounds. These rarities are kept in a separate section, known as The Archive, and there are special formalities for their use. Much of the library consists of 78 rpm records, which are easily broken, and so the formidable task is being undertaken of copying these hundreds of thousands of discs on to tape. It is the biggest library of commercially issued records in the world.

Waiting for us is a pile of discs, neatly done up with elastic bands. The size of the pile varies from week to week. In the case of a castaway who knows exactly what he wants, there will be just eight discs. If it's someone who knows what he wants but is uncertain of the details – for example, he lists the musical items without specifying orchestras, soloists or conductors – there will be three or four times as many, because he will have been given suggested versions from which to choose. (At the time of writing, the number of recordings of Beethoven's Fifth Symphony listed in the BBC index is thirty-seven.) For a castaway who is really vague – one of the 'Has Sinatra recorded any Gershwin?' people I mentioned – the pile may be enormous.

We carry the records up to the second floor, where a listening-room has been booked for us. These are cheerless little boxes equipped with reproducing apparatus for discs and tape, a record rack and two chairs. The walls are bare, the carpet is depressing, and there is a faintly frowsty smell. The window looks out into the well of the building and across to the windows of a vast open-plan office in which dozens of people are operating duplicating machines, presumably to keep up the Corporation's magnificent output of inter-office memoranda. The provision of just one picture, or reproduction, on the wall of a listening-room would make a great and humanizing difference, but doubtless, in officialdom's phrase, 'there is no machinery for this'.

Despite their austerity, listening-rooms are much in demand, and a lot of poaching goes on. Frequently one has to eject an intruder before starting work. I officiate at the record player while my guest sits and consults his notes.

'What shall we start with? Suppose we do the Beethoven first.' I put the disc on the turntable and await instructions. 'Which part of the symphony?'

'The big brass theme in the first movement', may be the reply, or 'The opening of the slow movement', or, if he is a musician, 'Let's start on the *sforzando* in the fourth bar of the tutti that follows the change into D minor,' – in which case he will be called on to translate, because my knowledge of music is modest, and his instructions will be noted by me as 'Start on loud wallop 3 minutes and 57 seconds after beginning of last movement', adding, as a precaution, 'This is 23 seconds after end of solo flute passage.'

At no time during the selection of records will I offer, or give, an opinion. 'Shall I choose the slow movement or the scherzo?' asks my guest. I keep quiet. 'Do you think Solti's is a better recording than Giulini's?' I suggest he listens once again and makes up his own mind. As soon as I allow my own opinions, likes or dislikes to become apparent, then the series will founder, because it will have lost its honesty. It is essential that each programme reflects only the personality of my guest, and any programme in the series which has my thumbprint on it is a failure.

Only on two occasions can I remember a castaway having been influenced. In the first instance, there was no alternative. It wouldn't be fair to name my guest: let it suffice that he is a writer, and a good one. He had been out of the country; the broadcast had been arranged with his agent during his absence. On the day of the recording, he turned up at Broadcasting House firmly under the impression that he was going to be interviewed on the subject of desert islands, about which he was something of an authority. When I began talking about discs, his face took on an expression of alarm. 'I think I ought to tell you,' he said, 'that I'm tone deaf and I don't know one piece of music from another.'

Thinking he was exaggerating, I began to question him, but it was soon apparent that he was indeed honestly incapable of making a list of eight discs: so the rules had to be broken and he had to be helped. Where had he been to school? What was the school song and has it been recorded? Good, that's one disc. He had been a regular soldier: which regiment, and what's the regimental march called? Fine, we've got two. Before he was married, was there any particular tune he and his fiancée used to dance to? Yes, there was, but he didn't know what it was called and he wouldn't recognize it anyway. A telephone call to his wife provided the information we needed. In that way we built a programme, but my guest had to take my word for it that the tunes he was hearing were ones he had heard before. The other occasion when the rules were broken was when a song by Frank Sinatra called 'One for my Baby, and One More for the Road' was chosen. As we were starting to record, Monica Chapman who was producing said: 'It's just occurred to me that this programme is going to be broadcast on Bank Holiday. It's going to be heard in pubs all over the country. I don't think "One more for the Road" is a good idea to suggest to motorists.' My guest chose another Sinatra song instead and it's very possible that at least one road accident was averted by Monica's quick thinking.

It has always been a point of honour with the gramophone librarian, Derek Lewis, and his assistants that, given time, they will produce any disc that is asked for, however obscure. If there isn't a copy on their shelves, they usually know where they can borrow one. I remember an occasion when I acted as go-between, so that a beautiful young actress could play a very rare record, of which the only known copy was in the possession of her ex-husband, with whom she was not on speaking terms.

The only time we have to refuse to provide a record is when there is a copyright 'stop' on certain music being broadcast. This sometimes happens in the case of songs from American or Continental musical plays which are scheduled for future production in this country, as for instance when James Agate was refused permission to play the Yvonne Printemps recording from *Les Trois Valses*. It is understandable that the producing manager wants to keep the music under wraps until the opening date, but by pointing out to him that if a distinguished person wishes to include an excerpt among the eight pieces of music to last for the rest of his life it can do the coming show nothing but good, we have been permitted to give a première broadcast performance of a number from a show which afterwards became famous. This happened in the case of *Fiddler on the Roof* and *Hello, Dolly*.

Similarly, in the days when the BBC was at its most 'Auntieish' and banned even the most minor impropriety in a song lyric, we were sometimes able to broadcast the unbroadcastable, on the plea that *Desert Island Discs* should be given special consideration. Mind you, we played ball by omitting verses that seemed particularly rough, but I remember arguing long and heatedly about Noël Coward's innocuous 'Don't Put Your Daughter on the Stage, Mrs Worthington', and asking why the hell we shouldn't broadcast the line '. . . the width of her seat would surely defeat her chances of success' if we were allowed to broadcast '. . . her bust is too developed for her age' – or was it the other way about?

During the war there was a curious piece of administrative woolly-mindedness, when it was ruled that there was no objection to the broadcasting of German and Italian vocal music providing it was sung in English. Sir Kenneth Clark, now Lord Clark, refused to take part in the series when told of this inspired lunacy.

But let's get back to that imaginary castaway who has, so far, settled on one disc, a Beethoven symphony. There are seven more discs to be dealt with.

We deal with the easier ones first, so that morale is kept high. The first difficulty arises when a familiar hymn is asked for, 'sung by an ordinary English church choir'. The library has sent us every available recording of the hymn. There are five – by a nasal Irish tenor, by a vast American evangelical choir, by two morose hillbillies, by a holier-than-thou soprano with organ accompaniment, and by a prize-winning brass band at a 1928 Crystal Palace competition. There is nothing by an ordinary English church choir. Disappointed, my guest decides to forego religious consolation on his island, and chooses a Fats Waller disc instead.

Despite the enormous repertoire of recorded music, there are still gaps. Apart from a paucity of good recordings of hymns, there are few good discs of Welsh choirs, of Scottish pipe bands, and of atmospheric flamenco songs and dances. With so many people adopting Spain as a holiday centre, flamenco music is frequently asked for. Most of the available recordings seem to have been made in studios and therefore sound inhibited . . . or it may be that the gipsies are losing their fire. Peter Ustinov told me recently that he was among the first clients to arrive in a Spanish gipsy cave one evening, to find the inhabitants preparing for the festivities by covering up a television set with a mantilla!

A kind of music that I find confusing to cope with is Scottish dance music. I quite like the sound of it; I just can't find my way about it. It is usually available only in medleys, and any Sassenach who can sort out a medley of half a dozen strathspeys is a better man than I am. 'That's it,' says my Scottish castaway, dancing away in the listening-room; 'start where "Poor Wullie" ends and "MacTavish's Sporran" begins.' But, to me, all the tunes sound exactly alike.

When the eight records have been decided upon, and the painful butchery of cutting them down to an average of less than two minutes has been completed, it sometimes happens that my guest has an afterthought and wants to change one of them. This is something I dread, because by now we shall be running out of time.

If he says, for example, 'I'm not very happy about the Haydn; it's too much in the same mood as the Mozart. May I take the Kyrie from Britten's *Missa Brevis* instead?', then there is no problem, because it takes only a few moments to have the disc brought up from the library; but it is agony when I hear something like, 'I've just realized I've chosen no Bach. Do you know a piece of Bach that goes tum tum tiddly tum tum tiddle?'

I don't know it, and neither do the six other people I bring in to listen to the tum-tum-tiddleing. At last, by tum-tum-tiddleing all over the building, we discover that the tune he has in his head is not by Bach but by Tchaikovsky, and he has decided against it after all, and by now we are forty minutes behind schedule.

I believe *Desert Island Discs* adds a dimension to a listener's mental picture of a well-known person, giving the same insight he would receive from visiting the celebrity's home and seeing the books, pictures and furniture with which he surrounds himself. Sometimes the programme is a revelation to the celebrity himself; I have had a guest say to me, as he looks down the list of his finally-chosen excerpts: 'I never before realized that I'm a slow movement man.'

The next step is the arrangement of the discs in the order in which they are to be played. Again, I will not interfere. There is a professional expertise in building record programmes, and I am well versed in this, and the last thing I want is for the programme to have a professional gloss. A good *Desert Island Discs* programme should sound sincere, casual and just a little bit of a ragbag.

By now, I hope, the producer's secretary will have looked in and offered us cups of tea – and here I must interject a line of tribute to Winifred Timmins, ('Tim') who was associated with the programme for almost twenty years, and without whom I believe the entire enterprise would have ground to a halt – and then it is about time for us to go to the studio to record. There are three small studios in Egton House, and normally we use one of those, but there is pressure on studios, as there is on listening-rooms, and we may have to go to a studio in Broadcasting House, which, if it happens to be raining, we can reach through a tunnel.

It is in the studio that the producer takes over. Over the years, a system has been evolved whereby the producer takes no part in the preliminaries, so that, at the recording, he, or she, will hear everything for the first time, just as our listeners will. Thus, he can take an objective view, pouncing on any obscurities, and demanding that we go back and re-record any passages that may sound verbose or dull. He will also edit the programme afterwards so that it runs exactly to time.

The producer and the recording engineer sit in a small control cubicle and survey us through a large glass window. The castaway and I sit on opposite sides of a table with a microphone between us. On the table are a jug of water and two glasses. There is something very distinctive about the water supplied in BBC studios. Basil Boothroyd tells a story of that splendid man, the late Gilbert Harding, who once took a sip of studio water, and exploded, 'This is the identical water that the Chairman of the Governors put his teeth into on the night of the Abdication broadcast.'

A number of staff producers have worked with me on the series, and the *doyenne* is Monica Chapman, who produced over seven hundred of the programmes, in the years from 1951 to 1967, during which time we never exchanged a cross word. The others with whom I have worked are Leslie Perowne, the late Frederic Piffard, Pat Osborne, Denys Jones, Anna Instone, Hilary Pym, Michael Hall, John Lade, Ronald Cook and the present incumbent, Derek Drescher.

The first two hundred programmes were scripted I believe I

became quite adept at going to my typewriter after a first meeting with someone, and writing a pastiche of his or her conversational style; but this was a poor sort of second-best, and it was a great improvement when, in the mid-'fifties, the BBC started the general use of recording on tape instead of acetate discs. That meant we could stop scripting and put the series properly to work to fulfil its function of revealing character.

When I am asked which are the records most frequently chosen, I can only reply that I don't know, because we have kept no figures, and it is unlikely that I am going to find time to collate ten thousand discs. Perhaps, one day, the Corporation will put its computer to work.

The following is a list of titles which turn up fairly frequently. I am sure there must be many omissions, and I have put them in no sort of order:

Beethoven's Fifth, Sixth and Ninth Symphonies.

Dvorak's 'New World' Symphony.

Mendelssohn's Fourth ('Italian') Symphony, and his music to *A Midsummer Night's Dream*.

Schubert's 'Unfinished' Symphony.

Rachmaninov's Second Piano Concerto, and his Rhapsody on a Theme by Paganini.

Beethoven's 'Emperor' Concerto.

Tchaikovsky's First Piano Concerto in B Flat Minor.

Mozart's Piano Concerto No. 20 in D Minor, and his Fourth Horn Concerto.

Bach's Double Violin Concerto.

Ravel's 'Daphnis and Chloe' Suites.

'Scheherazade' by Rimsky-Korsakov.

Mozart's 'Eine Kleine Nachtmusik'.

Vivaldi's 'The Four Seasons'.

Elgar's Enigma Variations, and his Violin Concerto (almost invariably the recording conducted by the composer, with the young Yehudi Menuhin).

Debussy's 'L'après-midi d'un faune'.

'On Hearing the First Cuckoo in Spring', and 'Walk to the Paradise Garden' (from *A Village Romeo and Juliet*) by Delius.

Handel's *Messiah* and Bach's *St Matthew Passion*.

Richard Strauss's 'Also Sprach Zarathustra', usually referred to as 'the 2,001 Music'.

From Opera, the favourites are:

The Love Duet and the Liebestod from Wagner's *Tristan und Isolde*, 'The Ride of the Valkyries', from *Die Walküre*, and the Immolation Scene from *Götterdämmerung*.

Dido's Lament, from Purcell's *Dido and Aeneas*.

'Che farò' from Gluck's *Orfeo ed Euridice*.

The Closing Trio, from *Der Rosenkavalier*, by Richard Strauss.

'Casta diva' from Bellini's *Norma*.

Arias from Bizet's *Carmen*, and from Puccini's *Madame Butterfly* and *La Bohème*.

The most popular excerpts from Verdi seem to be the Love Duet from *Otello*. the Fugue from *Falstaff*, and the Chorus of the Hebrew Slaves from *Nabucco*.

Of course, there are frequent items from Mozart's *The Marriage of Figaro*, *The Magic Flute* and *Don Giovanni*.

The most popular Gilbert and Sullivan operetta is *The Mikado*.

Ballet music is most often represented by Tchaikovsky's *Romeo and Juliet*, *Swan Lake* and *The Sleeping Beauty*, and by Prokofiev's *Romeo and Juliet*.

Johann Strauss waltzes appear on many lists, and so does Offenbach's *Gaîté Parisienne*.

Music on a smaller scale is represented by Bach's Air on the G String, Massenet's 'Méditation', from *Thaïs*, Borodin's Quartet in D Minor, Beethoven's supreme last Quartet in F Major, Opus 135, and Schubert's 'Trout' Quintet.

Perhaps the most frequently requested piano record is the Myra Hess arrangement of Bach's 'Jesu, Joy of Man's Desiring'.

The most popular organ pieces are Bach's Toccata and Fugue in D Minor, and Widor's Toccata, from his Fifth Organ Symphony.

Music to give courage includes 'Colonel Bogey', 'The Battle Hymn of the Republic', 'Onward, Christian Soldiers', 'Jerusalem', 'Land of Hope and Glory' (usually the recording of the audience singing at the Last Night of the Proms) and Jeremiah Clarke's Trumpet Voluntary.

Nostalgia for England is epitomized by 'Greensleeves', 'The
Eton Boating Song', and carols by the choir of King's
College, Cambridge.

From films: 'Lara's Theme' from *Dr Zhivago*, 'The Warsaw
Concerto' from *Dangerous Moonlight*, William Walton's
Henry V music, the Theme from *Lawrence of Arabia*, and
Chaplin's music from *Limelight*.

Regularly chosen 'personality' discs include Julie Andrews
singing 'I Could Have Danced All Night', from *My Fair
Lady*, Frank Sinatra, singing 'My Way', Edith Piaf's 'Non,
je ne regrette rien', Gene Kelly's 'Singin' in the Rain' and
Judy Garland singing 'Over the Rainbow'.

It's a much longer list than I thought it was going to be,
and already I notice that I've included nothing by Brahms or
Berlioz.

Whenever possible, we insist on working in a BBC studio.
We could capture many more world stars of the entertainment world if we were prepared to work in hotel rooms,
theatre dressing-rooms or airport lounges. But *Desert Island
Discs* is a programme which needs thought and concentration
if it is to be an honest expression of a person's tastes and
character; if that person is not interested enough to give us
the necessary time to do the job properly, then we are not
interested either. In fact we've worked outside a studio fewer
than a dozen times: with Sir Thomas Beecham, with Artur
Rubinstein, with Sophie Tucker, who was not at all well, with
Field-Marshal Viscount Montgomery, with Marlene Dietrich,
who is a law unto herself, with Bob Hope, who is such a
brilliant broadcaster that we were quite confident he could
do the job just as brilliantly in his dressing-room at Shepperton
Studios as anywhere else, and two or three others who, for
various reasons, could not manage the journey to Broadcasting
House. On a few occasions we have worked in BBC studios
in provincial cities.

'Are you ever going to run out of celebrities?' is a question
I am asked incessantly. There's no chance of that: celebrities
proliferate at a very much faster rate than one a week. We
have a working list of a hundred good names as yet untapped.
Every six or eight weeks, the producer and I have a meeting
to decide who our next castaways should be. Within a few
minutes we have thought of a list of a dozen or so exciting

personalities without even glancing at our working list.

I am happy to report that we have very few refusals. The reputation of the programme is jealously guarded, and many of our prospective castaways will have heard on the grapevine which operates in celebrity circles that in *Desert Island Discs* they will have an absolutely free choice of records, that the interview will not be embarrassingly probing, and that the interviewer will have done his homework. Anyway, there are few people, however busy, who will not be tempted to put aside an afternoon to have a pleasant lunch, listen to their favourite music, and then get paid a fee for talking about themselves for half an hour.

3

Luxuries and Books and Desert Island Lore

'Please, may I take a power station?'

The idea that each castaway should be allowed one 'luxury' on the island came from the castaways themselves, although the objects they suggested were usually extremely useful – such as motor-boats or guns or light aircraft – but there were a few modest and sensible requests, such as Joyce Grenfell's for pencil and paper so that she could write a play. It was after the first hundred or so programmes that I began regularly to invite the choice of a luxury, which is defined in the rules as 'an inanimate object which is purely for the senses; something to look at, or touch, or taste, or smell, but which is not going to help you to live. It can be something you've seen in a museum or art gallery and couldn't ordinarily hope to own, or a treasured personal possession, or something frivolous, like a mink coat or a bag of golf clubs.'

I suppose the most requested items have been musical instruments, with the piano at the top of the list (although I insist it shall be an upright model, as a grand is so useful for living under). Even so, there have been a few unscrupulous characters who, having been promised a piano, have indicated that they proposed taking it to pieces and using the wires to bind together materials for making a hut, and the woodwork as a basis for a boat. There is always a risk that I am going to be duped: it seemed quite reasonable that I should permit James Fitton, RA, to take an unlimited supply of paints and canvas – until he pointed out that the canvas could be stretched to make a canoe, the paint could be used to make it watertight, and canvas would also provide the sails.

I should have known better than to allow such a word as 'unlimited' to creep in. When the series started, back in the dear, dead days of the 78 rpm record, a hand-wound gramophone was envisaged, with which I promised 'an inexhaustible supply of needles' – until a bright castaway said he would start welding the needles together and so produce steel plates, with which he would make walls, and possibly even the hull of a ship.

Of course, if a castaway gives a solemn promise that a potentially useful luxury will not be used for practical purposes, then it is allowed. Hermione Gingold was permitted to take the Albert Memorial, after she had given her word that she would not take up residence; on the same terms, Anthony Asquith was allowed a fully-equipped seaside pier, with lots of pin-tables and penny-in-the-slot machines, including some of the 'What the Butler Saw' variety. I was even prepared to arrange for a supply of pennies.

Coming back to musical instruments, there would be the problem of maintenance in a hot climate, so it was a very good idea on Sir Michael Tippett's part to choose a harmonium, because it never goes out of tune.

Antoinette Sibley chose a comfortable bed: so did tenors Charles Craig and Peter Pears, and Baroness Summerskill stipulated that hers should be a large and luxurious four-poster with curtains. The latter choice produced an angry letter in *Radio Times* from a lady in Stroud.

Whatever has happened to Roy Plomley? [she wrote]. He has consistently denied castaways a grand piano, as it would provide shelter, and yet he did not object to a large bed complete with canopy, curtains, etc.

I replied:

If our correspondent cares to experiment, I am sure she will find that a grand piano, if properly sited, offers reasonable shelter from rain, if not from wind, whereas a four-poster bed, with curtains, will speedily become a dripping, flapping, depressing and useless encumbrance that shelters her from nothing.

As a plaything, Glenda Jackson chose the Queen's dolls' house, from Windsor Castle, while Harry Secombe asked for a collapsible concrete model of Broadcasting House, complete with plastic announcers and a cast-iron commissionaire, so that he could 'think of all the lads working their nuts off' while he was lazing in the sun. Luxury foods are allowed, on the premise that a diet of caviar would make you ill before it nourished you, but David Wynne's request for barrels of common-or-garden cocoa was so surprising that I let him have them.

Temperance campaigners will have noticed with sorrow how often alcoholic beverages are chosen. Sir Alec Guinness revealed a liking for apricot brandy; Edward Ardizzone requested a hogshead of the very finest Highland malt whisky; Sir Terence Rattigan opted for a dozen cases of Dom Perignon; while Robert Nesbitt suggested a year's output from the Moët et Chandon cellars. But the most popular request is for a still, so that the island's resources of coconuts or yams can be distilled into a potent and flavorous spirit.

That fine pianist, Benno Moiseiwitsch, who loved to gamble, chose a roulette wheel so that he could try out a few systems. Dr W. Grey Walter wanted a kit for making a transistorized computer powered by solar batteries (as is the Island's record player nowadays) which would be able to answer him back and take the place of a companion. Telescopes and binoculars are frequently asked for, ostensibly for bird watching but obviously they would be useful for scanning the horizon for a ship; a snorkel, while providing endless pleasure in watching underwater life, would also be useful in fishing.

Some would find comfort in the possession of extreme riches; Eric Robinson asked for £1 million in £1 notes, while Stephane Grappelli asked for the Koh-i-noor diamond. At the other extreme, G. H. Elliott, the music-hall performer who was famous as The Chocolate-coloured Coon, whose recording career began in the nineties and continued for over sixty years, chose an old waistcoat which he believed to be lucky. He had first worn it in 1903, and always put it on when trying out a new song.

An unorthodox and down-to-earth request came from Duncan Carse, for a rubber woman, an idea which has been echoed more recently by Oliver Reed and Vincent Brome.

The idea of inviting each guest to choose a single book, apart from the conventionally obvious choices of the Bible and the works of Shakespeare, did not strike me until I had broadcast about four hundred programmes, although earlier I had decreed that every actor and actress should be given a set of Shakespeare's plays, as so many Thespians had requested that as a luxury. It was decided that the word 'book' should be stretched to include any single work, even if it runs to a number of volumes, but we became tired of constantly advertising various multi-volume encyclopaedias, so we put the bar up on those too.

I don't know when the game of Desert Island Books was evolved, but William Wordsworth gave the matter some attention as long ago as 1799, when he began work on his immensely long poem, 'The Prelude' – although his castaway took his volume by chance rather than by choice. In Book VI, he wrote:

> 'Tis told by one whom stormy waters threw
> With fellow sufferers by the shipwreck spared,
> Upon a desert coast, that having brought
> To land a single volume, saved by chance,
> A treatise of Geometry, he wont,
> Although of food and clothing destitute,
> And beyond common wretchedness depressed,
> To part from company and take this book
> (Then first a self-taught pupil in its truths)
> To spots remote, and draw his diagrams
> With a long staff upon the sand, and thus
> Did oft beguile his sorrow, and almost
> Forget his feeling:

A century later, in 1900, a weekly paper called *Moonshine* ran a contest to decide which would be the most popular books to take for 'Five Years on a Desert Island'. Readers were invited to send in their personal lists of ten books; the volumes named most frequently, in descending order, were: The works of Shakespeare, the Bible, *Pickwick Papers*, the works of Tennyson, *Vanity Fair*, *Robinson Crusoe*, *Pilgrim's Progress*, *David Copperfield*, the works of Milton, Lamb's *Essays*.

A number of distinguished literary figures of the day were invited to submit lists, and Lord Avebury (Sir John Lubbock) wrote: 'I should advise for an Englishman – The Bible, Homer, Plutarch, Epictetus, Marcus Aurelius, Plato, Shakespeare, Milton, Scott, Ruskin' . . . which some Englishmen might regard as heavy going.

In *Desert Island Discs*, comparatively few works of fiction are chosen, but there are fairly frequent requests for novels which offer practical advice on desert island life, such as *Robinson Crusoe* and *The Swiss Family Robinson*.

Journalist Anne Sharpley had the bright idea of taking the official manual on survival issued to British forces, and telephoned the Ministry of Defence to ask if she could see a copy. To her astonishment, she was told that the book was classified and not available to the press or to members of the public, although presumably such persons are just as likely to be in need of the information as those in uniform. Anne therefore telephoned the GHQ of the American forces in this country, and they were positively delighted to present her with a copy of the book they use, called *The Raft*, and written for them by an Australian named Harold Gatty. It's full of details about tides and navigation and how to live on plankton. What is so secret about the British equivalent, I can't imagine.

Probably the favourite work for a good long read is Gibbon's *The Decline and Fall of the Roman Empire*, chosen by Sir Terence Rattigan, Sir Richard Woolley, Professor Asa Briggs, and the Rt Hon. Jeremy Thorpe, MP, with Proust's *A la Recherche du Temps Perdu* in second place. Tolkien's *The Lord of the Rings* is a frequent starter, and the Reverend Dr 'Tubby' Clayton shook us all by choosing a work called *Patrologia Latina*, which he said is in 198 volumes and is the longest single work in the world. I know he was not exaggerating, because when I looked it up in the British Museum catalogue to check the spelling, I found that their copy of Jacques Paul Migne's *'Patrologiae Cursus Completus. Series (Latina) prima'* (to give the full title) runs to 221 volumes. I should have made Dr Clayton promise not to build anything with it.

Christopher Chataway called for the complete works of Chaucer because they are 'so full of life and humour. I should get more enjoyment from him as I got to know him better.'

'In the original spelling?' I asked.

'Untampered with, and as difficult as possible,' he replied. 'Then I could puzzle over it as the weeks and years went by.'

Inspirational works, such as *Science and Health* and *The Power of Positive Thinking*, are high on the list, and Professor C. MacNeill Dixon's *The Human Situation* has been chosen by such diverse celebrities as Noël Coward, Lord Brabazon of Tara, athlete Robbie Brightwell, Tallulah Bankhead and mountaineer Eric Shipton.

Dennis Brain, the horn player, chose some bound copies of the motoring magazines which were his favourite reading during those sections of orchestral rehearsals which did not include horn passages; Alfred Hitchcock asked for a Continental time-table, so that he could go on imaginary journeys.

Henry Kendall, the comedy actor and revue star, asked for the latest edition of *Who's Who in the Theatre*, for 'memories of so many hundreds of plays and people – and it's always such fun looking up to see how old your friends are'. As an afterthought he added: 'And if it were allowed, I'd take an earlier edition of the same book as well – ten, fifteen or twenty years earlier – so that I could check up and see how old they said they were then!'

So far as desert island lore is concerned, I believe I have greater theoretical knowledge than anyone in the kingdom, for over one thousand three hundred and seventy brilliant people have told me their theories – but, of course, I have no means of knowing how many of those theories would work, and I have no ambition to find out.

Being a completely unpractical person who cannot knock a nail in straight, I am surprised at the number of people who have manual skills. Moira Lister, for example, a slender porcelain-like lady for whom a little light dusting would seem quite enough exertion, told me that, from her early years in South Africa, she knows how to trap wild animals and how to keep them at bay at night, how to cook in a sand oven, and how to build a rondaval, which is a round hut built of rocks and cemented with clay. 'If you have no clay, you use sand bound with grass; if no rocks, then lumps of coral.' She guarantees the hut to be warm and waterproof. To avoid having to hunt for fresh meat too often, she suggests building up a reserve store of biltong, which is strips of raw meat, dried and salted in sea salt. I suppose that could be done with fish too.

David Attenborough, who should certainly know something about camping out, favours a less permanent sounding hut than Miss Lister's – a ridge-pole hut, thatched with palm leaves. As additions to a castaway's diet, he suggests turtle eggs, sea slugs and snakes, which he says are edible and tasty. Joy Nichols, the comedienne, recommends that one should make damper, the Australian bushman's staple diet, if there is any wild grain on the island. Damper is a flour and water dough, cooked in ashes. 'It's a bit grubby,' she says, 'but it tastes very good.'

The majority of castaways claim that they could improvise fishing tackle, but say they would be too squeamish to take a fish off the hook. In fact, so many people have told me that they could not bring themselves to kill that I have a strong impression that if we had to kill for our own food, we'd all be vegetarians.

The number expressing confidence in their ability to construct some form of craft and sail it to safety is, not surprisingly, very small, but to Uffa Fox the problems seemed few. 'You'll have the hairs that protect the palm trees for your rope and sails; you'll have bamboo; and with that and the trees and the glue you'd make from fish you could make a catamaran. As for navigation, you get a coconut and poke some holes in it, and measure angles from the sun with that, because all navigation is a matter of angles and time.' It sounded too easy.

Ronald Searle, the artist and creator of St Trinian's, spent four years in a Japanese prison camp. He said that if there were enough grass on the island he'd be able to get all his essential vitamins from that. The next thing he would search for would be snails. Looking back on the horrors of those four years, he added, 'At least I shan't be competing with 7000 other for the food that I'm looking for.'

One of my guests has been a voluntary exile on a desert island. Journalist Macdonald Hastings, as a stunt for a Sunday newspaper, agreed to spend five weeks alone on a small island in the Indian Ocean. His living conditions were not as spartan as those to which I condemn my guests, because he was provided with a knife, some string and a dog, as well as a radio transmitter on which he could put out a distress signal if he found himself in real trouble.

The first hut that he built fell down, but the second was more successful and lasted the rest of his stay. There were many hazards on the island, including poisonous fish and sharp coral, which can be most dangerous. After about five days, he developed alarming aural hallucinations: he began hearing records playing in his head, one after another; the remarkable thing was he had no idea which disc was going to play next. Although he is not a musical man, he could hear orchestrations in great detail, and the lyrics of songs which he thought he had long forgotten. One of the discs which played over and over was Amelita Galli-Curci's recording of 'The Echo Song', which he hadn't heard since he was fourteen. The curious and disturbing phenomenon lasted seven or eight days, then stopped as suddenly as it had started. Afterwards, doctors told him it was a common experience in situations of that kind.

He found no shortage of food, because he could grab jungle fowl from their roosts at night, and spear fish in shallow water. Unfortunately there was no fruit and, as a result, he contracted scurvy, and had lost 32 lb by the end of his five-week stay. If he had done his homework properly, he would have known that he could have avoided illness by shinning up a palm tree and digging out some palm heart, or he could have eaten his fish raw instead of boiling it or frying it in coconut oil. The dog knew this instinctively, and spurned cooked food.

Norman Thelwell, the artist and cartoonist, who has made a fortune from his amusing drawings of plump little girls on plump little ponies, was the first to realize the benefits that castaways nowadays gain from the pollution of the seas. Every day the shore would be littered with a fresh supply of plastic bags and bottles, all most useful for storing food and supplies: if enough of them could be filled with air and tied together they would form an unsinkable raft of such dimensions that even the most timid castaway would be tempted to make a bid for freedom. There was also the likelihood of an oil slick arriving and providing a useful source of fuel.

It was a listener, the scientific journalist, Basil Clarke, who brought the best news to a modern castaway. There is no need, nowadays, to spend months and years languishing on a desert island: all you have to do is tramp out on the beach, in letters 100 feet high, SOS. This would be quite big enough to show up in the photographs which spy-in-the-sky satellites are sending back to earth the whole time, and before long suspicious sailors from one power or another would land from a warship to find out what was going on.

4
Writers

To interview Sir Sacheverell Sitwell, Ronald Cook and I took one of our rare excursions outside London. We drove to Towcester on a fine summer's day, and were given luncheon in a beautiful country house which has been in the family since the days of Queen Anne.

I knew that Sir Sacheverell is very interested in music because he has written books about a number of composers – Liszt, Scarlatti, Mozart, Offenbach – and is vice-president of the flourishing Liszt Society, but I didn't realize to what extent he is a record enthusiast. 'I play records nearly every night when I'm living here in the country,' he said.

For his programme, he chose four solo piano pieces, two by Liszt and two by Schumann, Mozart's Piano Concerto in C Major (K.415), Bach's Goldberg Variations, played on the harpsichord, and excerpts from Bizet's *Carmen* and Verdi's *Un Ballo in Maschera*.

Despite a background of aristocracy and wealth, the three young Sitwells, Edith, Osbert and Sacheverell, were all at the barricades in the post-First World War cultural revolution. Sacheverell's most useful contribution was probably his exhibition of contemporary French painting, which must have opened many eyes. It was the first time that Modigliani's pictures were exhibited in London, and Sir Sacheverell told me how he went to see him in Paris and bought two of his pictures for £4 each (one is now in the Tate Gallery). Eventually, he was offered the whole of the contents of the studio for £100, but being a very young man he didn't have that sum available. 'It makes me wild to think of poor Modigliani not having any of the money his pictures fetch now,' he said.

He has written eighty or so books, covering many subjects. His travel books on many countries form part of an early plan to see and assess every great work of art in the civilized world, but he has taken off at many splendid tangents, writing books about poltergeists, horticulture, porcelain figures or whatever has taken his interest.

His writing habits are disciplined. He works every morning

and evening ('and I make a point of always working on Christmas Day, Easter, public holidays and always on Sundays, all day Sundays'). When I asked him to choose one book for his solitary exile, he asked for *War and Peace* and *Anna Karenina* bound together.

A great deal of my leisure reading is English history, and two of my favourite historians have been my guests, Sir Arthur Bryant and Dame Veronica (C. V.) Wedgwood.

Sir Arthur, whose career has included becoming the youngest headmaster in the country at the age of twenty-three, some dabbling in politics, being called to the Bar but never practising, farming, and honorary posts in many learned and charitable institutions, said he was fascinated by English traditional tunes, so we arranged a preliminary meeting for him to hear what the Gramophone Library could offer in that field.

With the help of a librarian with a special knowledge of the subject, we began to explore. Piles of discs, most of them rare 78s, were brought into the listening-room. By the end of the afternoon Sir Arthur had looked through several hundred records, playing snatches of likely ones and putting aside a pile of forty or so to be considered in more detail at a later date.

When we resumed work, we found that some eager junior had put them all away, so we had to start again from scratch, trying to remember the titles of the missing discs.

In the end Sir Arthur chose only one true folk song, the Elizabethan 'Sweet Nightingale', sung by the counter-tenor, Alfred Deller. Most of his other discs were of seventeenth- and eighteenth-century music. He has a passion for dogs, and a sound which was new to the desert island was The Singing Dogs singing 'Pat-a-Cake'.

He likes to work with a background of rhythmic classical music. He described the endless re-writing which is necessary in boiling-down historical facts, taken from hundreds of slips of paper, into one easy-to-read paragraph. 'The harder it is to write', he says, 'the easier it is to read.'

Dame Veronica Wedgwood says she has never been able to manage a card-index or a system involving many slips of paper; she relies on working out an enormous chronology, and then going right into the source documents in order to fill it out.

At Oxford she was a medievalist but became very interested

in seventeenth-century literature, and did a lot of walking in the Oxford countryside, which was well fought over in the Civil War ('and finally, I sort of moved into the seventeenth century altogether'). In fact, only one of her books lies outside that century, a biography of the mid-sixteenth-century William the Silent. 'But,' says Dame Veronica, 'it's analogous – the counter-Reformation period, a period of the religious war.'

I asked whether, after sifting so much evidence, she was a Royalist or a Parliamentarian. She replied that she didn't think she was either, but was what they called, at the time, 'Mister Facing-Both-Ways'.

Although she spoke of the danger of taking too romantic a view of history, her choice of music was unashamedly romantic, and included five operatic excerpts by Massenet, Verdi, Mozart and Beethoven.

The first professional writer I ever met was R. C. Sherriff, who was Captain of Kingston Rowing Club, for which I rowed as a young man, and I felt a thrill of pride when the distinguished author of *Journey's End* took me out on the river and 'tubbed' me. We met again in a BBC studio.

Strange as it may seem, *Journey's End* was written for the club. As with most rowing clubs, there was a shortage of money, the most pressing need being a new set of oars for Henley, and it was decided to put on a show. If copyright material were used then a fee would have to be paid to the author, and that was something the organizers didn't approve of, so they looked round for someone to write something they could put on for nothing. Bob Sherriff took on the job. His first play ran for about fifteen minutes and had twenty-five parts in it, which was good because each of the players could be counted on to sell tickets to admiring relatives and friends.

Each year the show became longer and more ambitious, and always had plenty of parts in it. Then he wrote *Journey's End*, based on his own war experiences, and with a cast of only ten.

For some reason, the Rowing Club didn't produce it, and it was sent to an agent. After some re-writing and a halting start, it has become one of the most performed plays in the English language, and I have seen it stated in print that Sherriff made £300,000 out of it. He was a bachelor, lived in a handsome house in Surrey, and took an interest in rowing until the end of his life. His other hobby was archaeology, especially of the

Roman period, and one of his Oxford memories was of taking the Balliol College eight to dig up a Roman villa in Sussex. 'Very good training for them,' he said.

One of his discs was 'The Eton Boating Song', the rowing man's anthem. He also chose two Verdi excerpts, the Magic Fire Music, from Wagner's *Die Walküre*, and John Boles singing 'It Happened in Monterey', from the film *The King of Jazz*, as a memory of his first glimpse of Hollywood.

'Do you think it seems big-headed if I choose a disc of my own?' It's a question I have been asked many times, and one I always refuse to answer, because it would be breaking my basic rule of never influencing a castaway's choice. Sir Terence Rattigan chose a disc of his own, but it was very far from a solo performance; it was the whole of Harrow School singing the famous 'Forty Years On', recorded on Speech Day, 1928.

From Harrow he went up to Trinity College, Oxford, where he read History, which is still a major interest, and the shelves of his London flat are crammed with books on the subject. His father's idea was that young Terence should follow him into the Diplomatic Service, but he became fervently involved in the Oxford University Dramatic Society and, while still an undergraduate, had a play running at the Comedy Theatre.

Very soon there were about eight Rattigan plays circulating among London managers, while he earned a not very rich living writing film scripts for £15 a week. One of the plays, *French Without Tears*, a comedy based on a period in his life when he had been sent to Wimereux to learn French, was put on at the Criterion Theatre as a stop-gap, and stayed there for about three years. He is the only playwright who has had two plays run for a thousand performances in the West End – the other one was *While the Sun Shines* – and it's probably a record, too, to have had three plays running in three adjoining Shaftesbury Avenue theatres, the Lyric, Apollo and Globe.

His other discs included two arias from Puccini operas, Duke Ellington's Orchestra, Shirley Bassey, Edith Evans and John Gielgud in the Handbag scene from *The Importance of being Earnest*, and one of Noël Coward's songs from the New York production of *The Girl Who Came to Dinner*, which was based on Rattigan's play, *The Sleeping Prince*, and was the only Noël Coward musical never to be played in London.

Ben Travers, a small, twinkling man, was a cheerful eighty-eight when I interviewed him in May 1975. He has been a playwright for fifty-five years.

As a youngster, he was in the family wholesale grocery firm, which he hated, and then in publishing, which he liked. When the First World War broke out, he joined the Royal Naval Air Service: he was the first to drop a torpedo from a land-based aircraft, and during one of the first air raids on London he was sent up, armed with a rifle, to deal with a Zeppelin. He survived eight crashes, seven of which he walked away from.

After the war, he began to write plays and novels, hitting the jackpot with the famous Aldwych Theatre farces – *Rookery Nook*, *Thark*, *Plunder* and half a dozen others – written for the superb and incomparable team of Ralph Lynn, Tom Walls, Robertson Hare and Mary Brough.

One of the reasons why he was grateful for financial success was that he could afford to go to Australia to watch Test matches. Cricket has always been one of his great interests, and he remembers watching a match in which both W. G. Grace and Ranjitsinhji made a century.

After an interval of twenty years, during which he seems to have written nothing except a fascinating autobiography, *Vale of Laughter*, he returned to the West End with *The Bed Before Yesterday*, which has given him a success equal to his Aldwych days.

His discs included the Letter Scene from *Der Rosenkavalier* and the Prelude to Act 3 of *Lohengrin* (His interest in German opera persists since a six months' stay in Dresden at the age of seventeen in order to learn the language); Schumann's *Aufschwung*, played by Artur Rubinstein, Tchaikovsky's Fifth Symphony, some Gilbert and Sullivan, songs by Fats Waller and Maurice Chevalier, and Tom Walls talking about his 1932 Derby win with his horse, April the Fifth.

When I asked him what he would be happy to leave behind him when he set off for the desert island, he said, feelingly, 'My feet!'

When Denise Robins was my guest, she was working on her 166th romantic novel; she says she has slowed down a little nowadays, and no longer writes four a year. It was a need for money that started her writing love stories, otherwise she would have written historical novels.

She says she becomes much too emotionally involved with

her characters, and finds it hard not to burst into tears when her heroine is suffering. Obviously, I had to ask her if she suffered more with her heroines than with her heroes, and the answer was yes. A disciplined writer, she starts work at the same hour each morning, and dictates her books to a secretary. She says that she dictates fluently, the ideas flowing as she goes along. I told her I was going to put her to the test, and asked her to dictate to me the first paragraph of Romantic Novel No. 167, the one she would begin work on next.

She searched a moment for a title, and as we had just walked a long distance from the front entrance of Broadcasting House to a basement studio in the new extension, she hit on *The Long Corridor*. Then, without the slightest hesitation, she began: 'She was in the middle of the dreaded nightmare again. The sinister dream she had dreamed ever since she was a child. She called it "The Long Dark Corridor". When she woke up, bathed in sweat, and crying out, anybody who happened to hear her had come to her and would ask what was wrong, and she would sob *"It's the long, dark corridor again"*.'

If you want to know what happens next, the book has been published; it is now called *Dark Corridor*, because another author had already used the original title. I'm happy to say it is dedicated to me.

As the daughter of a celebrated music critic and singing teacher, Herman Klein, she was brought up with music, and thought little of finding such artists as Paderewski performing on the studio piano. The discs she chose included Bach's Air on the G String, Chopin's Fantaisie Impromptu, Rachmaninov's Rhapsody on a Theme by Paganini, and an excerpt from the first act of *Die Walküre*. Her mother was a writer, and her daughter, Patricia, is too. Her great hobby is her Sussex garden.

A very different sort of writer, from a different background, is David Storey, who was brought up in a mining family in the West Riding of Yorkshire. He decided he wanted to be an artist, so went from grammar school to art school in Wakefield, keeping himself by playing professional Rugby League football, which is a form of organized massacre. He also wrote two novels, which never saw the light of day. In due course he won a scholarship to the Slade School of Fine Art in London. He continued to play Rugby League football, travelling north on Friday evenings and returning to London to spend a couple of days in bed to recover from his injuries.

Having completed three years at the Slade, he became a mathematics teacher in the East End. He was still writing novels, and his eighth, *This Sporting Life*, was bought by the fifteenth publisher to whom he sent it. Both as a novel and as a film it was a success. After publishing two more novels and writing a few screenplays, he spent five years writing a very long novel, which he considered did not work out well enough, so he put it aside. He then wrote six more novels, which he also put aside as unsatisfactory. I asked him if he discarded those works entirely on his own opinion or whether he had showed them to other people. He replied: 'No, it's my own judgment. There should be a feeling of progression from one book to another or one intuitive statement to another, and if I feel there isn't one, then I tend to ditch it.' I have seldom come across such humility and dedication.

His plays he writes very quickly, in two or three days, more or less as by-products, although it seems quite wrong to refer in such a way to a play as sensitive and moving as *Home*.

His discs included music by Stravinsky and Prokofiev, and the third movement of Beethoven's last quartet, together with John Lennon's 'God', for its sense of anarchy, and Anne Shelton singing 'The Anniversary Waltz', to evoke his very early teens, when he started courting in Wakefield.

There are very few writers whose style is so distinctive that just three or four lines will serve to identify it immediately. That is the case with Harold Pinter, whose spare, stylized rendering of everyday speech is so wonderfully effective. In fact, to quote his own words, 'the more acute the experience, the less articulate the expression'.

Brought up in Hackney, in East London, Pinter did not set foot in a theatre until he was fifteen, when he went with a school party to see Donald Wolfit's Shakespeare Company. 'I had no idea what I wanted to be, then I played Macbeth at school, and I realized I couldn't do anything else, so I might as well have a go at acting.'

He was accepted for the Royal Academy of Dramatic Art, but found he could not cope socially with the other students, so he would leave home every morning, as if going to the Academy, but spend the day roaming the streets. That went on for a year. His first engagement was in an Irish fit-up company, playing the classics, followed by a round of English tours and reps. In between times, he was a postman, a book salesman and a chucker-out at a dance-hall. The whole time he was writing, mainly short prose pieces and poems, a few of which were published in magazines.

His first full-length play, *The Birthday Party*, was presented at the Lyric Theatre, Hammersmith, and it was savaged by the critics. His next play was *The Caretaker*, one of the great plays of our time. On this occasion, the critics overdid it. They recognized the worth of the play, but thought there must be much more to it than met the eye and ear. Was it, perhaps, an allegory? Was it a retelling of the Christ story?

I put the question to Pinter. 'Did you mean to say more than you set down?'

He replied: 'I can say quite definitely that I never intended any kind of allegorical significance. I wouldn't know a symbol if I saw one!'

Three of the records he chose were of Bach ('I think I could have devoted the whole programme to Bach'). There were four modern jazz discs. The eighth was the slow movement of the Beethoven Quartet No. 15 in A Minor, Opus 132.

Stephen Potter, ye onlie begetter of Gamesmanship, was a BBC producer, and for a number of years I had the privilege of being one of the 'select members of the *How* Repertory Company', which was how we used to be announced on the air.

The *How* series, on subjects such as 'How to Listen', and 'How to Appreciate Shakespeare,' was devised by Stephen, and Joyce Grenfell.

Stephen was a tall, fair, blue-eyed, good-looking man, with the boyish charm of an undergraduate or a junior don; he could have been cast for either. He was a good actor because his sense of timing was superb, but a limited one because his voice was flat and rather nasal. He liked to tell a story of having auditioned to Mary Hope Allan, in the hope of getting a job reading poetry, but she had turned him down 'because', she said, 'your voice is like Donald Duck's'.

He was a casual dresser and, in the studio, discarded his tweed jacket at the first opportunity, pulling the knot of his blue woollen tie half-way down his chest, so that he could open his shirt. There are some men whose hips are such that they need neither belt nor braces, but this was not the case with Stephen, and by the end of a day in the studio his trousers would have slipped down to the lowest possible limit of safety.

He was a very musical person, and a more than competent pianist. He said that music meant as much to him as writing. He chose Elgar, Beethoven, Stravinsky, Poulenc and Irving Berlin.

We began our *Desert Island Discs* programme with a little planned Gamesmanship.

'Here is Stephen Potter,' I said, then turned to address him. 'Stephen – if I may call you Stephen on this programme, because I think I've known you for about twenty-seven years.'

'Well, why not, Plomley?' he replied.

When I asked him if he were a gregarious man, I already knew the answer, because he was the only man I've ever known to belong to five West End clubs. He denied this, saying that he had resigned from one because the snooker table had been removed. He was an Old Boy of Westminster School, where he achieved the distinction of being the boy to catch the famous Westminster pancake, an achievement which was matched by his son. The chances against that happening have been worked out at eighty thousand to one.

One programme of the one thousand, three hundred and seventy-odd listed at the back of this book is marked 'Not Broadcast': it is the one I recorded with the novelist and broadcaster, E. Arnot Robertson. A few days before the recording was to go on the air, that tall, slim, youthful-seeming woman, still in her fifties, collapsed and died, and the BBC decided that the programme should be replaced by a repeat of a previous one.

Probably her best-known novel was *Four Frightened People*, which was set in Malaysia. The background was vivid and seemingly authentic, and the book was approved by many old Malaysia hands – but she had not visited the country when she wrote it.

An author who stuck to what he knew best was Henry Cecil, whose books and plays, almost without exception, concern the law in its more light-hearted and sensational aspects. In private life, Henry Cecil was His Honour Judge Henry Cecil Leon, a former County Court judge.

His first book, called *Full Circle*, was a collection of short stories which he had invented to tell the troops, to relieve the tedium of a long wartime voyage to the Middle East. He exceeded David Storey's record of perseverance in selling that first book, because it was bought by the seventeenth publisher to whom he sent it.

His first best-seller was a humorous novel called *Brothers-in-Law*, which became a successful play, film, radio series and television series – which is the literary equivalent to being dealt a royal flush. He also wrote on more serious legal matters, and was a campaigner for prison reform.

He and I worked together for some years on a radio series called *Your Verdict*, for the BBC World Service. Each programme features a panel of four listeners, mostly from the Commonwealth and mostly very nervous because they haven't been in a broadcasting studio before. Henry Cecil immediately put them at their ease, chatting to them with benevolent, rather owlish charm, and sometimes putting on a mock-severe 'rocket-from-the-bench' manner. To anyone with worries, he was generous with advice and practical help. We disagreed about music, because his taste was for chamber music and mine is for opera, and we argued amicably.

He freely admitted that he got the idea for his *Brothers-in-Law* series from the *Doctor* books by Richard Gordon.

Not surprisingly, Richard Gordon is the *nom de plume* of a physician, and he is another who uses his two Christian names. He says he wasn't a very good doctor, mainly because he didn't like patients, so he became an anaesthetist, dealing with patients who were asleep and therefore far less troublesome. He supposes the next logical step would have been to become a pathologist; in fact he took a job in charge of the obituary columns of the *British Medical Journal*. After an unfortunate incident in which he confused a living Doctor of Divinity with a defunct Doctor of Medicine, he decided to go to sea as a ship's doctor. He made half a dozen trips, all over the world, and out of sheer boredom sat down to write a comic novel based on his own experiences as a medical student. *Doctor in the House* was an immediate best-seller, and there have now been a dozen or more *Doctor* books, most of which have been filmed.

For him, the worst thing about a desert island exile would be the lack of opportunity to watch cricket, although he has never been much of a cricketer himself. The last time he played was as eleventh man in a team representing *Punch*, and he was very hurt when his captain put him to field behind a tree.

Music is not a great interest of his, but he assembled a list of items which have pleased him at various times. They ranged from the Overture to Handel's *Alcina*, which reminded him of a disastrous prep school production in which he had played Lady Macbeth for laughs and been beaten for it, to a rather bawdy rugger song. A Gilbert and Sullivan item was included because 'this desert island will, of course, be British, as I'm on it, and in all British possessions overseas they play a large amount of Gilbert and Sullivan.'

The book he chose is the *Michelin Guide to France*, which is probably the book I would choose myself. It would be pleasant to sit in the sunshine looking at the street plans of French towns, known and unknown, and imagine walks along picturesque streets. It would be pleasant, too, to choose a good hotel, and to decide which restaurant one would patronize, selecting one of the *spécialités de la maison* as a change from the inevitable boiled fish with coconut chunks. As Richard Gordon said: 'To enjoy all those meals without actually eating them would be very slimming.'

Following in the footsteps of the judge and the physician, a third highly-successful series of vocational comedy novels are being written by a veterinary surgeon. He, too, chose a *nom de plume*, but instead of using his own Christian names he took the name of a footballer he saw on television, James Herriot. ('I thought that was rather a nice name, and I pinched it from him.')

Born in Sunderland, he is the son of two professional musicians. He decided he wanted to work in the open air and, being fond of pets, resolved to be a vet, visualizing a cat-and-dog practice, but the first job that came along was among the hill farms of the Yorkshire dales, and he has now worked in that area for thirty-five years.

So many amusing and extraordinary things happened during his daily round that he kept telling his wife, 'One day, I'm going to write a book about it all.' When he was fifty, he was still saying it, and one day his wife replied, 'People aged fifty don't start writing books,' and he said, 'Oh, is that so?', and wrote one.

He wrote it in the evenings, after his day's work, with his family chattering around him and the television going full blast. He called it *If Only They Could Talk*, it had a better than average sale, and it produced an invitation from his publisher to write another. The second was called *It Shouldn't Happen to a Vet*.

An astute American publisher came across them, put them together in one volume – because the Americans like long books – and, under the title *All Creatures Great and Small*, they were on the American best-seller list for months. Since then, he has written several more books, still with the television blaring, and three or four of them are usually in the list of the top ten paperback sellers. Two of them have been made into films, and Mr Herriot is making a great deal of money, but he says he is still 99 per cent veterinary surgeon and only 1 per cent author and, with the exception of moving into a larger house, he hasn't changed his style of living at all.

All his stories are set in the late 'thirties and early 'forties, before the days of antibiotics, when 'we were always making up our own medicines, trying a little bit of this, a little bit of that . . . when everything was bathed in a touch of witchcraft and black magic.' Nowadays, he says, it's all very scientific and not nearly so amusing.

As a youngster, he played the piano, and later he taught himself the violin, so it was understandable that he chose Schubert's Trio in B Flat Major and 'The Maid and the Nightingale', and Elgar's Violin Concerto in B Minor. His vocal discs were 'Porgi amor', from *The Marriage of Figaro*, Gigli singing 'Panis Angelicus' and Michael Halliday's 'The Story of My Life', and he completed the list with Bob Newhart's 'A Friend with a Dog' and Louis Armstrong and Duke Ellington playing 'Mood Indigo'.

He is devoted to good draught beer, and doesn't have a good opinion about the gaseous stuff which is served in most of the pubs round Broadcasting House.

One of the most successful British authors may well be unknown to you unless you are in touch with children. The Reverend W. Awdry, who writes books about railway engines, such as *Thomas, the Tank Engine* and *Gordon, the Big Engine*, is another who can count his sales in millions.

Tall, gaunt, white-haired, Mr Awdry inherited his love of railways, as well as his vocation for the Church, from his father. Having the good fortune to live within sight of the main line from Paddington to Bristol, they would train-spot together with a telescope. In those days, it wasn't a matter of collecting engine numbers, which seems dreary, but engine names which is much more fun – and, of course, they were steam engines. 'Of all the mechanical contrivances made by man,' says the Reverend Mr Awdry, 'the steam engine is most human.' When I asked him to justify that statement, he said, 'Unless he's at rest, with his fires drawn, a steam engine has always got something to say; he likes you to know how he's getting on and what he's feeling about things.' He went on to describe the boastful, bustling express engine, hauling a train of calm, female carriages who, like dutiful wives, say: 'Just-as-you-say; yes-dear-of-course; just-as-you-say; yes-dear-of-course', in order to make him think that they're listening to what he's saying; and the hard-done-by goods engine which, whether it's got one truck or fifty behind it, always complains that it's very badly treated. And again he lapsed into a steam engine rhythm, but this time it was a dispirited 'I-*can't*-do-it; I-*can't*-do-it'.

Mr Awdry began telling his stories about personalized steam engines to his son, when he was three and had measles. He then had the idea of writing the stories down. All are technically accurate; they have to be, because there are no more demanding classes of reader than children and railway enthusiasts – and when your readers are both at the same time, they are doubly demanding.

He chose a recorded excerpt from one of his own stories, 'Edward and Gordon', read by Johnny Morris, and a number of railway records, such as the sound of a two-cylinder engine, Stanier class, going up a gradient, and a goods engine hauling a train up the one-in-thirty-seven Lickey incline, between Birmingham and Gloucester, followed by a banking engine, which Mr Awdry affirmed was saying 'Don't-be-silly; don't-be-silly; don't-be-silly'. We finished with the sound of the first engine built for the Talyllyn Railway over a hundred years ago, but that one didn't seem to be saying anything – or it may have been saying it in Welsh.

Another celebrated railway buff is Sir John Betjeman who, on the occasion of the first of his two appearances in the series, recorded on a sunny afternoon in 1954, chose a collection of railway noises as one of his discs as well as songs by Randolph Sutton and John McCormack, and the bells of Thaxted Church in Essex. He and I had already done a lot of broadcasting together in *We Beg to Differ*, in which he was a reserve member of the gentlemen's team. One day, a member of the ladies' team was talking about the drab clothes habitually worn by men, and she was obviously getting at John Betjeman, who was wearing a dark suit and a sober tie. After enduring the jokes patiently for a while, he rose to his feet and said: 'Things are not always what they seem,' and threw open his jacket to show that it was lined in crimson. It was hardly good radio, but it was beautifully timed and brought a whoop of delight from the studio audience. It also revealed a facet of a delightful but complex nature.

After our *Desert Island Discs* recording, we came out of Broadcasting House at about a quarter past five. 'It'd be nice to have a drink,' I said, 'but it's a quarter of an hour before opening time.'

'Let's walk up to Marylebone Station,' said John. 'By the time we get there the buffet will be open.'

'All right,' I said. 'Er – why Marylebone Station? Are you catching a train?'

'No,' he replied, 'but the station is a beautiful example of Victorian railway architecture, and it's the only buffet in London where one can hear birdsong.'

They seemed two excellent reasons, so we set off in the sunshine up Portland Place, feeling relaxed and cheerful, having finished our day's work. Another of the discs he had chosen was a catchy May Day song, sung by Cornish villagers, and after a while we both began to sing it. Then, because we felt like it, we began to dance as well.

We sang and danced our way along the pavement, which was almost deserted. Then, bearing down on us, we saw the dignified figure of a very senior BBC official indeed, wearing, as all very senior BBC officials should, an Anthony Eden hat and a double-breasted dark blue Crombie overcoat, and carrying a briefcase and a rolled umbrella. We saw his eyebrows shoot up as he observed the two broadcasters come dancing towards him.

But the future Poet Laureate wasn't in the least abashed. 'Ah, my dear fellow,' he called, 'Come and dance with us.'

And, bless his heart, he did. We all three sang and danced together, belatedly celebrating May Day in far-off Padstow, and then John and I continued on our way to Marylebone Station, which is indeed a beautiful example of Victorian railway architecture and where one could, and please God still can, hear birdsong in the buffet.

5
Musicians

During the early days of *Desert Island Discs*, Ernest Newman, the music critic, devoted several of his *Sunday Times* articles to the series, and wrote that any musician worth his salt would insist on taking scores rather than discs.

I have questioned a number of distinguished musicians about this, and almost unanimously they declare that Mr Newman was right. 'You can give yourself the ideal performance from a score,' said Sir Charles Groves, and Sir Malcolm Sargent, Sir George Solti, Raymond Leppard and Sir Adrian Boult have agreed with him. Not so Sir Arthur Bliss, who said: 'I much prefer sound. Reading scores is rather a dry, musicological occupation. No, I'd like to hear the real stuff.'

Sir Malcolm Sargent shared with Yehudi Menuhin the distinction of being the most efficient castaway among musicians. He knew exactly what he wanted – he had sent in a list of records with full details – and told me the exact sections he required: 'If you start at the beginning of the last movement and play to the end of the tutti, it will be one minute and twenty seconds' – and it was. He was brisk and cheerful, and not a speck of dust marred his neat, dark suit.

On five of his discs, he was conducting himself: *Messiah* ('modesty forbids me mentioning the name of the recording which I think is the best so far'), *The Dream of Gerontius* ('Elgar was a friend whom I loved very dearly'), the Elgar Violin Concerto, with Heifetz ('which for me has associations of great value'), Dohnányi's Suite for Orchestra in F Sharp Minor ('a critic once wrote that this is café music; he must have gone to some jolly good cafés') and one of the Beethoven Piano Concertos, with Schnabel as soloist ('quite magnificent'). The others were the Sanctus from the Bach Mass in B Minor and Beethoven's Ninth Symphony, both conducted by Herbert von Karajan, and Kreisler playing 'Caprice Viennois'.

Mr Menuhin's approach was different. The list he sent us was vague, so we had a huge pile of discs waiting for him. He attacked them with great enthusiasm and enormous speed; his first sorting was like watching a terrier at a rabbit hole, expect that it was discs flying to either side instead of earth. His sense of enjoyment of music was shown by his decision to follow Brunnhilde's Immolation, from the last act of *Götter-dämmerung*, by an excerpt from Anna Russell's irreverent telling of the *Ring* story. He also chose an excerpt from Bach's *St Matthew Passion*, Georges Thill singing the Flower Song from *Carmen*, Irmgard Seefried singing Schubert's 'Heiden-röslein', Bartok's Quartet No. 2 in A Minor, Beethoven's Seventh Symphony, and Dylan Thomas reading his own poem, 'And Death Shall Have No Dominion'.

He described his first meeting with Elgar, in the summer of 1932, before recording his Violin Concerto. Young Yehudi had prepared it on his own, and he was to play through the work, with Ivor Newton at the piano, so that he could receive the composer's last admonitions. 'We'd only played about two or three minutes of it when he got up and said that he had heard enough, that it was quite satisfactory, and that he was off to the races.'

I believe that *Desert Island Discs* has made one positive contribution to the nation's musical history. I was interviewing André Previn, whose early career encompassed countless Holly-wood film scores and some first-rate jazz piano discs. I asked him; 'If the telephone were to ring tonight with an offer, a suggestion, what would you like it to be?' Without hesita-tion he answered, 'That's very simple. I'd like to be offered the post of Conductor in Chief of the London Symphony Orchestra.' It was only a few months later that the news of his appointment to that post was announced. Of course, it could have been coincidence, but it's nicer to think that it wasn't.

Although, at that time, he was associated to a large extent with twentieth-century music, he chose only one work by a contemporary composer, the Dies Irae from Britten's *War Requiem*. His other discs consisted of three pieces by Mozart, two by Beethoven, and one each by Brahms and Debussy.

An unexpected choice of discs was made by Leopold Stokowski. After Bach, Mozart, Beethoven, Brahms, Debussy and Tchaikovsky, he wanted a jazz disc of 'Are You From Dixie?' and an Argentine tango.

I found him a rather aloof man and, at that time, a lonely one. In the studio he was unhelpful; when the programme engineer asked for more voice, he refused and asked pointedly if the BBC could not provide amplification. We were recording in the evening, and we left Broadcasting House quite late. He asked me if I would care to have supper with him, as he had nowhere to go and he did not want to return to his hotel. I accepted with pleasure, and he asked me to suggest a restaurant. It was too late to take him to one of my clubs, where I could have offered him the cheerful companionship of other artists, so I suggested Verreys because it was near at hand. It happened to be an off-night, and the restaurant was deserted, but his mood had changed and he was a most entertaining host.

When I was a young actor, I took singing lessons, and I used to hang around the Royal College of Music. I wasn't enrolled there, but I used to pick up odd crumbs of knowledge and, a more important reason, I had a more than passing interest in a dark-haired soprano in the Opera Class. Among my acquaintances of those days was a tall, round-faced student whose principal study was the organ, but who changed direction to be an accompanist. In fact, he used to accompany the dark-haired soprano. More than thirty years later, I met him again when Sir Charles Groves, the rubicund conductor of the Royal Liverpool Philharmonic Orchestra, visited the desert island.

Almost the first job he obtained when he left the College was as a rehearsal pianist for Toscanini, and for Sir Thomas Beecham.

'How did they compare?' I asked.

'They were both fire and brimstone people, but Beecham had more charm. Toscanini used to call Beecham "Arlequino" or "Pagliacci", and Beecham used to refer to Toscanini as "Poor old Toscanini" or "a military bandmaster".'

A piece of modern music which Sir Charles chose struck me as especially suitable for a desert island – Messiaen's 'Quartet for the End of Time'. It was written in a prisoner-of-war camp in Poland, and shows amazing tranquillity under such circumstances. His other choices included Schubert's Ninth Symphony, conducted by Furtwängler, Beethoven's Ninth Symphony, conducted by Beecham, Jon Vickers singing Sigmund's 'Spring Song', from *Die Walküre*, Diana Maddox singing Polly Garter's song, from *Under Milk Wood*, Heddle Nash singing the Dream Song, from Massenet's *Manon*, and Guy Oldham's 'Alleluia on a Plainsong Melody' by the Choir of King's College, Cambridge.

Sir George Solti has also acted as rehearsal pianist for Toscanini – at Salzburg in 1936. This ebullient Hungarian is a man of decided views: he told me he doesn't like Bellini and Donizetti very much, and when I ventured to suggest that there should be more French opera in the repertoire of the Royal Opera House, Covent Garden, of which he was then Musical Director, he replied, scornfully: 'What French opera? There is no French opera.' It seems strange that a man holding such views should go on to become Musical Adviser to the Paris Opéra, which is one of the posts he holds at the moment. I can only assume that he advises the Parisians not to perform French opera, because of eleven new productions announced as I write, only two (by Massenet) are French, against nine from the Italian and German repertoires. Obviously, there is nothing by Bellini or Donizetti.

He is a man of relentless energy, but when I asked him if there was any truth in the famous story that when conducting *Götterdämmerung* he had spent the interval in his office getting on with the casting of *Moses and Aaron*, he denied it. He had not been casting the other opera, he said, he had been getting on with some urgent work for the next day!

For his desert island, he chose Toscanini conducting the Verdi Requiem, Mozart's String Quintet in G Minor, the Love Duet from *Tristan und Isolde*, Schumann's Piano Concerto in A Minor, Mahler's Tenth Symphony, an excerpt from Verdi's *Falstaff*, and two spoken records, John Gielgud reading the Shakespeare sonnet, 'When my love swears that she is made of truth', and Sir Winston Churchill's wartime speech including the words 'I have nothing to offer but blood, toil, tears and sweat'.

A distinguished conductor whom I have known for many years is Charles Mackerras, now Musical Director of the English National Opera. In the early 'fifties we worked together on a series of musical-comedy programmes, for which I wrote the scripts and he conducted the BBC Concert Orchestra. In the Australian musical scene, in which he spent his early years, there was little scope for specialization, and he began his career in commercial radio, scoring everything from jazz jingles to concert pieces, and playing the oboe in his own arrangements. He is a fiercely dedicated worker and, on the first of the two occasions on which he appeared in *Desert Island Discs*, he insisted on carrying through the recording, although suffering agony from an impacted wisdom tooth.

In both his programmes, he chose three operatic excerpts: in the first, from Mozart's *The Marriage of Figaro*, Verdi's *Nabucco* and Bellini's *Norma*; in the second, from Verdi's *Otello*, Janacek's *The Makropulos Case* and Wagner's *Die Walküre*. Each time, Mozart was featured among his other records: the Clarinet Concerto in the first programme, the Quintet for Clarinet and Strings in A Major, K. 581, and the 'Prague' symphony in the second.

On the first occasion, he included his own recording of Handel's 'Music for the Royal Fireworks', for which he had assembled the wind ensemble originally envisaged by the composer. It includes twenty-six oboes and fourteen bassoons.

'Where did you find twenty-six oboists?' I asked.

'There are about fifty in London. To get the best ones we made the recording late at night, when all concerts and broadcasts and operas were over.'

It's a splendid piece of music, and sounds even better in its original version.

Another conductor to strike a blow for the wind instrument is Raymond Leppard. As Musical Adviser to the Royal Shakespeare Theatre, he decided that the music to the Shakespeare plays must be integrated into the performance, so he formed a wind band, which frequently appears on stage and which is admirable at providing music on the move.

Mr Leppard's main musical interests lie in the seventeenth and eighteenth centuries. While on a sabbatical term from an academic post at Cambridge, he went to live in Venice, hoping to find Monteverdi manuscripts among the huge piles of unsorted material in the libraries. No lost works of Monteverdi turned up, but he discovered two operas by his pupil Cavalli, which had not been performed for three hundred years and which, restored and orchestrated, have proved much to the taste of modern opera-goers. 'And there are lots more,' says Mr Leppard. 'It's just a question of finding them.'

Such research work, through manuscripts undisturbed for hundreds of years, must be unimaginably exciting. Just think what could turn up! Monteverdi's manuscripts, yes – but possibly even a play in Shakespeare's hand, because many scholars are convinced he travelled to Italy as a young man.

He included no Cavalli among his discs but a Monteverdi madrigal, 'Chiome d'Oro'. He also chose excerpts from Bach's

The author, cast away on the Thames foreshore

above Harold Pinter in the studio

below Sir Noël Coward

B Minor Mass, Verdi's *Falstaff*, Hugo Wolf's 'Italian Serenade', 'When Corals Lie', from Elgar's *Sea Pictures*, sung by Janet Baker, the Liebestod from *Tristan und Isolde* sung by Kirsten Flagstad, 'Le Marteau sans Maître' by Pierre Boulez, and a Eudosia Welty short story.

Few musicians can have been given a more challenging assignment than Sir Adrian Boult when, soon after he had been appointed BBC Director of Music, he was invited to form a symphony orchestra of a hundred and twenty musicians. He was its conductor for twenty years, and as it is virtually a national orchestra, he had the responsibility of covering the whole musical repertoire, as well as giving first performances of works by most of Britain's foremost composers.

Early in the war, the orchestra, based in Bristol, was bombed out. Sir Adrian remembers a performance of Borodin's Second Symphony by the light of a few hurricane lamps.

A gentle, quiet man, whose background is very English, he studied music in Germany. His desert island choice seems to match his personality faultlessly. He selected two pieces by Mozart – Bruno Walter conducting the Columbia Symphony Orchestra in a rehearsal of the 'Linz' Symphony, and his own recording of the Horn Concerto in E Flat, with Aubrey Brain as soloist – Weber's Overture to *Der Freischütz*, conducted by Arthur Nikisch, for whom he has a great admiration, and Elena Gerhardt singing a Brahms song. 'The Blacksmith', with Nikisch at the piano; part of the Silver Jubilee Message to the Empire by King George V, and a Vaughan Williams Anthem from the Coronation Service of Queen Elizabeth II; an excerpt from *Job*, A Masque for Dancing, also by Vaughan Williams, and the Overture to Rossini's *The Silken Ladder*.

If Rossini seems slightly out of place in that list, it fits in better when I explain that Sir Adrian chose it as an example of the sounds that Toscanini produced from the BBC Symphony Orchestra, as guest conductor, and obviously Italian music suited the Italian guest best.

Sir Michael Tippett chose nothing by Beethoven, or Mozart, or Brahms – 'I would have them inside myself'.

At the Royal College of Music, he studied composition and conducting and the piano. He decided that he wasn't good enough to earn a living as a conductor, so he took a job as a schoolmaster, teaching French, so that, by living simply, he could find time to compose. He thought of himself as a slow developer and, because of that, withdrew his early works, including his First Symphony. It wasn't until he was nearly thirty that he wrote anything which he considered worthy of publication.

During the war he became Director of Music at Morley College, an activity that was interrupted by a spell in prison for his pacifist principles. It would have been easy for him to avoid going to prison, because the work he was doing was considered important enough to exempt him from military service, but he elected to serve the sentence.

From his experience of a prison cell, he could visualize the ordeal of desert island existence, but he declared that the inner life is so strong that through inner feelings and, he supposed, music, he would feel that every human being could be present to him; he would not feel deeply alone.

He left Morley College in 1951, to become a full-time composer. He was then half way through his opera, *Midsummer Marriage*, and it needed his whole attention. It took six or seven years of such hard work that his health suffered.

The records he chose were of the Schubert Quintet in C Major ('fascinating and beautiful'); Dido's Lament, 'When I am laid in earth' from *Dido and Aeneas*, by Purcell ('the great English figure, the one great composer'); 'Siegfried's Journey to the Rhine', from Wagner's *Götterdämmerung* ('where you are spellbound from sound to sound'); the Monteverdi madigral, 'Chiome d'Oro' ('delicate, gay and yet virile'); Bessie Smith singing 'St Louis Blues', with Louis Armstrong ('This is where I learned nearly everything'); the opening of his own Second Symphony ('this sort of virility, which I value in myself'); Charles Ives's 'The Fourth of July' ('extreme tenderness, extreme apprehension') and Stravinsky's 'Symphonies of Wind Instruments' ('a sort of hieratic Russian element').

If he were allowed to take only one disc, it would be 'St Louis Blues', and the one book he chose was Homer's *Odyssey* 'because that's about the sea, and about islands, and then he did, after all, come back again to Ithica'.

I asked him, 'If a few minutes, and a few minutes only, of your work were to be preserved for posterity, which section of which composition would you choose?' He thought for a moment, and decided that it wouldn't be from one of his big works, but a song, such as his setting of 'Full fathom five thy father lies', which he had made for an Old Vic production of

The Tempest, 'partly because Shakespeare and *The Tempest* mean so much, partly because it is a very tender and a very small, but perhaps almost forgettable, song'.

As I have mentioned, we do not like recording *Desert Island Discs* in hotel rooms or, in fact, anywhere away from BBC premises, so when Liberace, on his first visit to London, said he would appear in the programme only if we would record it in his suite at the Savoy Hotel, we said, 'Thank you very much; some other time', because being young and active, there seemed no reason why he should not get into a taxi and travel a few hundred yards in a north-westerly direction. The second time he came to London he didn't argue; Mahomet came to the mountain.

An amusing man with a talkative charm, born in Winconsin of Italian, German and Polish stock, he began his career as a child vaudeville artist, playing the piano, singing and dancing. When he was sixteen he played the Liszt A Major Piano Concerto with the Chicago Symphony Orchestra, but the rewards in the lush fields of light music looked greater. He was given a television series, and the flamboyant clothes, the candelabra on the piano, and the rest of the gimmicks were built up as a running gag, becoming more outrageous each week. He is modest about his success and claims to be no more than a competent pianist who has been lucky enough to strike it rich. 'Nothing was ever handed to me,' he said. 'I had to fight for it.' He it was who, when asked if he worried about poor notices from the critics, coined the famous phrase: 'I cry all the way to the bank.'

There is a curious ingenuousness in Liberace's character; for example, he chose Richard Strauss's 'Death and Transfiguration' as one of his discs because he associated it with a painting of the Crucifixion, commissioned by Paderewski, in Forest Lawns cemetery in Los Angeles. ('It's a hundred and twenty feet long, it's a magnificent masterpiece, and the music that is interpolated during the narrator's description of this painting is "Death and Transfiguration" '). His other discs included music by Tchaikowsky, Rachmaninov, Rimsky-Korsakov and Puccini, together with three show tunes.

He defended his habit of getting through condensed versions of such works as Tchaikovsky's First Piano Concerto in four minutes flat ('I feel that half a loaf is better than no bread').

An artist we gladly went to the Savoy Hotel to record is Artur Rubinstein, whom John Lade and I found practising in his suite overlooking the Thames. White-haired and gentle, he still gets through a concert schedule that would tire a man half his age. He is wonderfully well preserved, his skin white and clear. 'I am grateful to have reached my age in this condition,' he said, 'I can still run, even. Yes, I made a race with a young lady and outran her.'

He has three homes – in France, Switzerland and Spain – but he is at home almost everywhere in the world. There is one country, however, which he will not visit: he never goes to Germany, 'out of respect for the dead' – and among those dead are his whole family.

He was born in Lodz, in a part of Poland then under Russian domination. Seeing that he had musical talents, when he was four years old his parents bought him a violin, but he deliberately broke the instrument because he was devoted to the piano. At the age of fifteen he went to live in Paris.

The first years of his career were inevitably a mixture of success and failure. At the age of twenty, being lonely and bitter and completely without money, he seriously considered suicide. When he was first established, he almost threw away his career by acquiring a reputation as a playboy. As a young man he did not take much pride in being a pianist because, in past times, pianists had usually been composers who happened to play the piano too, and to be a pianist without being a composer seemed inferior.

Remembering that he had lived in Hollywood for a number of years and had appeared in several films, I asked him if the world of films intrigued him. He assured me that it had, very much indeed, and that he is still a passionate filmgoer, able to endure three features in a day.

He said he did not take kindly to the idea of *Desert Island Discs* because it expected him to limit himself, instead of enriching and adding something to his life. Most of the music he chose is chamber music, which he believes is more suitable for recording than concert music, because records are usually played in the home. At his request, I did not specify the artists who were performing.

His list comprised the Brahms Piano Quartet in A ('it goes deeper than the other two'), the Beethoven String Quartet in F, Opus 59 No. 1 ('I cried when I heard it for the first time'), a

song from Schubert's *Winterreise* ('I heard it as a young boy'),
Bartok's Concerto for Orchestra ('it's a great work'), Mozart's
Piano Concerto in C Minor ('it shows the real Mozart, not the
Baroque Mozart'), Chopin's Nocturne in E Flat Major, Opus 9
No. 2 ('to listen to on a lovely night, with the moon shining
and a lovely girl next to me . . . better still, my wife, of
course'), Schubert's Piano Sonata in B Flat ('I love to play it.
Each time, it's a great experience and an honour to put my
fingers on it'), and Schubert's String Quintet in C. That last
piece has first place in his heart. He remembered evenings in
Chelsea, many years ago, when he and his friends, Ysaye,
Thibaud, Kreisler, Casals and Lionel Tertis, would make music
until seven or eight o'clock in the morning, and the Schubert
Quintet was always the highlight. He said that at the moment
of his death he would like his wife to play to him a record
of the second movement.

For his one luxury to take to the island, he could only think
of a revolver, because he was sure he would kill himself after
a few days of isolation.

It was Erich Leinsdorf who explained to me why the supply
of great Jewish virtuosi is now diminishing. In the years of
tyranny, musical prowess was a way out of the ghetto, and
Jewish mothers would force a child through hours and hours
of daily practice on the violin or piano in the hope that even-
tual international recognition, which transcends all racial
barriers, would provide a way of escape. In our more enlightened days, it is likelier that bright young Jewish boys will be
put to such surer fields as accountancy or economics.

Obviously, the programmes I enjoy most are those with old
friends. In introducing Spike Hughes, I was baffled by what to
describe him as, because he has fulfilled most functions in the
musical and literary worlds. He had the good fortune to
spend his childhood being dragged about Europe by a splen-
didly eccentric mother, so he is able to operate in three or
four languages.

For some years, he concentrated on jazz and, in the early
thirties, produced a number of discs, with British musicians,
which were far ahead of their time and which still have many
admirers. (Some of the discs, made for Decca, were recorded
under the inspired name of Spike Hughes and his Deccadents.)
A number of his compositions were linked to form the score
of the first jazz ballet, *High Yellow*, which the Camargo

Society presented at the Savoy Theatre in 1932, and which provided the unprecedented spectacle of brass players of the London Symphony Orchestra using bowler hats to mute their instruments.

In January 1933, he went to New York, planning to spend a couple of weeks looking round the city and listening to a few bands, but he plunged into hectic musical activity, which culminated in three recording sessions at which he directed such jazz greats as Benny Carter, Coleman Hawkins, Luis Russell, Chu Berry and Henry Allen in a dozen of his own compositions. Returning to London after four months, he decided that there were no higher jazz pinnacles to be reached, so he resolved to clear his mind of the subject and turn to serious music criticism and, later, the composition of *Cinderella*, the first opera ever to be written for television.

When I first knew Spike, during the latter years of the war, he was living in All Souls Place, a cul-de-sac between All Souls Church and Broadcasting House, which was very handy and enabled him to broadcast a whole week of *Housewives' Choice* programmes in his pyjamas (with sweater and trousers over them) before breakfasting. His immediate neighbours were Constant Lambert and Michael Ayrton, and the social life of all three centred on a pub called The George, just round the corner in Mortimer Street. Spike liked to refer to it as his permanent address, and even had mail addressed there. Leaning on the bar, with a pint of mild-and-bitter at his elbow, he kept the nearest to office hours that our foolish licensing hours allow. It was a convenient arrangement, because everybody knew where to find him, and anyone wishing to book him for a broadcast or a magazine piece could seal a contract in beer, which is more binding than ink.

Grey-eyed, balding, with a shy smile that charmed extra guineas from tight-fisted editors and booking managers, Spike was going through a non-sartorial phase, and his overcoat and jacket were frayed and torn. Perhaps he thought that even further guineas could be extracted by signs of apparent need.

He was at that time married to Barbara McFadyean, a pretty, dark-haired girl who broadcast regularly on the Overseas Service. Barbara's tastes in social life were more formal than Spike's. and she tried to prise him away from The George to put on untorn clothes and preside at dinner parties In fact, she insisted that they move to a large house in St John's

Wood, where they could give larger dinner parties, but all it meant was that she had further to go in order to fetch him home.

I believe it was a deliberate affectation of his that he never allowed anyone actually to see him working. His output was prolific, and included two wise and witty volumes of autobiography, and every script or article that was commissioned arrived precisely on deadline, but whether he wrote late at night or early in the morning, nobody knew. His afternoons he used to spend in an inexpensive and excellent Italian restaurant, known as Soave's, in Great Portland Street, and an expensive and scruffy backstreet club. I once persuaded him to go back to All Souls Place in the middle of the afternoon to knock out four hundred words which I needed in a hurry for a magazine programme. He put on an old cricketing blazer as his working costume before he sat down at the typewriter and by the time I had drunk one glass of his claret the piece was finished, and he hadn't even stopped talking while he was writing it.

Cricket was important to Spike in those days, and he ran a team of his own. The club tie was a pattern of the Roman numbers VII and XIII on a green ground, because XI players had never turned up for a match. Only Away matches were played, all on the strict understanding that stumps would be drawn sharp at Opening Time.

Early in the nineteen-fifties, Spike and Barbara parted, and he married Charmian Newton, known as 'Chim'. For the past nineteen years, they have lived in a 1603 farmhouse near Glyndebourne Opera House, and he has settled down to writing books on music and, with Chim, food. I wish he would do more broadcasting, because he is one of the best in the business, and I wish he would write a third volume of autobiography, and I wish he would come more often to London to see his friends.

His discs for the island comprised Mozart, Johann Strauss, Verdi, Duke Ellington, Ravel, Beethoven, his own jazz orchestra, and the voice of Dinah Shore.

A jazzman who provided me with a really first-rate programme is Count Basie. It was in 1957, during the Count's first visit to Britain. His sponsors had given him a murderous schedule : within one period of forty-eight hours he played concerts in Glasgow, London, Southend and Cardiff. As a result, the only time he was available to come to Broadcasting House was in the early morning, a time when the Count is not at his best. He was not fully awake, but he revived after we had sent out for what he claimed to be his usual breakfast, several bottles of Coca-Cola.

Through the years, ever since he started his band, in 1935, as Bill Basie and his Orchestra, he has ignored all passing crazes and stuck to what he describes as 'Kansas City style, with four heavy beats to the bar, and no cheatin' '. He selected for his exile discs by Ella Fitzgerald, Fats Waller, Tommy Dorsey, Billy Eckstein, Louis Armstrong, Sarah Vaughan and Duke Ellington.

The reason why he had never played in this country before was because of an idiotic Trade Union ban which had kept out all American bands since 1934, seemingly on the rather insulting premise that British bands couldn't compete with them.

The very first American band to play here, after the twenty-two years' interdiction, had been Stan Kenton's, the year before. In contrast to Basie's cheerful conservatism, Kenton had evolved a jazz sound all his own, and was innovating and experimenting all the time. I found him a strange man, claiming to be absolutely devoid of any feelings of sentimentality or nostalgia. He travelled with one suitcase, and the brown suit he wore was the only suit he possessed, and when it was worn out he would throw it away and buy another. He wanted no possessions.

His mother was a piano teacher, who tried many times during his childhood to persuade him to take an interest, but without result. Suddenly, when he was about fourteen, he became obsessed with the idea of learning to play the piano and of making a living by doing so. At sixteen he was playing in a café for fifty cents a night. The music he liked playing best was jazz, and he decided that the best way to develop a good jazz style was to listen incessantly to Louis Armstrong.

As soon as he could get some money together, he formed his first band; but he didn't just build a commercial group with which he could experiment slowly; he wanted to start straight away with a fresh sound. After many growing pains, he achieved what he wanted – challenging, contemporary music. 'It's like a modern painting. I don't think you can ever absorb it all, because there's too much going on.'

His desert island music was an unusual mixture; Bartok's Concerto for Orchestra, Louis Armstrong, Duke Ellington, Frank Sinatra, Jacques Ibert's 'Escales', Tennessee Ernie Ford, and his own band.

To interview Louis Armstrong, the greatest jazz figure of all, I went to Leeds. Satchmo was playing at one of the big northern clubs in near-by Batley, and, together with his musicians and entourage, had been given the nearest the Queen's Hotel could get to a soundproof wing, because he enjoyed listening to his own old discs – at top volume.

We were to record in the BBC studios in Woodhouse Lane, and I waited in the hotel lobby while his manager went up to his suite to collect him. This was in 1968 and Louis, already sixty-seven, had begun to take a great interest in his health; he travelled with his own doctor, and was keeping to a strict diet. He had slimmed down to about half his former weight, and was a great believer in speedy elimination. 'As soon as you've tasted it, man, get rid of it,' he told me. His manager had warned me that I would probably be offered one of Louis's special pills, which I was to accept but under no circumstances take, as it would very likely blow me inside out.

He came out of the lift, and his manager escorted him across the lobby. He was indeed a slight figure compared with the portly Satchmo I had seen on stage and screen. We were introduced; Louis was distantly polite. It was obvious that he would much rather be up in his suite playing his old records, and had no desire to take a taxi-ride across Leeds to be interviewed. He was only to be with me for an hour or so, and I saw that I would have to win his confidence quickly if our recording was to be a success.

'You and jazz were both born in New Orleans,' I said. He acknowledged the familiar line patiently.

'My mother was raised in that city,' I said.

He nodded politely. 'Is that so?'

'I believe, as a kid, you used to sell the *Times-Democrat* in the streets. My grandfather and my uncle were on the staff of that paper.'

'You don't say?'

'Fact. So that means we're practically related.'

He grinned – and we were friends.

Five of the records he chose were his own. He liked playing his old ones.

6

Artists and Designers

I have found artists to be modest people. Whereas the conversation of writers is inclined to centre on the number of copies sold, and that of actors on the numbers of performances played, it is seldom, if ever, that an artist will tell you how many pictures he has sold, or even where they may be seen on show – and, much more than among writers and actors, there is gratitude and acknowledgment to the great ones of the past.

Pietro Annigoni is completely in the thrall of the old masters. While admitting that the French Impressionists were great artists, he looks on Impressionism as the sunset of a great period, and not the dawn of anything worthwhile. He dismisses most modern art as symptomatic of the diseases of our present society, and it is appropriate that his studio in Florence should be in a fifteenth-century building. Using what he believes to be the methods of the old Venetian masters, he makes his own paints.

He was only six when he decided that painting was to be his life. He studied in Florence, but found formal art training of little use, and worked mostly on his own. I asked him if he remembered the first picture he ever sold, and he told me his first remuneration was fifty lire for sketching a few figures on a large architectural drawing of a proposed new building. At that time, Annigoni was going through a phase of sketching beggars, and the architect wasn't very pleased to see beggars all around his fine new creation.

There was little response to his work by London dealers until his striking self-portrait was shown at the Royal Academy. The next year, he gave his first one-man show in London, and a few years later he was commissioned to paint his first full-length portrait of the Queen, bare-headed, wrapped in the blue mantle of the Order of the Garter, with the Order blazing at her breast.

Nowadays, there is always a queue of rich and famous people waiting to commission portraits, but he paints only three or four a year. Many of his finest paintings are of religious subjects. Knowing that he had been brought up in an anti-clerical household, I asked him about this.

'Anti-clerical doesn't mean anti-religious,' he said. 'I am myself rather agnostic, but with a great nostalgia for religion.'

On the east side of Broadcasting House is a narrow one-way street, running into Langham Place. Traffic shoots round the corner very quickly, and it is not a place to linger. We were crossing that street, when Annigoni stopped with a gasp of admiration. He had caught sight of Nash's beautifully proportioned spire of All Souls Church. I took his arm to lead him on, because we were both likely to be mown down at any moment. He shook off my hand and looked his fill.

The music he loves is by Beethoven, Corelli, Mozart, Vitali and Verdi.

Michael Ayrton was another artist who owed little to formal studies. 'I studied in a sort of vague way in Vienna and Paris and London, but really I studied in the museums, and studied the great masters, who taught me everything I know.' He certainly studied the great masters thoroughly, because one of the most impressive feats of memory I have seen was his performance in a television series called _Animal, Vegetable and Mineral_, in which a panel was shown objects from the past and asked to identify them. Ayrton was shown photographs of details from paintings that are far from well known, and would immediately give the names of the artists, the subjects of the whole pictures, the galleries in which they are to be found – and he probably threw in a description of the frames as well.

His talents matured very early; he was only nineteen when John Gielgud invited him to design a new production of _Macbeth_. His great ambition was to emulate a Renaissance artist and plan an entire building from start to finish, designing the structure in association with architects, then painting it, doing frescoes in it, placing sculpture, and designing and making everything to embellish it. He was very much a Renaissance man, and Italy was his second home.

Since his early years, he had a musical obsession, being irresistibly drawn to everything about the life and works of Hector Berlioz. He drew fanciful portraits of Berlioz many times, wrote and presented a fascinating television programme about him, and had a collection of almost all of his music which had been recorded. He restrained himself sufficiently to allow Berlioz only a quarter of his desert island listening time, in the form of an excerpt from the scene in Dido's garden by the sea, from *Les Troyens*, and the mightiest moment in the *Grande Messe des Morts*.

He also chose two arias from Mozart operas – *The Marriage of Figaro* and *Don Giovanni*. I remember being very impressed when, one evening, I was dining with him and Wynford Vaughan-Thomas as guests of the late Pat Dixon. The conversation turned to Mozart, and Wynford mentioned one of the Don's arias in *Don Giovanni* as being a favourite. Michael began to sing it, in Italian, and Wynford joined him. Together, they sang it all the way through in clear, true voices and, especially as we were dining by candlelight, the effect was delightful.

To complete his eight records, Michael chose items from operas by Bellini, Gluck and Purcell, and a Baroque piece for double brass choir by the Venetian composer, Gabrielli. For his luxury, he chose a piece of Greek sculpture of a man carrying a calf. 'It's about three thousand years old, it's not very large, and it's rather fragmentary; and it has in it all the mystery, all the timelessness, all the absolute silence which an ultimately great work of art has.'

John Piper started in his father's solicitors' office, for which he was quite unsuited, and he confessed to having spent much of the firm's time visiting the Leicester Gallery and queuing for the ballet.

As a small boy, he developed a great interest in topography and architecture, and by the time he was fourteen he had bicycled to practically every church in Surrey.

Having given up the law, he studied at Richmond School of Art and then at the Royal College. He says his greatest early influences were Braque, Picasso and Cézanne. For some years, his paintings were abstract, but 'at the beginning of the war it was impossible to go on painting completely abstract pictures in isolated ivory towerism. I think that's why I started looking at architecture with such intensity, thinking that one might not have any architecture left once the bombs started raining down.' With a number of other artists, he became engaged on a project called Recording Britain, making pictorial records of historic and interesting buildings which might become war casualties.

Then he joined the RAF, only to be whisked out and told to

go to Windsor to make some drawings of the castle. He made a fine series of studies, in the dramatic style for which he is famous, and afterwards was invited to show them to the King and Queen. His Majesty looked at them, reacting to the stark outlines and lowering clouds, and said, mildly, 'You had very bad weather while you were working here.'

In recent years, his painting has moved into the abstract again, 'but it's always veering between the abstract and the non-abstract, especially the topographical. This seems to provide the two poles in my painting life, and one gets some kind of tension going between them, which occasionally produces something.'

Mr Piper has designed a number of Benjamin Britten's operas, so it was natural that he should choose an excerpt from one of them, and also natural that the one he selected should be *The Turn of the Screw*, for which his wife, Myfanwy, wrote the libretto.

His very favourite composer is Mozart, and he chose the Sinfonia Concertante and the opening bars of *Don Giovanni*, 'the greatest opera of all time'. He is also devoted to Stravinsky's music and asked for an excerpt from *Apollon Musagète*. His lighter tastes were catered for by Fred and Adele Astaire singing a Gershwin song, and the Earl Hines Trio playing 'A Cottage for Sale'. For his book, he chose James Joyce's *Ulysses*, and as his luxury 'a whacking big Turner landscape . . . that great view from the drawing-room windows of Petworth Park, with the sunset, and the stags in the foreground'.

John Bratby chose eight pieces of pop sung by, among others, Anne Shelton, Elvis Presley and Shirley Temple.

Mr Bratby paints with great vigour and gusto and vitality, and he likes to work on a large scale. He had a wonderful opportunity to do so when he was commissioned to provide the huge pictures Alec Guinness was supposed to have painted in the film of Joyce Cary's novel, *The Horse's Mouth*.

He was one of the first artists about whose work critics used the words 'kitchen sink', because he was painting, with earthy realism, the mechanics of life around him. He explained that phase of his life with the logical statement that, as a poverty-stricken young painter, there was nothing around him to paint but a poverty-stricken interior. He still likes to paint what, or who, is near to hand, so when he was asked to paint the Nativity, the obvious choice of model for the Virgin Mary was his wife, and when he portrays the face of God, 'the easiest, convenient, malleable object is myself'. He paints quickly and, in the single day before our recording, he had completed a picture three feet by four feet.

In contrast, David Hockney tells me he can complete only about ten pictures each year. His portraits are unorthodox, and that of the late Sir David Webster, which has probably been reproduced more often than any other of his pictures, shows his subject sitting on a spindly metal-legged chair, looking across at a bunch of tulips set on a glass table, and Sir David occupies only about ten per cent of the canvas. 'I probably spent longer painting the tulips than I did him,' said Hockney thoughtfully. 'You see, I really didn't know him, and I really didn't get to know him – and it makes a difference to me.'

The first time he came into the public eye was as a student at the Royal College of Art, when he went up to receive a gold medal wearing a gold lamé coat. 'Well, the coat's not really gold, but their medal wasn't gold either.' Shortly afterwards, he decided that his hair should be gold, and he continues to wear it that way.

It is unusual for an artist in his thirties to be accorded a retrospective exhibition, but in 1972 it happened to Hockney. He had nothing to do with the organization or arrangement of it, and he went to the opening very apprehensively. 'I thought the early pictures just wouldn't stand up, and they'd be a bit thin.'

'Did the pattern of change through the ten years of your painting life seem to have a regular curve?' I asked him.

'I must admit I was slightly impressed with it, because I saw there was a continuity in the work.'

He moves in a male world, and that's the world he likes to paint. Women rarely feature in his work.

His records included Jeannette MacDonald singing 'San Francisco', because the song is about California, and because he had heard it sung in a San Francisco bar by a drag queen sitting on a swing, who looked exactly like Miss MacDonald. His other discs included Poulenc, Satie, two Wagner arias, the opening of Giordano's *Fedora*, and Marilyn Monroe singing 'I'm Through With Love'.

He is the only castaway, to date, who as his one book has chosen a pornographic one. It's American, is called *Route 69*, by Floyd Carter, and I don't think you will find it in your local library.

Helen Bradley, who paints the events in the lives of Grandma, and Mary Ellen, and Florrie, and the Aunts, and Miss Carter, who always wore pink, in the bountiful year of 1908, did not begin to paint seriously until she was sixty-four.

She was originally to be a pianist, but her father objected to the prospect of having her trailing round the world, and said 'No'. She had also won an arts scholarship and, when she was seventeen, was paid sixty pounds for painting a fresco for a local library, the excellence of which brought her the chance to study in Paris, but once again her father said 'No, we're having no artists.'

However, she married an artist, Thomas Bradley, and raised a daughter, and took up weaving rugs. Then, at the age of sixty-four, despondently surveying a world confined to domestic chores, she heard a voice saying 'Paint!'

She went out and bought a piece of hardboard, and set to work with her husband's paints – but she didn't dare to use his brushes, so she used a kitchen knife instead.

Right from the start, she painted only childhood memories, with lots of detail and lots of little figures, mostly painted in profile and always without shadows – just as the early painters from Persia, who travelled up the silk roads into Northern India, put in no shadows because their subjects were fantasies.

She was persuaded to send some of her pictures to a local art show, and she priced them at a modest £3.50 each. Nowadays, there are people competing to buy them at almost any price.

She is a charming lady, and when I met her at Euston Station, where she arrived from her Cheshire home, I had to wait at the ticket barrier while she went to thank the train driver for a safe and comfortable journey.

Four of her discs were to evoke memories of 1908, the ballad, 'When You Come To the End of a Perfect Day', Satie's Trois Gymnopédies, Debussy's 'Jardins sous la Pluie', and 'All on an April Evening', sung by the Glasgow Orpheus Choir. Then followed a piece of Chinese music, the Serenade from Bizet's 'The Fair Maid of Perth', sung by Heddle Nash, who was a personal friend, an excerpt from Stockhausen's 'Kontakte', which for her is Earth music, with the sounds of worms and ants and the grass growing, and 'Nimrod', from Elgar's Enigma Variations, which evokes *her* England, 'of all that time ago'.

In 1951, or thereabouts, I became Chairman of a BBC radio game called *One Minute, Please*, which had been devised and was produced by an enthusiastic young ex-conjuror named Ian Messiter. Ian's idea was that the two teams should be composed of experienced professionals leavened by one or two 'discoveries', people of promising talent who had individual voices and unusual personalities. He cast his nets wide, and held frequent auditions, emerging triumphantly with such captures as a Belfast journalist who could speak more rapidly than almost any mind could comprehend, a cheeky, squeaky Windmill girl with a great sense of fun, a young French actress who gurgled when she laughed, and Gerard Hoffnung.

He had found Gerard up a ladder, where he was painting a mural for an exhibition. I don't suppose it's very easy to get into conversation with someone who is eight feet up a ladder, but Ian is a sociable man, and I dare say Gerard felt like a breather. I don't know whether he went through the indignity of an audition, but we were all enchanted with him when Ian brought him into the studio. He was small and bald and rolypoly, and he beamed at the world through his spectacles. He was in his mid-twenties, but looked very much older. (Some years later, I heard Michael Flanders introduce him in a television programme as 'Britain's only thirty-three-year old octogenarian'.) He had a voice that swooped and soared through several octaves, from a bass rumble to a bat-like squeak, and he could be splutteringly and comically indignant.

The first time I met him outside the studio was, I think, when Ian gave a party. Gerard happened to have brought his tuba, but nobody had asked him to play. Gilbert Harding and I came across him, disconsolately nursing the instrument in a spare bedroom and, rather sportingly, we offered to be an audience. After a little while, Gilbert accused him of being a studied eccentric, which didn't go down well, especially from Gilbert.

. It was quite a long time before I saw any of Gerard's work, which was part of the modesty thing I mentioned at the beginning of this chapter. His work was inventive, but sometimes grotesque and macabre in a Teutonic manner: he was at his funniest in his books of musical drawings. With the Hoffnung

Music Festival, he took caricature into music most successfully.

For his eight discs, he chose Ravel, Richard Strauss, Debussy, Gershwin, Peter Warlock's 'Corpus Christi', Stravinsky and Honegger. For his one luxury, he chose his tuba, but had to promise not to live in it.

Gerard died in 1959, at the age of only thirty-four. Dennis Dobson put together a book called *O Rare Hoffnung*, consisting of tributes and reminiscences by his friends. The autobiographical part of our broadcast, on a small plastic disc, was enclosed in it.

A friend and colleague of Gerard's was Roland Emett; in fact, Gerard met his wife, Annetta, for the first time in Emett's Sussex house, and offered her a lift home. The fact that he didn't have a car with him and Annetta wanted to go to Folkestone meant nothing to Gerard: he could talk anybody into anything, even a taxi-driver into driving fifty miles across country to the Kentish coast.

I'm sure that in your travels you've come across the Far Twittering and Oyster Perch Railway. Well, Roland Emett is the chap who runs it. He was born in London on the very day and month and year that Cézanne died, but doesn't think that affected his artistic career. His first bent was mechanical rather than artistic: when he was only twelve or thirteen he invented some improvements for the hand-wound acoustic gramophone, and patents were filed for him. When he left school, he went into an advertising studio. Envious of the fact that a copywriter in the studio had sold a humorous story to *Punch*, he countered by sending some humorous drawings to the same magazine; he has been contributing to it ever since.

During the war, he was impressed into designing aircraft, and that gave him the technical knowledge to design such benefits to agriculture as the Hogmuddle All-Purpose Rotatory Niggler and Fidgeter, which has the very neat feature of a large hole in the centre to let the hunt go through.

Mr Emett claims no musical skill, but he likes to conduct Mozart records. Unfortunately, he is not allowed to do this at home, because of one or two incidents involving pieces of Dresden, but on his desert island he was planning to conduct not only Mozart but Brahms, Rachmaninov, Bach, Beethoven and Handel. For his book, he chose Burton's *Anatomy of*

Melancholy ('It's the biggest book I know, and just the right size for a podium'). Generously, he offered to design a new cage for the BBC seagulls.

It has always interested me how a painter sometimes allows himself to be possessed by a single subject: having painted a first picture, which touches off a particular response, he then feels he has to paint that subject to exhaustion. I remember Ayrton's series of drawings and maquettes of balancers and acrobats, and John Bratby's temporary obsession by sunflowers. I discussed this artistic manifestation with the Australian painter, Sidney Nolan. In the first years after the war, a number of young Australian artists were trying to express the essence of their country on canvas, both the landscape and history. For some reason, Ned Kelly had become fixed in Nolan's mind, perhaps because his grandfather had told him some legends about him, and because Kelly's armour was on view in Sydney Aquarium. To Nolan, Kelly was neither a romantic Robin Hood figure nor a mere thug: the prompting for the long series of pictures which Nolan painted of him was the social injustice he represented. As he told me, 'There were two or three hundred police after him for three or four years, so he must have had a certain amount of support for his views to have been able to keep clear that long. Also, he was a very good bushman, and he was very brave.'

Less easily explained was Nolan's later preoccupation with Leda and the Swan: nearly every canvas at one of his major London exhibitions depicted a different treatment of the subject. It followed his sequence of paintings of Gallipoli, a subject to which he afterwards returned, and some art critics surmised that Nolan was thinking of Helen of Troy, born of the coupling of Leda and the Swan, who caused the hideous carnage of the Siege of Troy, which was associated in his mind with the Anzac landing at Gallipoli. It seemed an ingenious piece of psychological detective work, and I asked Nolan for his views. He assured me that it wasn't consciously true, but that there must have been some connection. The workings of inspiration are unfathomable.

His choice of music was interesting: a piece of Aboriginal music, and some classical music from India; poems by Dylan Thomas and Coleridge; Britten and Stravinsky; a late Beethoven quartet and Bix Beiderbecke playing 'Somebody Stole my Gal'.

Probably the principal influence on design in Britain during the 'thirties was Vincent Korda's art direction of the film *Things to Come*, which portrayed H. G. Wells's ideas of life in the future. No further shot in the arm was to come until the Festival of Britain, in 1951. The art direction of the Festival was in the charge of Sir Hugh Casson, whose official title was Director of Architecture and Chairman of the Design Group.

He was given three years in which to get everything ready. He gathered round him a group of young ex-Service men, short on experience but full of ideas. The budget was limited, and there was a lamentable shortage of materials, but the highest standards were insisted on, and every single object was submitted for approval by the Design Board, right down to the smallest ashtray. Even the texture of paving stones was considered.

Little emerged that was revolutionary, but the influence of the Festival architecture on our new towns, and on such amenities as shopping centres, has been very considerable. It was unfortunate that, having been presented by Sir Hugh and his associates with the makings of the magnificent South Bank arts centre, the Greater London Council permitted it all to be boxed in by some of the ugliest office blocks in the city.

After the Festival closed, Sir Hugh went on to design some buildings for Cambridge University, the street decorations for the Coronation route, and some state rooms for the Royal yacht. He then became Professor of Environmental Design at the Royal College of Art, where he was surrounded, he says, by the best design brains in the country. He is now President of the Royal Academy.

One of the young architects working on the Festival team, was the late Sir Basil Spence, recently out of the Army, where he had been engaged on tactical deception and camouflage. A masterly piece of tactical deception, which had been his own idea, was the provision of a dummy beach, to be towed-in to the D-Day landing area in order to draw the German fire. It worked beautifully, and for forty days German shells and mortar bombs rained down on the beach and on Spence, who was in charge of it. It is likely that at the end of the forty days he wasn't so keen on his idea as he had been at the beginning.

After his work at the Festival, he landed the most important architectural assignment of post-war years, the building of the new Coventry Cathedral. To design a cathedral is every architect's dream, and 219 architects spent nearly a year in preparing speculative designs in open competition. Like the other contestants, he went to look at the site and, he said, had his design clearly in his head within five minutes. When his plans were finished, he felt that the months of designing had been an act of worship, and that he would be denying this if he handed in his work to make money – but he realized that a building on paper is no building at all, so he submitted his plans.

In designing a project of such vast size and complexity there were bound to be snags. He told me that at one point, when he was held up by a particular technical difficulty, he had an abscess on a tooth, and went to his dentist, who proposed to remove the molar under a local anaesthetic. As soon as he had the injection, Spence passed out. During the short time he was unconscious he had a very vivid dream of walking through the completed cathedral, with the choir singing and the organ playing, and the sun shining through stained glass windows *towards* the altar – and that is the way he subsequently planned it. Another inspiration was received when, flipping through the pages of a natural history magazine, he came across an enlargement of the eye of a fly, and that gave him the general lines for the vault.

A cathedral takes a long time to build; in the case of Coventry Cathedral, about ten years, with costs rocketing the whole time. It was obviously going to cost more than had been anticipated, and the winning architect found that one of his first duties was to go on a fund-raising tour in Canada. He told me that one of the most rewarding features in the building of the cathedral was being able to invite the help of some of this country's greatest artists, including Graham Sutherland, John Piper and Jacob Epstein, to design specific items for the decoration of the building.

While working on his plans, Sir Basil played discs of Bach's Brandenburg Concertos over and over again, and on his desert island he chose to hear again No. 3. He also chose the opening of Britten's *War Requiem*, which had its first performance in Coventry Cathedral.

It's a big jump from designing a cathedral to the delicate, small-scale glass engraving done by Laurence Whistler.

Mr Whistler published two volumes of poetry while still

reading English at Oxford. When he came down, he took an office job, which didn't last very long. 'I wasn't sacked actually but I managed to get out.' He settled down to writing, but didn't make much out of it. One day, he wrote a sonnet about an old house in Northumberland, and knowing that in Elizabethan times couplets were sometimes scratched on windows, he thought it would be pleasant to inscribe his poem at the house. There was no other diamond-point glass engraver working at that time, so he had to teach himself the craft.

Most of his work nowadays is on wine glasses and goblets, and the curved surfaces give special problems of perspective, but there are four surfaces to work on, and it is sometimes possible to use all four. Most of the things an ordinary pencil can do in the way of stippling and shading can be done with a diamond point, but it is slow and finely detailed work, and each piece takes weeks. The effects Whistler obtains are really beautiful.

It is a great delight to him that the succession is assured, and that his son Simon, whom he has taught since the age of ten, is now a professional glass engraver as well as a musician.

He believes that the eight discs he chose have in common the qualities of tenderness and compassion. They are Mozart's Piano Concerto No. 20 in D Minor, Flanagan and Allen's 'Underneath the Arches', 'Dido's Lament' from Purcell's *Diao and Aeneas*, an excerpt from 'Under Milk Wood', by Dylan Thomas, Charles Trenet singing 'La Mer', 'Garden of the Sleep of Love', from Messiaen's Turangalila Symphony, Beethoven's Septet in E Flat, Opus 20, and Stanley Unwin's inspired address on musical matters, 'Classicold Musee'.

Most of the artists I have interviewed have told me that they like to have music playing while they work. As Sidney Nolan said: 'Life is short, and if I couldn't paint and listen to music at the same time, I'd never get through all the music there is to hear.'

7

The Stage

In my experience, actors and actresses are not the best at expressing themselves fluently; they are used to working from a script which someone else has written – and, in the main, they are shy people. It is that shyness which prompts many of them to take to the profession, because to act is to retreat from the problems of reality by hiding behind make-up and false noses, and pretending to be someone else. There are many exceptions, of course, and it would be hard to find better off-the-cuff speakers than Sir John Gielgud, and Renée Houston, and Robert Morley (who confided to me that he had been named Robert after a favourite sheep dog).

John Gielgud appeared in our twentieth birthday programme, in 1962. He is a very musical person; a good pianist, and a good light vocalist, as those who saw him as Inigo Jollifant in either the original stage or screen versions of *The Good Companions* can confirm. Only once has he sung more seriously in public, when he took over, for one performance only, the part of Macheath in his own production of *The Beggar's Opera* at the Haymarket Theatre. 'By stamping my foot and waving my hand in the air at the top note, the audience imagined I'd hit it', he said. 'I'm told this is a very celebrated operatic trick, but I didn't know it at the time.'

Despite the fact that there is theatre blood on both sides of his family, it was not a foregone conclusion that he would act. His father wanted him to go up to Oxford and then become an architect, but the boy was stage-struck and an agreement was reached that he should go to drama school but, if he hadn't succeeded by the age of twenty-four, he would switch to architecture. As he played a highly promising Romeo in London at the age of only nineteen, there was no question of that.

One of his chosen discs was 'Wohin', from Schubert's *Die Schöne Müllerin*, sung by Peter Pears. He said that in listening to the best singers of Schubert and Schumann, one discovers not only the composer's arch of shape in a song, but also the way the singer can decorate it with colours and tones without

)

losing the shape, and that this had taught him a great deal in speaking verse.

Strangely, considering his success in directing opera, he chose nothing from that field, and his only other vocal disc was Dvorak's 'Die Bescheidene', sung by Elisabeth Schwarzkopf and Irmgard Seefried. He chose three pieces by Mozart, the Rondo for Piano and Orchestra in D Major, the Piano Concerto No. 20 in D Minor, and the Clarinet Concerto in A Major, and his remaining discs were the Bach Double Violin Concerto, the Brahms Third Symphony, and Purcell's Tune and Air for Trumpet and Orchestra in D. For his one luxury, he would take a Raoul Dufy watercolour of Versailles, with the palace in the background, and the statue of Louis XIV on his great horse vividly portrayed in a few brilliant strokes of the pen.

A year or so previously, to celebrate our five hundredth programme, we had invited Sir Alec Guinness ashore, and I will now break the news to Sir Alec that, in fact, he celebrated the four hundred and ninety-eighth programme. I'm afraid arithmetic was never my strong subject!

Sir Alec's first job, when he left school, was in advertising, but he was inclined to confuse the signs for feet and inches, and once sent a surprised *Daily Mail* a half-tone block four feet square. This gives me added hope that he will have understanding and forgiveness for my own mathematical lapse.

His first professional appearance was at the King's Theatre, Hammersmith, in a play called *Libel*, in which he walked on, and understudied a one-line part, for twelve shillings a week. He then went into a play by Noel Langley called *Queer Cargo*, in which he understudied the six leading men, and walked on and had a line to say as a Chinese coolie, an English sailor and a French pilot. For all that, he picked up £3.

What he called his 'first proper job' was playing Osric to Gielgud's Hamlet, at the New Theatre. He stayed with Gielgud for about four plays, then went to the Old Vic for a season, and then returned to Gielgud. 'I owe my proper start to him entirely.' He was only twenty-four when he played Hamlet at the Old Vic, in Tyrone Guthrie's modern-dress production.

He is one of those who have experienced shipwreck in real life. During the war, as a naval officer, the craft he was captaining was blown on to the Italian coast in a hurricane. There was no question of taking records ashore, but he did grab one

book from the little library he had on board and stuffed it into
the pocket of his duffel-coat. Instead of taking a classic, he
took a thriller, 'and delighted I was I took it, because when
I did get the chance to read, it absorbed me more than anything else would have done'.

His discs included two pieces of religious music – Gregorian
Chant by the monks of St Pierre de Solesmes, and the Agnus
Dei, from Verdi's Requiem Mass – as well as Haydn's 'Surprise'
Symphony, Schumann's Piano Concerto in A Minor, some
Spanish guitar music, one piece of jazz and a dance tune.

To celebrate our twenty-first birthday, we were honoured
by a visit from Noël Coward, surely the most talented man in
the history of British theatre. One could not hope to work
with anyone more concise, inventive, witty and thoroughly
professional. I asked him which of his many plays were his
own favourites; he named *Private Lives*, *Hay Fever* and *Blithe
Spirit*. On looking up his volumes of autobiography, I find
that those three glittering successes were written in four days,
three days and six days respectively – and I don't think many
people can match that in terms of productivity. He asked that
his island should be one of those in the Somolan Archipelago,
'somewhere between Fiji and Hawaii', which he invented for
use in several of his plays and in his novel, *Pomp and Circum-
stance*.

Like Alec Guinness, he chose an excerpt from Verdi's
Requiem Mass, and also the love scene from *Private Lives*,
which he recorded with Gertrude Lawrence, for whom he
wrote the play, ('as I was deeply fond of her, and we worked
together so much in our lives, and I shall miss her always, I
thought I'd like, on my desert island, to be able to hear her
voice occasionally'). His other discs were the Rachmaninov
Second Piano Concerto, with the composer as soloist ('I used it
as the background music in *Brief Encounter*, and I love it and
I know every note of it and I very often play it'), Frank
Sinatra singing 'All the Way' ('he phrases beautifully, he sings
with great charm, and he means – or apparently means –
what he's singing about'), Maria Callas singing 'Casta diva',
from Bellini's *Norma* ('I was immensely moved by this very
great artist'), Dame Edith Evans speaking the Shakespeare
sonnet, 'Shall I compare thee to a summer's day?' ('to my
mind, our greatest actress'), Peter Sellers and Irene Handl as
'The Critics' ('one of the most brilliant bits of satire I've ever

heard on a disc') and Bernard Cribbins singing 'A Hole in the Ground' ('this is to me a classic'). For his one luxury, he chose painting materials.

As we walked out of Broadcasting House, I told him how interested I had been to read in his book, *Future Indefinite*, that it had been mainly due to his efforts that a French radio station called Radio International had been taken off the air in the early days of the Second World War. Although the station had been backed by the French Government and its main intentions had been the entertainment of British troops in France and the transmission of propaganda to Central Europe, it had not conformed to the security regulations requiring the synchronization of transmitters, and furthermore there had been suspicions of a profit motive in the background. I told Coward that I had been employed on the station as producer and announcer, and had seen the results of his activities from the other side.

Coward stopped abruptly and looked at me with concern. 'So I put you out of a job?'

'Not me, because I was moved to another French station,' I replied, 'but most of us were sacked.'

'I'm terribly sorry.' He looked really worried. Obviously it had never before crossed his mind that the success of his battle against politicians and business men had resulted in some performers being put out of work, and this thought, to such a kindly and dedicated 'pro' as Noël Coward, was a serious one.

Almost as talented, if not so versatile nor so industrious, is Peter Ustinov. He is the easiest person in the world to interview, because you just sit back and let his rich, comic monologue roll over you, and the only problem is how you are going to shut him up.

I admire him not only for the lively qualities of his mind but also for his independence. As a playwright, he insists that his works be presented as he wrote them: at least two of his best plays failed because they needed cutting, and I am sure that he preferred they should fail honourably rather than be presented in versions which he considered to be incomplete.

He is a great gramophile, and his first call in any foreign capital is always at a record shop to enquire what is new and what is unusual. 'Records are essential,' he insists. He has appeared on the programme twice; I find that on the second occasion his musical enthusiasms were for composers from

France, Mexico, Spain, England, Austria, Germany, Russia and Czechoslovakia.

His first screen appearance, he told me, was in a thirty-five-minute film called *Hello, Fame,* which was made in a studio just off Baker Street. All the cast were shown climbing ladders to success, Peter's ladder being next to Jean Kent's. Unfortunately, he missed a rung and fell to the bottom. I don't see that happening in real life.

One of the most consistently romantic lists of records was Ruby Miller's; it was all soft piano music and soaring violins. As a Gaiety Girl, Miss Miller had known the era of Stage Door Johnnies. In fact, from her slipper a Russian Grand Duke drank champagne – at a private party at Romano's. He asked for the slipper, ordered a waiter to fill it with champagne and drank from the heel. When it was returned, Miss Miller laughingly said, 'You've left it a little damp, sir.' A day or two later six dozen pairs of shoes, in every colour and material, were delivered at her flat, with a note saying, 'That was the best champagne I ever drank.' Things were done in the grand manner by Grand Dukes.

She told a story about her friend, Evelyn Laye ('the most lovely girl I'd ever seen in my life'), and chose one of Miss Laye's recordings from *Madame Pompadour*. 'I had a letter from her – I was in New York at the time – and she wrote: "Darling, you'll be delighted to hear I've made a big success in *Pompadour*. I based the character entirely on you, because you're the only bad woman I know."' I asked Miss Miller to elaborate, but she declined!

Another distinguished veteran of the great days of the Gaiety Theatre was Ellaline Terriss, who was to live to reach her century. In the eighteen-eighties, there was no actors' trade union, and Miss Terriss's introduction to the stage was a telegram from Beerbohm Tree inviting her to take the place of an actress who had been taken ill, and for whom there was no understudy, in his production of *Cupid's Messenger* at the Theatre Royal, Haymarket. Apparently her father, the actor William Terriss, who was later murdered outside a backstage private entrance to the Adelphi Theatre, had casually mentioned to Tree that his daughter was occupying herself with drawing-room theatricals. Young Ellaline, who was only fifteen, had no chance to rehearse and nobody to help her with her costume. 'The clothes for the part included tights. I'd

never worn tights before, and I put them on over my petti-
coats, which were lacy and starched. I got a very big laugh
on my first entrance; I must have looked a very funny shape
indeed.'

She was invited by Sir Henry Irving to play Elaine to his
King Arthur, and it would have meant a very different career
for her if she had been free to accept – but she had signed a
contract for three years at the Gaiety Theatre.

We were recording in a studio with a piano, and I broke all
precedent by asking her to finish the programme by playing
and singing a chorus of one of her old songs. She chose 'The
Honeysuckle and the Bee', and she was enchanting.

A contemporary of hers – in fact, just over a year older –
was the dapper and debonair actor, A. E. Matthews, who chose
a record Ellaline Terriss had made with her husband, Sir Seymour Hicks. The majority of his records were of musical
shows of his youth. Leaning back in his chair and addressing his
remarks to the ceiling, he gave us a glorious flow of reminis-
cence. A good athlete as a young man – he once swam from
Southsea Beach to the Isle of Wight – he still kept in trim
by riding.

His great-uncle had been Tom Matthews, one of Grimaldi's
favourite pupils, who had become Clown at Drury Lane and
Covent Garden, and this link with the theatrical past obviously played its part in influencing Matty's career.

As a youngster, he was apprenticed to a bookseller at 87
Newgate Street, in the City of London, working in the office.
'I didn't like it very much, but the awful part of it was they
didn't like me.' Quite speedily he was sacked. His employer
said, 'Don't worry, my boy, the young man who sat at that desk
some years ago was sacked and he isn't doing badly. He's in the
theatre now. By the way, his name is cut in the desk. Haven't
you ever noticed it?' The name cut in the top of the desk was
Brodribb, which was the real name of Sir Henry Irving.

Matty went round to the Princess Theatre, in Oxford Street,
and took a job as call boy at fourteen shillings a week.

In 1889 he was a member of the first theatrical company to
go to South Africa. The journey from Kimberley to Johannes-
burg took two days and a night, using a span of sixteen horses,
with a change of horses every twelve miles. They were the
days of the Gold Rush, and things were wild. Every male carried a revolver.

'Including you actors?' I asked.

'Oh, yes. The audience, of course, had much larger ones. We did forty-two plays in a year, and I was getting around and enjoying myself. I didn't always know my part as I should have done, but the audience were very nice; when I dried up, they'd shout "Stick it, Matthews", and fire a couple of shots through the roof.'

Similar hazards during his early days were reported by Fred Emney. At the age of nineteen, he was playing the piano in a bar in Tijuana. One day a general swaggered in ('They're nearly all generals in the Mexican army; there must be more money in it') and demanded that Fred should play 'La Paloma'. Fred wasn't feeling too good that day, and he resented the general's tone. Furthermore, he didn't like 'La Paloma'. So he refused. The general took out his gun and fired three bullets into the piano. Fred played 'La Paloma'.

His first job in the theatre had been as a page-boy, with Doris Keane in *Romance*. After about six months he found he was growing out of the suit, so he went to the manager and asked if he could have a new one. The manager looked at him and shook his head. 'No! Cheaper to get a new boy.'

At the weigh-in before the broadcast, Fred tipped the scale at twenty-one stone two pounds – but he had decided to go on a diet. He was going to give up prunes.

His choice of music was light and tuneful: Frankie Carle at the piano, Bing Crosby, Bud Flanagan, Max Miller, Carol Carr, Jack Buchanan – and Rachmaninov's Second Piano Concerto.

I have long ceased trying to forecast what kind of discs my guests are going to choose. In the case of actors it is even more difficult, because one is inclined to superimpose the stage character on to the real one. Take the case of the late Gordon Harker, for instance, who was renowned for his Cockney roles. What would he choose? 'Knocked 'em in the Old Kent Road'? 'Down at the Old Bull and Bush'? or perhaps the 'Cockaigne' Overture? Not a bit of it. In private life, he was 'a Wagner maniac'. In addition to the Siegfried Idyll and the quintet from *Die Meistersinger von Nürnberg*, he chose music by Mozart, Schumann, Dunhill, Dvorak, Verdi – and Flanagan and Allen. And would you have guessed that Dame Edith Evans was a fan of television Westerns and especially devoted to the theme music of a series called *Rawhide*? – and that Dame

Flora Robson used to be a fan of a Rock 'n' Roll singer of the 'fifties named Frankie Lymon?

One of the happiest sessions I remember was with Tod Slaughter, the King of Melodrama. Nobody knows how many murders he committed in public, playing his villainous roles in *Maria Marten, or the Murder in the Red Barn, Sweeney Todd, the Demon Barber of Fleet Street*, and *The Crimes of Burke and Hare*, but it must have been many thousands. He was a great raconteur, and told hilarious stories of his early days, playing in fit-up companies in the north-east. Incredible as it seems nowadays, a young actor could then get a bed and a good breakfast for a shilling.

A large repertoire of old melodramas was played, and if a company ran short they'd get hold of a best-selling novel, cut out everything except the dialogue, and map out a roughly constructed play. On one occasion, they were about to play *The Silver King* when the manager came running backstage and said, 'The author's agent is in front, and we haven't paid any royalties : we'll do *Maria Marten* instead.'

That presented problems for young Tod. Everyone else in the company had done the play before but, at that time, he hadn't, and he was to play the leading man. He protested.

'What are you worried about? You know the story of the play, don't you?' said the manager.

'Yes,' said Tod.

'Then make it all up. I'll be on the side and if I see you're getting lost, I'll send someone on with a letter.'

'A letter?'

'Yes, then you open the letter, and that'll tell you what to do next.'

For a professional murderer, his musical tastes were astonishingly gentle and sentimental : 'Cornish Rhapsody' from the film *Love Story*, Dame Clara Butt singing 'Home, Sweet Home', Hutch singing 'Alone With My Dreams', and Max Bygraves singing 'Mr Sandman' – but things livened up with 'The Post Horn Gallop' and Rob Wilton's Police Station sketch.

Jon Pertwee, also, remembers a tricky moment during his early days, when he was playing in repertory on the West Pier, Brighton. It was one of those theatrical treadmills, with the company performing two different plays every week, and twice nightly. For the first three days of the week, Jon had played the old gardener in *Love From a Stranger*, and on Thursday he was to start playing the young curate in Shaw's *Candida*. After the Thursday morning dress rehearsal, his brother Michael took him out for a splendid lunch, which went on for most of the afternoon, and Jon got to the theatre only just in time for the first house. Absent-mindedly, he put on the heavy character make-up of the old gardener, donned his corduroy trousers and green baize apron, and went up to the side of the stage, ready for his first entrance. He listened for his cue, then suddenly realized that it was his cue in *Candida*. Quickly, he rubbed the character make-up into his face, shouted: 'I'll be with you in a moment, I'm just doing a little gardening', and played the curate's first scene dressed as the gardener.

It was in Australia that Jon made his unofficial attempt on the world's water-skiing speeed record. He happened to have had a few glasses of plonk ('the more expensive kind, at five shillings a gallon') and that and the encouragement of the pilot of a shark-spotting plane put him in the mood. Adjusting his skis, Jon hitched himself on to the back of the plane, which took off and reached seventy miles an hour, with Jon still upright and enjoying the ride. Then the plane hit a thermal, and started to rise and to veer to the right, where the land was. To ski over the beach at that speed would probably have proved singularly painful, so Jon decided to let go. He was undoubtedly right.

The records he chose included two Mozart arias (but one by Florence Foster Jenkins), Russian church music, Ray Charles, Miriam Makeba, Lonnie Donegan, and a flamenco song. For his book, he chose *Culture of the Abdomen: A Cure for Obesity and Constipation* by F. A. Hornibrook ('It would help me to know how to digest the strange foods I would discover on the island, and how to get over a surfeit of fish, and how to sit properly while eating').

Robert Atkins was the first man in this country to produce the whole thirty-seven of Shakespeare's plays. He had no doubts about their authorship. 'It was the man from Stratford,' he said, firmly.

Of Welsh descent, he had a natural love of music, and if he had been given the choice, he would have preferred music as a career, instead of the straight theatre.

Corpulent, red-faced, deep-voiced, Robert Atkins was a

power in the theatre for over sixty years. When he was a boy, his uncle had made up his mind that Robert was going to become the best manufacturer of straw hats that Luton had ever known, but Robert had other ideas and set out for London, with six guineas in his pocket.

Seven of his eight discs were to remind him of past productions: Grieg's *Peer Gynt* music, because he had been the first man to present Ibsen's play in a public theatre in this country; 'The Cobbler's Song' from *Chu Chin Chow*, because he had revived that great First World War success during the Second World War, although for security reasons the elephants and camels and other animals which had graced the original production were not allowed. (I remember meeting Jerry Verno, who played Ali Baba, during the rehearsals of the 1941 production, and he was a very sad man. 'Because I served in the Camel Corps during the 1914-18 war, I'm the only actor in London who can manage a camel,' he said, 'and Robert won't give me one.') His third disc was the Love Duet from Wagner's *Tristan und Isolde*, which he had produced at the Old Vic; 'The Dance of the Clowns' from Mendelssohn's music to *A Midsummer Night's Dream*, to remember many performances of the play, especially at the Open Air Theatre in Regent's Park, (He was renowned for his portrayal of Bottom, and he gave a graphic description of the occasion when a bee got into the ass's head while he was wearing it); the Welsh song, 'David of the White Rock', which he always introduced into his productions of *Henry IV*, Part One; The Fugue from Verdi's *Falstaff*, which he assisted Sir Thomas Beecham to produce at Covent Garden; the Shakespeare song, 'Blow, Blow, Thou Winter Wind', and, finally, 'Land of Hope and Glory' ('I know that it's not amongst the greatest music that Sir Edward Elgar wrote, but to me he represented such patriotism, and that music always thrills me').

He told an amusing story about Elgar. One sunny afternoon, they were sitting together beside the river at Stratford-upon-Avon, when some friends drifted by in a punt. They invited the two distinguished gentlemen aboard, but Elgar said, 'No, thank you, I am contra-puntal.'

Cathleen Nesbitt can also claim to have established a Shakespearean 'first' – in broadcasting. Before the BBC was born, she broadcast a scene from *The Merchant of Venice*, playing Portia to Arthur Bourcier's Shylock, from Marconi House. This gave her the idea that a complete Shakespeare play should be broadcast, something which nobody had attempted before, and she made a radio adaptation of *Twelfth Night*, which went on the air in June 1923.

As a girl, Miss Nesbitt was inspired, by seeing Sarah Bernhardt, to learn to speak French and to become an actress. The first ambition was more easily fulfilled than the latter, but eventually she made her début, playing a suffragette in a play called *The Cabinet Minister*.

I asked her about her friendship with Rupert Brooke: with his good looks, could he have been an actor? She said she doubted it, because he didn't have a very good voice, and he didn't read poetry very well. 'He might have been a good modern actor – because he had great ease of movement, and distinction. But he did want to be a playwright.'

They planned to marry, but he was sent to the Dardanelles and died of blood poisoning. 'What were his feelings about the war?' I asked.

'At first he was always depressed: he was very fond of the Germans; he'd been in Germany a great deal, and he thought that war never settled anything . . . And then they suddenly got the feeling that their business now was to crush the Germans . . . They went off with gaiety, feeling that it was romantic. I have such a romantic letter from the Aegean, saying that he had seen Parnassus.'

Few actresses have covered such a wide range. She has toured with the Irish Players, played Yasmin in Flecker's *Hassan*, Madam Goddam, who managed a brothel in China in the notorious play, *The Shanghai Gesture*, Julie in T. S. Eliot's *The Cocktail Party*, in many plays by Shakespeare, in thrillers by Edgar Wallace and Agatha Christie, and in the first American production of *My Fair Lady*.

She asked for a song from *My Fair Lady* as one of her discs, as well as numbers from *Oklahoma!* and *The Rise and Fall of the City of Mahagonny*. Her more serious choices were by Brahms, Chopin, Mozart and Tchaikovsky.

One actor who'll never need a press agent is Derek Nimmo; he knows all the tricks. He told me that at one time, when things weren't very bright in the acting business, he decided to promote some Rock 'n' Roll concerts in provincial theatres. To publicize them, he hired an alligator's head from a theatrical property shop and, a few days before each concert, would visit the town and walk round the shopping centre, wearing the head and carrying sandwich boards reading: 'See you later, alligator, at the Whateveritis Theatre'.

'If you've ever walked round as an alligator', he said, 'you'll have discovered what a large percentage of passers-by stuff chips and cigarette ends into your mouth.' Having had his walk round, Derek would telephone the editor of the local newspaper and say: 'Look here, my wife was walking along the High Street today, and she happens to be pregnant, and she saw a man dressed as an alligator, and it gave her a nasty shock, and are people allowed to walk about the High Street dressed as alligators?' Then, within minutes, the editor would send a photographer out to get a picture of the alligator sandwich-man for the next edition.

Derek began his career in repertory at Bolton, at a salary of £4 a week. He didn't possess a large wardrobe, and used to buy clothes from a local undertaker, who had a suspiciously large supply of partly-worn clothing. He still wears a blue smoking jacket he got from the undertaker for half-a-crown.

A Liverpool man, one of the discs he chose is the Beatles song, 'Penny Lane', because he was born just round the corner from that celebrated thoroughfare.

Most theatre people stay young and live long, because they relish the excitements each job brings, and because they stay busy and active. Matt Halton, the Canadian journalist, once told me that he divided people into two categories – 'Gee Whizz' people and 'So What' people – and actors and actresses are almost invariably 'Gee Whizz' people, preserving the same sense of wonder they had as children.

One wonders what went wrong in the life of Tallulah Bankhead, so that she couldn't stay the course. What was the reason for the strange compulsion to burn herself out? She was a popular and beautiful and successful actress, and the theatres of two continents were open to her; she loved her work and she loved life. When I recorded a programme with her, she was a very frail and ailing lady, and I was shocked to see how old and ill she looked as I helped her out of a taxi. She had come from her hotel wearing a mink coat slung over a pair of lounging pyjamas, and she leaned heavily on my arm as I supported her to the lift. Her eyes were still fine, and there was still beauty in the bone structure of her face beneath the wrinkles and ravages of hard living. Her hands shook, and when she wished to go to the loo she had to ask Monica Chapman to accompany her to help her with her clothing. She was only sixty-one, an age at which most actresses are reluctantly considering whether the time has come to start playing mothers.

During her eight years in London, in the 'twenties, it was said that she and Steve Donoghue were the two most newsworthy people in the country. The gallery girls mobbed her at the stage door. Hers was the kind of success and adulation echoed in our days only by the Beatles. Then came Hollywood and equal triumphs in the New York theatre.

Her programme was a poor one, for she rambled on and on, and much of what she said was incoherent. Sadly, when I asked her if she had any remaining ambition professionally, any part she wanted to play, she said, 'No, just to retire.' She told me that her visit to Broadcasting House was the first time she had left her hotel, except to go to the film studio where she was making *Fanatic*.

I hesitated when I approached my usual question about how well she could cope with the practical problems of being a castaway, but then decided that it was, after all, only a game, a fantasy, and asked it. She looked at me helplessly and said: 'I can't even put a key in a door, darling. I can't do a thing for myself.'

8

Singers

A programme I look back on with affection is one I recorded with Elisabeth Schwarzkopf. Her list of records was as follows: 'Ye Who Now Sorrow', from the Brahms Requiem, sung by herself ('the record which began my career'); the duet from the second act of *Wiener Blut* by Johann Strauss, sung by herself with Nicolai Gedda ('which I think is something very loveable'); the quintet from *Die Meistersinger von Nürnberg*, sung by herself and four others at a Bayreuth Festival ('a very great occasion in my life'); Mozart's 'An Chloe', sung by herself, with Walter Gieseking at the piano ('just to hear what he does with the accompaniment'); Hugo Wolf's 'Elfenlied', sung by herself, with Gerald Moore at the piano ('a very romantic affair'); the Fugue from Verdi's *Falstaff*, sung by herself and six others ('a very wonderful memory'); a duet from the second act of *Hansel and Gretel*, sung by herself and Elizabeth Grümmer ('going back to childhood memories'); and the Prelude to *Der Rosenkavalier*, played by the Philharmonia Orchestra.

The last record didn't seem to match the others, but then I remembered having heard it rumoured that Madame Schwarzkopf had once been a viola player, so I wondered if perhaps she was to be heard again in that capacity. She assured me however that her only reason for taking it was her affection for the Philharmonia Orchestra – and, incidentally it was the opening of a new complete recording in which she took part.

The list was a piece of colossal nerve: it obviously lacked sincerity; moreover, self-advertisement was not the object of the series. However, she presented it with such aplomb and such charm – at one moment, she murmured to me, 'I'm being outrageous' – that Monica Chapman and I let her get away with it. The programme was a great *succés de scandale*, and it is very rarely that I find myself talking about *Desert Island Discs* with people in musical circles without someone mentioning it sooner or later. But it was a gimmick that could be effective only once.

The American singer, Regina Resnik, wanted none of her

own records. This cheerful lady confessed that she had been inspired to become a singer by seeing Deanna Durbin at the movies and, at the age of only eighteen, had sung Verdi's Lady Macbeth, under the baton of Fritz Busch. Admittedly, she went on as an understudy, but to have tackled the role at all at that age was no mean feat. She progressed to ten years of leading soprano roles at New York's Metropolitan Opera House and elsewhere, then suddenly decided she would be a mezzo, so took a year off to re-think things. She already had a repertoire of forty-five roles, and it meant abandoning the whole lot, except *Carmen*.

Among her eight chosen discs were three vocal recordings – by Bidu Sayao, Caruso and Rosa Ponselle. Of Rosa Ponselle's recording of the aria 'O nume tutelar' from Spontini's *La Vestale*, she said it was 'the greatest singing lesson of all time'.

Another Rosa Ponselle aria from *La Vestale*, 'Tu che invoce con onore', was chosen by Joan Cross, who told me she had been warned against specializing in opera because her sense of humour was too lively. For many successful years she managed to keep a straight face – but she failed to do so while we were recording. We were talking about her early career with what was then the Old Vic Opera Company, when suddenly I noticed she was going red in the face and making alarming facial contortions while staring over my left shoulder. After a moment, failing to suppress it any longer, she let out a roar of laughter. Behind me on the wall was a large clock, and she had suddenly noticed the one word printed on the face of it, the name of the manufacturer. 'Gents!' she spluttered. 'It says "Gents" on the clock.' And so it does, on every clock in every BBC studio, but Joan Cross was the only one of the many who have noticed it to be tickled into irrepressible laughter.

The first major part she had been given at the Old Vic was Cherubino, in Mozart's *The Marriage of Figaro*. For her, it was a great occasion, but the only comment she received afterwards from the daunting Lilian Baylis was 'You sing very nicely; what a pity you can't act.' She took that criticism very much to heart and, as the Old Vic Shakespeare Company shared the theatre, she began attending every performance she could. She recalled that, in one season, she saw John Gielgud's Richard

II thirty-six times.

Marilyn Horne chose the same Rosa Ponselle aria, and said of it, 'I learned a great deal about vocal technique from listening to this woman's great, great art, and I think this aria is the absolute tops in vocal line and breath control.'

Whether Miss Horne is a soprano with an exceptional lower register or a mezzo with an exceptional top, nobody knows, including Miss Horne, but she has an extraordinarily wide range. She can look back on a wide range of recordings, too, because, while studying at the University of Southern California, she made some pop records (which are nice collector's pieces, if you can find them) and, at the age of twenty, provided the singing voice of Dorothy Dandridge in the film, *Carmen Jones*.

Knowing of Marilyn Horne's close friendship with Joan Sutherland, I was not surprised to find that Rosa Ponselle aria turning up yet again in Miss Sutherland's list. This was an unusual list as, apart from her own recording of the Mad Scene from *Lucia di Lammermoor*, all her discs were by female singers who were no longer active. They were Gina Cigna, Chloe Elmo, Amelita Galli-Curci, Luisa Tetrazzini, Marion Telva, Eva Turner, Elvira de Hidalgo and Claudia Muzio. Elvira de Hidalgo was one of Maria Callas's teachers, and Miss Sutherland pointed out the similarity between the two voices, especially in the lower register. She continued her single-minded approach to the desert island situation by choosing, as her one book, *The Memoirs of Jenny Lind*.

Dame Maggie Teyte had the good fortune to be heard singing in a church in Maiden Lane, when she was only sixteen, by a wealthy benefactor who sent her to Paris to study with Jean de Reske. He was one of the most expensive teachers in Europe, charging eight guineas for a fifteen-minute lesson, a fantastic sum in the years before the First World War. She made her début as Zerlina, in *Don Giovanni*, at Monte Carlo and, before she was twenty, was singing leading roles at the Opéra Comique, in Paris.

She studied Debussy's *Mélisande* with the composer himself, whom she described as a big, sombre-looking man, who told her, 'Wagner and Mozart and everybody else – they don't know anything about music. You can tear up their music.' Her own advice to young singers was: 'You must learn Mozart, and learn tradition.'

Some little-known facts about Dame Maggie are that she invented a fire extinguisher, that she was an expert mechanic, and that she knew a great deal about acoustics.

As a teacher, she numbered among her pupils the musical comedy star, Binnie Hale, who told me that Dame Maggie was inclined to put a clothes peg on a pupil's nose, so that the voice was placed where nature intended it to be. At lessons, they would act scenes from opera, putting in stage movements. She remembers singing Mimi in the love duet from *La Bohème*, with Dame Maggie as Rodolfo. At the end of the duet Rodolfo shows Mimi out of the door, and that is just what Maggie Teyte did to Binnie Hale, who found herself, still singing lustily, on the pavement in Wigmore Street, with a clothes peg on her nose.

Maggie Teyte's chosen records included her own enchanting version of 'Tu n'es pas beau', from Offenbach's *La Périchole*, Kirsten Flagstad's Immolation Scene from *Götterdämmerung* and, rather unconventionally, Harry Secombe singing 'Nessun dorma' from *Turandot*.

The operatic disc which has been chosen most frequently is, without doubt, the trio from the last act of *Der Rosenkavalier*, recorded in 1930 by Lotte Lehmann, Elisabeth Schumann and Maria Olszewska. When Kirsten Flagstad chose it, she said: 'I think this is my favourite part of any non-Wagner opera. It is most beautifully performed – lovely.' Both Lotte Lehmann and Elisabeth Schumann included it among their eight discs.

Madame Schumann chose two discs from the *Der Rosenkavalier* set, the other being the monologue of the Marschallin, sung by Lotte Lehmann. Of the trio, she said that it is the most fascinating piece of music Richard Strauss wrote, and that it was played at his funeral. She described the three singers as 'a very happy trio'.

I called to see Lotte Lehmann at the Wigmore Hall, where she was giving a reception to talk about a series of master classes. Part of the occasion was to be the introduction to the press of a young protégée, but by half way through the proceedings the young lady had not arrived. A telephone call to her hotel revealed that she claimed to know nothing about the function, and that she had her hair in curlers. 'Never mind,' said Madame Lehmann, sternly. 'Come just as you are – and at once!' And that is how I first saw the future international prima donna, Grace Bumbry – with her hair in curlers.

Apart from the *Der Rosenkavalier* trio, Lotte Lehmann chose no vocal excerpts from opera, although she asked for the Prelude to *Die Meistersinger*, conducted by Toscanini. Her other vocal discs were Mahler's 'Um Mitternacht', sung by Kathleen Ferrier, Richard Strauss's 'Freundliche Vision' sung by Elisabeth Schumann, a Hugo Wolf song by Dietrich Fischer-Dieskau, Duparc's 'Serenade Florentine' by Gérard Souzay, and her own recording, in German, of 'Vienna, City of my Dreams'.

Carrie Tubb lived to celebrate her centenary, and when she recorded with me in 1970 she was a very sprightly and up-right ninety-four. It was incredible to think that she had begun her career before the turn of the century. She recalled an occasion, at the beginning of the First World War, when she was touring Britain with Ben Davies and Clara Butt, and they were living in a railway coach, which was moved on from day to day. Despite the cramped quarters, Clara Butt had with her a small dog and a parrot. In those days, lady singers wore dresses with long trains, and one evening Madame Butt swept on to the platform unaware that her dog was sitting on her train.

I asked Carrie Tubb if she proposed to include one of her own discs, and she replied modestly that she had never recorded well, and did not posses a single one of them. I showed her a list of several dozen titles which had been compiled for me by one of the BBC librarians, and she said she could remember having made hardly any of them.

She still had a keen ear and eye on the musical scene, and felt that while the standard of musicianship was much higher there was a lack of outstanding personalities. She was yet another to choose the Lehmann-Schumann-Olszewska trio from *Der Rosenkavalier*.

Richard Tauber's broadcast was a very early one in the series, in September 1942. It was in the depths of the war, when transport was exceedingly difficult and the posts were even more unreliable than they are today, so I had a great deal of leg work to do. I was living in Edgware, in Middlesex, and I slogged right across London to see Mr Tauber at Wimbledon Theatre, where he was playing a singularly unconvincing Chinese prince in Lehar's *The Land of Smiles*. He was geniality itself, and we had an enjoyable chat, but he was a very busy man as he was also rehearsing his own musical play, *Old Chelsea*, which was to start on tour in two weeks time. That meant that any further discussion, and the recording, must be fitted between rehearsals. Before I was able to get from him a list of records and some notes about the reasons for his choice, together with his final approval of the script, I had to make another interminable journey to Wimbledon and two trips to his flat in Hampstead.

His opening disc was Beethoven's *Egmont* Overture. His first musical studies were not as a singer but as a conductor, and that work was the first for which he ever waved a baton, at Frankfurt Musical Academy in 1912. 'Were you very nervous on that occasion?' I asked.

'I have never been nervous in my life, so long as I have known my work.'

He then chose Caruso's recording of 'Ave Maria', in the setting by Percy Kahn, who had toured all five continents as Tauber's accompanist. This was followed by a song by Marlene Dietrich, whom he had known in Berlin long before she achieved international fame. 'She played a very small part in my first talking picture – a vamp in a waterfront café in Marseilles – but the picture ran too long, and her one short scene was cut out.'

He then chose a composition of his own, a Symphonic Prologue and Epilogue to an Imaginary Play. The recording was by the Vienna Philharmonic Orchestra, conducted by himself, but the record had never been issued and, so far as he knew, his was the only copy in existence. His remaining discs were of Grieg's 'Spring', 'These Foolish Things', Tchaikovsky's Sixth Symphony and the Prelude to *Tristan und Isolde*.

When I recorded with Peter Pears, we were renewing an acquaintanceship that dated back many years. On an earlier page, I referred to having developed an interest, as a young actor, in some of the activities of the Opera Class at the Royal College of Music. As a result, I found myself working – and working very hard – on a production of Mozart's *Il Seraglio*, presented in the Parry Opera Theatre, for a single performance, during the vacation. I was the business manager, assistant producer, adapted the dialogue, helped to make the scenery and played the non-singing part of the Bashaw. We had a working capital, raised from friends and relatives of £25: if ever there was a shoestring production, that was it.

Peter Pears was our Belmonte and, in order to rescue his Constanza from the Bashaw's palace, he had to climb a ladder set against a large plywood cut-out representing the front of the seraglio. The entire cast was behind that piece of scenery holding it upright. I shall always remember hearing our handsome, romantic tenor hero uttering his lovelorn cry of 'Constanza, my beloved!' followed by an anguished wail of 'For God's sake, don't let it go over.'

Despite his eminence as one of the most highly regarded singers in the country, Peter Pears still finds time each year to spend a week or two working with his teacher. His plan in choosing his records was 'to be reminded of old friends, old sounds and voices'. He began with 'Brigg Fair' by Delius ('which recalls to me, as nothing else does, the countryside of Suffolk or Sussex in early May'), and then chose Dowland's 'Captain Piper's Galliard' ('because Dowland and the Madrigalists are my great love, and I would like one disc, anyway, of the finest lutenist we've ever had since Dowland's day, Julian Bream'). His other discs were of 'Et in unum' from Bach's B Minor Mass, the Moonlight Interlude from Britten's *Peter Grimes*, a song from Schubert's *Winterreise*, Shakespeare spoken by John Gielgud, a Scarlatti sonata played by George Malcolm, and a piece of Indian music.

One of the very few singers to have made two appearances in *Desert Island Discs* is Isobel Baillie. She has sung Handel's *Messiah* more than a thousand times, and must have appeared in every town and city in the United Kingdom. It is not surprising that her programmes brought in an extra large mail, from listeners who remembered, gratefully, hearing her in person in their own part of the country.

She began to sing at the age of five and, performing in church choirs and choral societies, had learned most of her oratorio repertoire by the time she was twenty. In her second programme, with the exception of a Chopin Piano Concerto and a Brahms Symphony, all the music she chose was vocal, and all of it composed in the British Isles. One of the discs was a chorus from *Messiah*, to remind her of all the performances she has sung. She chose 'Worthy is the Lamb', ('because it comes at that point when I've done my work. I've sung my solos, and I can sit back and really enjoy the rest of it — and that's one of the choruses that used to thrill me').

Tito Gobbi was my guest in the summer of 1958, while he was appearing at Covent Garden in Verdi's *Don Carlos*. Already, at that time, he had ninety-five roles in his repertoire.

He was originally destined for the law, and began his legal studies. One day, playing tennis with a musician who was a friend of his father's, Gobbi, who delights in clowning, was singing while playing, and his opponent was so impressed with the young man's voice that he persuaded his father to arrange that he should study singing. Eventually, he dropped his law studies, and made his début in Rome, singing the part of Alfredo's father in *La Traviata*. Right at the beginning of his career, the man who was to be one of the great actors of the operatic stage was playing a character part.

His English was charmingly approximate. I talked to him about his films, some of which had been operatic, while others had been comedies with very little singing. He grinned in agreement. 'Yes, with very little sing-song in them,' he said. 'Not so good, not so bad.' Later, when we were discussing how he would manage for food on his desert island, he announced, 'I will throw some stones against birds.'

His records included songs by Caruso, Gigli and Marilyn Monroe, 'Stormy Weather', the Italia section of Verdi's 'Song of the Nations', and the Fugue from the same composer's *Falstaff*, the opera in which he had made his greatest success. As his luxury, he chose 'a very expensive ivory back-scratcher'.

The most forthcoming singer in my experience is Beverly Sills, currently the highest-paid opera star in the world. Tall, with red hair and an hour-glass figure, she has a great sense of fun and can rattle on amusingly for hours. Born in Brooklyn, she began her professional career at the age of three, in the days of the kiddie cult started by Shirley Temple. There were years of radio work, in soap opera and singing commercials, until she was fifteen, when she was featured as 'The Infant Prima Donna' in a touring operetta company. Then came variety work on 'the bortsch circuit', playing in holiday hotels in the Catskill Mountains, and long, late nights in smoky Manhattan nightclubs, until an opera career opened up for her.

Her first introduction to opera was hearing her mother's Galli-Curci discs, which she played while doing the housework, and young Beverly could sing a dozen or more of the arias by heart, without knowing what any of them were about, so Galli-Curci's 'Una voce poco fa', from *The Barber* of *Seville* had to go with her to the island, as did Ljuba Welitsch's closing aria from *Salome*, and Birgit Nilsson's 'Liebestod'. She also chose that familiar Trio from *Der Rosenkavalier*. First, she asked to hear the version by Elisabeth Schwarzkopf, Christa Ludwig and Teresa Stich Randall, but rejected it because, she said, the three singers sound as if they were competing rather than blending. She preferred the older and more popular Schumann-Lehmann-Olszewska version – but only the beginning of it. 'Don't go on too long, because one of the ladies goes very flat.'

Beverly Sills's career has been curiously paralleled by Robert Merrill's. He, too, comes from Brooklyn, was a child performer on radio, and is an alumnus of the bortsch circuit. His first musical inspiration was Caruso's disc of 'Vesti la giubba', brought into the home by his father.

As a youngster, he worked on a Brooklyn radio station which ran a profitable little sideline by which children paid a dollar to be taught a song, and if they sang it well enough they were allowed to sing it on the air. Robert established a reputation as a reliable Bing Crosby imitator, and became a regular. However, there didn't seem much future in a job where you had to pay to get in.

Right from the beginning his ambition was opera, and during the years when he acted as straight man to Danny Kaye, Red Skelton and The Three Stooges, he dreamed of the Metropolitan. He made his first operatic appearance in some performances of *Aida* in Newark, New Jersey. He was twenty-three, and he sang Amonasro, the father-in-law of Radames, played by Giovanni Martinelli, who was then sixty-eight. Then came an audition at the Metropolitan Opera House, and the first of thirty seasons there.

He is another to have chosen a disc by Rosa Ponselle, 'Voi lo sapete', from *Cavalleria Rusticana*, which he used to hear her sing from the fifty-cents seats in the top gallery – and, of course, he chose Enrico Caruso's 'Vesti la giubba'.

That same disc played a formative part in the early days of a singer on this side of the Atlantic. Charles Craig was seven when his brother brought it to their home in the East End of London. On first hearing it, he said to himself that one day he wanted to be able to sing like that. The state of the family finances made any kind of musical education an impossibility, but the ambition was always at the back of his mind during the years after he left school, when he went aimlessly from job to job.

His chance came during his war service in the army, when he was called on to display his natural tenor voice by singing ballads in the unit concert party. Later, he was transferred to a full-time entertainments post, and toured India and Burma with a symphony orchestra made up of Italian prisoners of war, which seems a sensible use of captured enemy man power. As soon as he was demobilized, he auditioned for the Royal Opera House chorus, where he spent three or four years.

In 1951, Sir Thomas Beecham was looking for a tenor to sing in his Festival of Britain production of Balfe's *The Bohemian Girl*. Somebody suggested Charles Craig, and Sir Thomas auditioned him. After hearing him sing his audition piece, Sir Thomas pushed the accompanist off the piano stool and took over. He gave Charles several scales to sing, and then said: 'You must leave Covent Garden. We must find you a scholarship or something.' In fact, Sir Thomas sponsored him himself, paying him a salary to live on during two years of training.

Afterwards came three years with the Carl Rosa Company, guest appearances at Sadler's Wells, and then the supreme excitement of returning to Covent Garden to sing Pinkerton in *Madame Butterfly*, just eight years after he had left the chorus there. Nowadays, he spends most of his time abroad, and has a great reputation in Italy, singing the roles that Caruso sang.

Apart from 'Vesti la giubba' and 'The Ride of the Valkyries', conducted by Alexander Gibson, he chose no opera, but asked for two recordings by Heifetz, the Beethoven Violin Concerto and 'Gypsy Airs' by Sarasata, Beethoven's 'Pastoral' Symphony, and Mozart's 'Eine Kleine Nachtmusik'.

Soprano Rita Hunter was stage-struck from her very early youth, and was Principal Boy in a touring pantomime at the age of fifteen, having assured the management that she was seventeen. After that, she toured in the chorus of *Gay Rosalinda* and *The Chocolate Soldier*.

Edward Renton, who was conducting, recognized the quality of the girl's voice and suggested that, instead of going home to her family in Cheshire, she should go to London and help his wife in the home in return for coaching by him. He taught her several roles, and arranged an audition for her with the Sadler's Wells Opera Company. She was accepted as a chorister. After two years, she moved to the Carl Rosa Company, where there was a better chance of being promoted to small parts. She remembers, with affection, playing *The Tales of Hoffman* in unsuitable little provincial theatres where the stage had a steep rake and the gondola used to get stuck, 'so we used to have to walk up the canal'.

She was awarded a scholarship, which enabled her to study with Dame Eva Turner, and then with Redvers Llewellyn, which meant going to North Wales each weekend for her lesson. Her first big part was Musetta in *La Bohème*, for the Sadler's Wells Company. Then she sang some mezzo roles, and, eventually, Senta in *The Flying Dutchman* ('I sang two Sentas a week, and maybe a Mother in *Hansel* and two Marcellinas in *Figaro*').

Her big opportunity came with Brunnhilde in the Sadler's Wells *Ring* – and the same role at the Metropolitan, New York. Physically, she is a powerful lady, which rather limits her to powerful parts, but she says that to lose weight affects her voice, and the voice must come first.

Her discs included four Wagner items, the Prelude to *Lohengrin*, the Love Duet from *Tristan und Isolde*, sung by Kirsten Flagstad and Ludwig Suthaus, 'Wotan's Farewell' from *Die Walküre*, sung by George London, and her own recording, with Alberto Remedios, of 'Zu neuen Thaten' from *Götterdämmerung*. Others were 'Deh! vieni' from *Don Giovanni*, sung by Ezio Pinza, Beniamino Gigli singing the Ingemisco from Verdi's Requiem, and the title song from *Cabaret*, sung by Jill Haworth.

It frequently happens that a guest brings a husband or a wife to the studio, or, sometimes and less welcome, an agent or a manager : Miss Hunter was the first to bring not only her husband but her five-year-old daughter as well. I viewed this innovation with mild alarm, because we had a lot of work to get through in very little time, but the five-year-old was as good as gold, took a lively interest in all that was going on, and was absolutely enraptured by the music.

9

Dancers

I fear that *Desert Island Discs* has been the cause of at least one car crash, but mercifully a slight one in which nobody was hurt. One day in 1965, Charles Murland, who is a power in the City and also a Governor of the Royal Ballet School, was driving down King's Road, Chelsea, while listening on his car radio to the programme in which I questioned the South African ballerina, Nadia Nerina.

'They did say, one time, I was the greatest technician in the West,' said Miss Nerina, and there was a bump as Mr Murland's car hit the one in front.

He climbed out and surveyed the damage, as did the puce-faced, angry driver of the other car.

'I'm sorry – that was my fault,' said Charles. 'I was listening to *Desert Island Discs* and I didn't brake fast enough.'

'I was listening to it, too,' said the other driver, calming visibly. 'I had to brake hard to avoid a pedestrian. It was something that Nadia Nerina said.'

'You mean, when she said that she was the . . .'

'Yes, that was the bit.'

The anger had passed and, as horns honked from behind, the two ballet enthusiasts shook hands and went their separate ways.

The name, Nadia Nerina, sounds very Russian, but in fact Nadia is her Christian name, Nadine, in the form in which her father always used it when she was a child, and Nerina is her mother's Christian name, and a variety of lily which grows on Table Mountain.

She had great difficulty in deciding between acting and dancing. She won a scholarship to come to Britain to study drama, but decided to come, under her own steam, to dance. She arrived in London, knowing nobody, auditioned at the Sadler's Wells School ('they were thrilled, I believe'), and was taken straight into the Sadler's Wells Ballet Company.

She chose only one piece of ballet music, Elihu's Dance of Youth, from Vaughan Williams's *Job*, to remind her of her ex-partner, Alexis Racine, and of Dame Ninette de Valois, who choreographed the ballet. As a memory of South Africa she chose the Kurt Weill song, 'The Hills of Ixopo', from *Lost in the Stars*, and as a souvenir of meeting her husband, Charles Gordon, at Cambridge University, where he was an undergraduate, she chose an excerpt from Evensong for Ash Wednesday, by the Choir of King's College. For no reason except enjoyment she chose Albinoni's Adagio for Strings and Organ.

She is a lady who takes life seriously, which was shown by her early decision to perfect her technique before allowing herself to develop the emotional qualities in her dancing.

Her parents were not musical, and the only reason she started dancing was because, as a schoolgirl, she hurt her ankle, and the doctor recommended dancing classes to strengthen it.

Of such minor accidents are great dancers made. If little Alice Marks had not suffered from flat feet as a child, then Alicia Markova would not have been born, because her training was started as a cure for fallen arches.

She made her first professional appearance in a pantomime at the Kennington Theatre, London at the age of ten. Later Diaghilev saw her working in a studio and engaged her for his company. She joined them on her fourteenth birthday, in Monte Carlo, and one can imagine what a day of enchantment that must have been for her.

When Diaghilev died and his company dispersed, she felt that she did not want to dance any more. At that time, of course, there was no British ballet. Eventually she went back to Monte Carlo for a season, but was not very happy. Then Frederick Ashton wrote to her from London that he had been asked to choreograph some dances for a Dryden play at the Lyric Theatre, Hammersmith, and invited her to dance with him.

She accepted, then moved on to the Ballet Club, which was started by Marie Rambert and which was the first permanent home of ballet in England. Then came the creation of the Vic-Wells Ballet, and Alicia Markova was its first prima ballerina.

'What was your salary there, when you started?' I asked.

She smiled. 'I think it was five guineas a performance – but there wasn't a performance every week.'

Later she formed her own company with Anton Dolin. Of the two, she claimed that she was the practical one.

Three of her records had associations with dancing; the first was the Overture to *The Merry Widow*, because of a childhood memory of her father waltzing her round to it, then the Panorama from Tchaikovsky's *The Sleeping Beauty*, because it reminds her of Diaghilev, and because it was the first great classical ballet she ever saw, and Gluck's 'Dance of the Blessed Spirits', to which she has danced many times. She chose vocal records by Renata Tebaldi, Amelia Rodrigues and Marion Anderson.

All artistic occupations are financially hazardous, and none more so than dancing. At any point in a dancer's career, from the first year in ballet school onwards, the axe may descend. A dancer may become too tall, too heavy or too similar in style to a leading dancer who is already established; the result is polite dismissal. Christopher Plummer told me that of the twelve boys at the Sadler's Wells Ballet School when he joined he was one of only two or three to work eventually with the company.

In 1970 we invited the late Graham Usher, as one of the best of the Royal Ballet's leading dancers, to take part in the series. I met him, for the first time, at Verreys Restaurant. After we had ordered our meal, he turned to me and said : 'I'm sure this is the first time you've featured one of the unemployed in your programme'.

I lifted an eyebrow or two, enquiringly.

'I've got the sack,' he said. 'I'm thirty-one and my career as a dancer is finished. There's a reorganization going on in the company and some of us have got the push, including me.'

'The Royal Ballet isn't the only company in the country,' I said.

'It's the senior company, and I've been a leading dancer in it. I've danced a leading role on the stage of the Maryinsky Theatre in Leningrad, and that really means something. I'm at the peak of my career, and it's better to take up something else rather than start going down the slope.'

'What will you do?' I asked.

He shrugged. 'I might open a bookshop, if I can raise the capital.' Unlike most of his colleagues, he had no desire to teach or to choreograph or to act – he wanted a clean break.

The fact that a British company could achieve success on equal terms with the Russians on the hallowed boards of the

Maryinsky Theatre is mainly due to the determination of an Irish woman of Huguenot descent, Dame Ninette de Valois. She was Principal Dancer at the Royal Opera House, Covent Garden, in the 'twenties, but as the opera season lasted only three months in the year, she had to earn her living for the rest of the time in revues and pantomimes and musical comedies.

She joined Diaghilev for two years, watched how he administered his great company, decided that such an organization would be possible in this country, gave in her notice and set to work to build one. She had a very important meeting at the Old Vic Theatre with Lilian Baylis. For four years, she worked there, helping Miss Baylis with her drama students, and preparing the dances that were needed in the operas and plays. She was waiting for the great day when the rebuilding of the Sadler's Wells Theatre would be completed, because she had been promised facilities for a company which would be capable of presenting a complete evening of ballet.

There was very little money, and a desperate shortage of male dancers. There is a story that Madame de Valois borrowed young Frederick Ashton from Madame Rambert for five shillings a performance – but Dame Ninette thinks it was a little more than that.

Strangely, Ninette de Valois chose no ballet music. She asked for excerpts from two Britten operas, *Peter Grimes* and *The Rape of Lucretia*, Mahler's *The Song of the Earth*, Dinu Lipatti playing 'Jesu, Joy of Man's Desiring', Mozart's Piano Concerto No. 20 in D Minor, the Gretchaninoff setting of The Creed, the final chorus of Rimsky-Korsakov's *The Snow Maiden* and a Greek song by Hadjidakis.

Dame Marie Rambert said she has been told that she jumped out into the world with a dancing step. First inspired by Isadora Duncan, she studied at the Dalcrose School, leaving it when Diaghilev and Nijinsky invited her to help with the first production of *Le Sacre du Printemps*. After the First World War, she started her school in London. Apart from Frederick Ashton, the talented youngsters she gathered round her included William Chappell, Harold Turner, Anthony Tudor and Diana Gould. At Madame Rambert's school nobody disguised a British name under a Russian *nom de théâtre*. Hers was the first British company to dance abroad – in France, Belgium and Germany.

She chose a record of the Pavane from Peter Warlock's *Capriol* Suite, conducted by Constant Lambert, because that music played a part in their first season. She had gone with Frederick Ashton to an evening of folk dancing at the Albert Hall, and when he heard Warlock's music, which is based on folk tunes, he decided to devise a ballet to it. Another early ballet memory was evoked by Chausson's 'Poème', which was used by Anthony Tudor.

To complete her eight discs, she asked for the voices of Chaliapin, Kathleen Ferrier, Mistinguett and Henry Ainley, the Sanctus from Bach's B Minor Mass, and a Polish folk song.

Sir Frederick Ashton, now our greatest choreographer, was born in Ecuador, and the first dancing he saw was one of Pavlova's South American tours. He began a business career in the City of London, where he was very unhappy. His initial dancing lessons were from Léonide Massine on Saturday afternoons.

Massine told him that one lesson a week was useless, he needed one every day, so Ashton staged a nervous breakdown, and the family doctor advised that he should be allowed to follow his wishes. His first professional appearance was in a short ballet, which he arranged himself and which was included in a revue called *Riverside Nights* at the Lyric Theatre, Hammersmith.

He heard that Ida Rubinstein was starting a company in Paris, so he borrowed five pounds, flew over to give an audition and was accepted. He said that trip was really the best thing he ever did in his life, because he had the opportunity of working under two very great choreographers, Massine and Nijinski, and really learned his craft. Then he returned to England and worked with Madame Rambert, later joining the Vic-Wells Company as principal choreographer, working with such talented young dancers as Margot Fonteyn and Robert Helpmann.

He chose his records mainly nostalgically: the Panorama from Tchaikovsky's *The Sleeping Beauty*, the Gretchaninoff setting of The Creed, Yvonne Printemps singing 'Air de la Lettre' from Reynaldo Hahn's *Mozart*, Poulenc's *Les Biches*, Ethel Waters singing 'I Can't Give You Anything But Love', César Franck's *Symphonic Variations*, Prokofiev's *Romeo and Juliet* and Ravel's *La Valse*.

While a pupil at the Imperial Ballet School in Moscow,

Léonide Massine played small parts in straight plays at the Bolshoi Theatre, where he had a family 'in', because his father was a horn player in the orchestra and his mother a soprano in the opera company

For a while he pursued the two careers of drama and ballet, and when Diaghilev invited him to join his company, some of his drama colleagues told him he would be foolish to accept because he was in line to play leading parts.

Soon, however, he was dancing leading parts in Diaghilev's company, and the young man's feeling for drama, painting and music inspired Diaghilev to give him a trial as a choreographer. He went on to choreograph such great ballets as *The Three-Cornered Hat*, *La Boutique Fantasque* and *The Good-Humoured Ladies*. After Nijinsky got married and quarrelled with Diaghilev, Massine took Nijinsky's place as leading dancer of the company.

Later he was to work in a lighter vein in the London theatre, in a Noël Coward revue and in Charles B. Cochran's production of *Helen*, and to make the films *The Red Shoes* and *The Tales of Hoffmann* with Michael Powell and Emeric Pressburger.

There has been no completely satisfactory way of recording the movements and groupings of a ballet other than by filming, which is expensive. Massine told me that, after many years of work, he has now perfected a method which will preserve choreography on the written page, in the same manner as a musical score.

For many years he has lived on his own small island near Naples, so he didn't view the prospect of a desert island sojourn with any particular alarm. As his desert island music, he required Mozart's Symphony No. 40 in G Minor, Stravinsky's *The Rite of Spring*, Hindemith's 'Nobilissima Visione', an excerpt from Bach's *St John Passion*, Beethoven's Seventh Symphony, and three excerpts from opera, the Prelude to Wagner's *Parsifal*, an aria from Mussorgsky's *Boris Godunov*, sung by Chaliapin, and the opening of Verdi's *Falstaff*, with Geraint Evans.

Another second-generation Bolshoi Theatre performer is Tamara Karsavina, whose father was also a dancer there. When I went to visit her in her Hampstead home in 1957, she must have been as upright and almost as agile as on the day in 1910 when she took over from Pavlova as *Première Danseuse* at the Imperial Opera House. She was the star of the Diaghilev company which first revealed the splendour of Russian ballet to Western Europe, and few artists can have been accorded such adulation.

Her father had not wanted her to work in the theatre because, he said, it was full of intrigues, but her mother took her side and she began her dancing training at the age of eight. She danced her first major role in St Petersburg. When I asked her if there was much rivalry between the two great companies in St Petersburg and Moscow, she answered: 'There was a little difference in outlook. We believed in more classical forms, and Moscow was more exuberant, which we thought perhaps overstepped good taste.'

When speaking of Diaghilev, she said that he was very offended if referred to as an impresario: he was a man of good family and a lover of art, and his only wish was to blend the best of Russian design, music, dancing and stagecraft.

Since settling in Britain, Madame Karsavina had done a great deal to help and encourage British ballet, and would make guest appearances with the young dancers at the Ballet Club. When I asked her to single out one British dancer for special praise she chose Margot Fonteyn ('She can't do wrong, and I simply love her, because the line is so beautiful from head to toe.')

Madame Karsavina's discs included two with ballet memories: Victoria de los Angeles singing 'Le Spectre de la Rose,' because Gautier's words inspired the happiest ballet she has ever danced ('and every time, before going on, I recited the poem to myself, because I loved the words'), and the 'Fête Populaire', from *Petrouschka*, not only to remind her of the ballet but because, as a child in Russia, she would see the big fairs, with dancing bears, big wheels, booths and peepshows.

Her other discs were Mozart's 'Eine Kleine Nachtmusik', Schubert's 'Trout' Quintet, Holst's *The Planets*, the Don Cossack Choir singing 'Along the St Petersburg Road', Laurence Winters singing 'I Got Plenty of Nuttin'' from Gershwin's *Porgy and Bess*, and Tito Schipa singing 'Che farò', from Gluck's *Orfeo ed Euridice*. As her one luxury, she chose a carved wooden figure of St Florian, which she had found at Salzburg ('because he is very beautiful and he seems to dance').

Dame Margot Fonteyn honoured us by being our seven hundred and fiftieth castaway. She told me she doesn't play records very often in leisure moments because she is never completely relaxed when listening to music. 'Music is so much a part of my dancing that if I'm listening to music I'm, in a way, working,' she explained.

Born in Surrey, she is a quarter Brazilian, on her mother's side. She took her first dancing lesson at the age of six, and spent quite a lot of her childhood travelling. When she was twelve, she and her mother came back to England to see her brother, who was at school, and she saw the Camargo Society dance the first ballet performance she had ever seen ('I saw Markova dancing, and I saw *Les Sylphides*, and I saw some of the early performances at Sadler's Wells – and I think from that moment I knew what ballet was, and then knew that I would like to do it, although I never thought I had any possibility of succeeding'). At fourteen she was accepted for the Sadler's Wells School, and the following year started to dance with the company.

She chuckled to remember how small the Sadler's Wells Company had been when she first joined them. In the same evening she would be in two or three ballets, dancing a principal role in one and being in the *corps de ballet* in the next. When Alicia Markova left the company, there was no one dancer of sufficient stature and experience to take over as prima ballerina, so her roles were divided among five young soloists, of whom Miss Fonteyn was one.

She chose only one disc from the ballet repertoire, 'Daybreak' from Ravel's *Daphnis and Chloe* ('it would be so marvellous in the early morning on a very beautiful island'). She followed it by Mozart's Sinfonia Concertante in E Flat Major, and Bach's Passacaglia in C Minor. For her Latin blood she chose a Spanish song by Guridi, 'Mãnanita de San Juan' sung by Teresa Berganza. Then came the 'Dies Irae' from the Berlioz Requiem, Chopin's Etude in E Major, Opus 10 No. 3 played by Richter, and the Invocation to the Moon from Puccini's *Turandot*.

She has always delighted in dancing in nightclubs when the day's serious activities are over, and she chose a disc by Lena Horne to provide a late-night atmosphere. ('I would probably discover how to ferment coconuts and make coconut wine.') When I asked her what she would be happiest to have got away from on her desert island, she thought for a moment and then answered, 'Should I say ballet critics?' As her luxury, she wanted a skin diver's mask ('I love swimming, and I would have a whole new world to explore under water').

I never cease to be amazed at the dedication shown by dancers. No matter how exhausting the previous evening's performance, 10.30 a.m finds a dancer at the *barre*, ready for the daily ninety minutes of limbering-up. In the afternoon, there will probably be a rehearsal, and in the evening another performance. It is hard to estimate the number of hours of gruelling work that go to produce those few rewarding moments when the audience are cheering, and flowers are raining upon the stage.

'Do you sometimes wish you weren't a dancer?' I asked Antoinette Sibley, after she had been telling me of the rigorous self-imposed discipline that must never be relaxed.

'Quite a few times,' she admitted, 'but you must remember that I don't know any other life; I have done this since I was nine years old.'

In her case, her early years had been dogged by ill health, so it had needed even greater determination and grit than usual to stand the strain. 'I've taken lots of knocks; I know how to take them. I don't think I do at the time, but I usually seem to.'

She confessed to me that she has an enormous appetite and likes lots of solid food, such as steak and spaghetti and suet puddings, but not an ounce of it is visible on her slender body: she burns up every calorie.

She talked of the choreographers she had worked with, and their different approaches to creating a ballet. For example, Kenneth Macmillan knows every note of the music at the first rehearsal and has evolved the actual steps that he wants, whereas Sir Frederick Ashton has a more poetic approach, with merely an overall picture in his mind, the steps being almost incidental.

She spoke with gratitude of her partnership with Anthony Dowell ('We're very great friends, and because we've been through so many awful things and so many good things together, we can be absolutely honest with each other – we don't have to act'). They find great inspiration in each other's work, and if one happens to be particularly on form, the other will react and find an effortless technical ease which normally is impossible. It was an inspired thought on the part of someone in high places that the two partners should be summoned together to Buckingham Palace, each to be invested as C.B.E.

I don't remember anyone suffering to the extent that she did in narrowing down her choice of discs to a meagre eight. At one point she had a list of fifteen in her hand and assured me, almost with tears in her eyes, that each was indispensable. It was like losing loved ones for her to leave behind Mozart and Verdi.

The one piece of ballet music she chose is from a ballet in which she had never danced, Stravinsky's *The Rite of Spring* ('I think the world started with that music; to me, it is the beginning of life'). Her one piece of opera – and opera and reading are her main interests outside ballet – was part of the closing duet from Puccini's *Turandot*. For a restful mood, she chose the Villa-Lobos Bachianas Brasilieras No. 5 ('to put me to sleep'). She asked for one poem – e. e. cummings reading his own 'What if a much of a which of a wind', and she described cummings as 'the David Hockney of poets'. The remaining four discs were in lighter vein – songs by Dionne Warwick and Frank Sinatra, a comedy sketch by Tony Hancock, and 'Rock around the Clock' by Bill Haley and the Comets.

Of the many dancers who have successfully made the transition to straight acting, Sir Robert Helpmann was probably the first. Quite early in his days with the Vic-Wells Ballet he decided that, because a dancer's performing life is so short, it would be taking out an insurance policy for his mature years to learn to act – although he had already played a small part in *The Barretts of Wimpole Street* in his native Australia, and appeared in a play called *I Hate Men* at the Gate Theatre when he had first arrived in London. With the acute shortage of male dancers, he knew that Lilian Baylis, who controlled both the Old Vic and Sadler's Wells Theatre, would not take kindly to the idea – so he decided to use guile. Every year, each principal member of the opera, ballet and drama companies had an interview with Miss Baylis at which the next year's salary was discussed. Robert walked in and shook the old lady rigid by saying that he wasn't going to ask for more money. Nobody had ever said anything like that to her before, and when he asked permission to play Oberon in the Old Vic production of *A Midsummer Night's Dream*, it was granted.

He is another dancer to have been first inspired by Anna Pavlova, whom he saw dance in Melbourne. It was arranged that he should take lessons with her, and that he should go on tour with her company to fill odd corners of the stage when necessary. It was she who gave him the second 'n' at the end of his surname. She was interested in numerology and told him the extra 'n' would bring him luck, although it gave a rather Teutonic look to a surname derived from an ancestry three parts Scottish to one part English.

It was Margaret Rawlings who encouraged him to come to London, and she once told me of a temperamental scene she had with the young dancer when she said she was going to send him for an audition at Sadler's Well. Angrily, he declared he hadn't come 13,000 miles to dance in a provincial company. It transpired that he was confusing Sadler's Wells with Tunbridge Wells

In May 1940, on the night the Germans launched their *Blitzkrieg* on Holland, Helpmann was dancing with the Vic-Wells Ballet in Arnhem. The instructions were that the company should finish the performance and then leave at once – fast. He, Margot Fonteyn and Ninette de Valois were lined up for a quick curtain call when a woman, with a little girl in Dutch costume, came on to the stage with bouquets of tulips and made a very long speech, in Dutch and then in English. Desperate with anxiety, Robert grabbed the bouquets from the little girl's hands, and the company fled into the waiting buses. Years later, in Hollywood, he was introduced to Audrey Hepburn, who revealed that she had been the little girl, and that the woman who made the speech was her mother, who was afterwards to become a leader of the Dutch underground movement. Four hours after the company left Arnhem, the Germans occupied the town. Dame Margot told me she saw the parachutists coming down. It took the dancers four days to reach England, crossing the North Sea in the hold of a cargo boat. Costumes, scenery, music and many personal possessions were left behind.

Helpmann was another dancer to choose the Panorama from Tchaikovsky's *The Sleeping Beauty*, and he also asked for the same composer's *Hamlet* Overture. Opera was represented by the Love Duet from *Madame Butterfly* and an aria from Verdi's *The Force of Destiny*, and lighter music by a Cuban rumba, and songs by Josephine Baker and Judy Garland. An unusual choice was a piece by Sibelius called 'The Bard'.

10

Films

What happened to the film business is sad. For those of my generation, films were an important part of our lives. For a shilling or two the cinema provided luxury and instant balm, an escape from worry and perplexity and an assured happy ending. Furthermore, we went to the cinema to see friends, those dimpled heroines and handsome heroes, and swarthy villains, and gormless or knowing comedians; all under contract to one studio or another, and drawing impressive salaries in exchange for the excitement and reassurance they gave.

Nowadays, cinemas are few and far between, and most films are aimed at a specialized audience of under-25s. Little comfort is to be had from the restless brightly-coloured reels of crude violence and overt sex, and there are few familiar names and faces. We are tempted to sit at home and look at old films on 'the box' – and that makes us lazy and sedentary and sentimental.

When *Desert Island Discs* started its run, the film industry was in the midst of a wartime boom, to be succeeded by an even bigger post-war boom, and the capture of a British or American film star for the series was a guarantee of a big listening audience.

The first star in a long list was Leslie Howard, in a programme transmitted in July 1942, when he was completing work, as actor and director, on *The First of the Few*, his film biography of R. J. Mitchell, the designer of the Spitfire. He selected a recording of William Walton's 'Spitfire Fugue', written to accompany a montage sequence of the prototype Spitfire being assembled.

Most of his discs were nostalgic. They included an Irving Berlin tune from one of the Music Box revues, to remind him of his early years in the New York theatre, and of the brilliant bohemians who assembled at the Round Table in the Algonquin Hotel; Charles Trenet's 'J'ai ta main dans ma main', as a souvenir of the South of France and sunshine and a world that seemed very far away; and the Grieg Concerto in A Minor, which was featured in his last Hollywood film, *Escape to Happiness*. Another disc recalled a facet of his talents which I have not seen referred to elsewhere: he loved to write songs. He chose a Bing Crosby record because, he told me with pride, Crosby had sung a song of his, called 'Without You', on a Hollywood radio programme.

Leslie Howard had an easy friendliness, and I recall his slim, casual elegance and the bright blue of his eyes. Although radio is a blind medium, his expressive face was acting every line of his script. The following year, this gifted man was to be killed when a plane in which he was flying from Lisbon to London was shot down by the Germans.

Many years later, Evelyn Rothwell, the oboist, told me that she and her husband, the late Sir John Barbirolli, were in Lisbon, on their way from New York to Manchester, where Sir John was to take over and reconstruct the Hallé Orchestra. They had crossed the Atlantic in a Portuguese ship of only seven thousand tons, and were waiting for air passages to London, which had been promised to them for the following Wednesday. On Saturday they were asked if they would care to exchange tickets with Leslie Howard and his manager, who had been allotted seats on a flight leaving that morning but who wished to stay a few days longer so that they could attend the Portuguese première of Howard's film, *The Gentle Sex*. As Sir John was anxious to get to work with the Hallé, they jumped at the opportunity Had they waited until Wednesday, they would have been on the plane which was shot down.

The first film director to be cast away was Michael Powell, who had had practical experience of being marooned on an island with a few records, although the island wasn't a deserted one. In the summer of 1936, he made a film called *Edge of the World*, inspired by a newspaper article about the gradual depopulation of the outer Scottish islands. His location was the little island of Foula, the westernmost of the Shetlands; his unit consisted of twenty-four men and two women, with an average age of twenty-five. In four months, they shot two hundred thousand feet of film, of which about seven thousand were used. By the end of October, several vital scenes still remained to be shot, and every day brought the winter gales nearer, with a good chance of the unit being marooned on Foula until spring. In fact, they were cut off for several weeks, with no fresh meat, bread, vegetables or cigarettes. They finished the picture in a hundred-miles-an-hour gale. Then came a lull, when a relief ship was able to take them off.

While on the island, their only music had been provided by Michael's portable gramophone, and he chose two discs which had stood the test of constant repetition under trying circumstances, Bax's 'Tintagel', and 'The Campbells are Coming', sung by the Glasgow Orpheus Choir.

At the time of the broadcast, Powell was directing his memorable tragi-comedy, *The Life and Death of Colonel Blimp*. When I saw the film I noticed that he had christened one of the characters in a War Office scene Plomley. I still haven't made up my mind whether he meant it as a compliment or not.

Perhaps the most musical of Britain's film directors was Anthony Asquith, whose first ambition was to be a composer. When he was seven, someone told him that Mozart had composed an opera at the age of eight, so he decided it was time he started, and began an opera based on his favourite book, H. Rider Haggard's *Allan Quartermain*, a subject which might present difficulties in staging. As he didn't get very far with the score, the problem did not arise.

While an Oxford undergraduate, he decided he wanted to make films, and his first job in the business was on a film about Boadicea, for which he made the tea, made-up Ancient Britons with woad, and, in a long blond wig, doubled for one of Boadicea's daughters, in a chariot. 'Puffin', as he was nicknamed, had a dreadful memory for names and faces, and a story is told that shortly after completing *The Browning Version*, a film set in an English public school, he was on Paddington Station when he was hailed by a distinguished and scholarly-looking gentleman. Asquith, who was well aware of his failing, was delighted that, although he couldn't remember the gentleman's name, he knew him immediately as the actor who had played the Headmaster.

'My dear fellow, how nice to see you,' he said. 'I congratulate you on a perfect piece of characterization; I've never seen anyone look more like a headmaster.'

It was only later in the day that he realized that he had been talking to the man who had been his real-life headmaster at Winchester.

Asquith's choice of discs showed his appreciation of all sides of life, and ranged from Bach and Monteverdi to 'Knocked 'em in the Old Kent Road', and 'If You Were the Only Girl in the

World', sung by George Robey and Violet Lorraine.

A George Robey disc, 'The Fact Is – ', was chosen by Alfred Hitchcock, who told me how he had begun in the film world, after a spell in engineering, by drawing what were known as 'art titles' in the days of the silent movies. 'The subtitle would read "John was leading a very fast life" and underneath I would draw a candle with a flame at both ends.') This is a fine example of a completely lost art.

I went to make his acquaintance in his suite at Claridges. He is the only film director to be readily recognizable to the public, because of his astute self-publicizing gimmick of appearing briefly in every one of his films. Even in *Lifeboat*, he was glimpsed, as the 'Before' photograph in an advertisement for a slimming preparation on a torn scrap of newspaper. After many years in Hollywood, he retains his London accent, and he has a kind of cocky complaisance that is endearing.

Shrewd publicist that he is, he was not going to lose an opportunity to advertise his latest picture, and I was amused to see how he twisted his answer to one of my questions to do just that. 'How well could you stand up to loneliness?' I asked.

'It's rather coincidental you should ask that,' replied Hitchcock, 'because I've expressed my feelings in a picture I've just finished, called *North by North-East* . . .' He went on to describe how he had decided to place his hunted hero, Cary Grant, not at the corner of a dark alley, but in the loneliest part of a desert. One might think all that had a tenuous connection with the desert island situation and extended loneliness – but that's film business.

As is well known, he is a director who has every shot of a picture clear in his mind before he starts production, his script illustrated with neat sketches for each set-up. So far as he is concerned, by then all the work has been done and it is merely a question of getting the actors to go through the required motions. Believing that the film is a visual medium, he tells his story with his camera rather than through dialogue.

He told me that from boyhood he has been a devotee of symphonic music. ('The Albert Hall on Sundays, and the Queen's Hall during the week.') He chose orchestral music by Roussel, Elgar and Wagner, Dohnányi's 'Variations on a Nursery Suite' ('because it opens like the most grandiose, huge, spectacular movie, probably by De Mille, and then reduces itself to a little tinkling on the piano. It's always appealed to my sense of humour') and Artur Rubinstein playing Schumann's 'Carnaval'. He also chose Gounod's 'Funeral March of a Marionette' ('because it does rather express my own attitude of treating the macabre with a sense of humour').

One of Hitchcock's earliest associates was Sir Michael Balcon, whose choice of discs showed him to be a complete romantic. It consisted of music by Donizetti, Ravel, Chopin, Richard Strauss, Puccini and Brahms, together with Shakespeare's sonnet, 'Shall I compare thee to a summer's day?' Sir Michael has been concerned with well over three hundred films, and will always be remembered for two particularly rich periods in his career, his adventurous Gaumont-British pictures of the early 'thirties, and the documentary-orientated Ealing pictures of the war years and the late 'forties. Sir Michael's job, as producer, was mainly in the office, and he controlled the financial side. He told me an amusing story of going to buy Islington Studios during the 'twenties, as a production centre for Gainsborough Films. The owner of the studios said to him: 'I've got a bit of a shock for you; we want £100,000 for the lease of the plant and equipment.'

Balcon replied: 'I've got a bigger shock for you; I'm offering you £14,000.'

The owner said, 'I'll take it.'

Balcon added, 'But I want to pay over seven years.'

And the deal was done.

He has a genius for collecting round him the best young directors and writers and technicians, and welding them into teams. To visit Ealing Studios during his regime was not like visiting any other film studios. Coming from the road, one crossed a lawn beside a white-painted house, through the french windows of which the boss kept a benevolent eye on what was going on. There was a bee-hive on the lawn, which seemed a symbol of the ordered activity which permeated the whole place. There was, too, an atmosphere of permanence which was missing in other studios; and the red-faced White Russian who was Publicity Director for many years, satirized this by putting his name on his office door reading: This week: Monja Danichewski. (It is the same excellent man who says that he wrote his publicity releases with the aid of a bottle of Veuve Cliché.)

A producer with a very different approach to his job is

Peter Rogers. He does not have to search for new talent, new stories, new ideas, or even new audiences; he produces a standardized product, made by the same people on the same production belt – and very nicely he does out of it.

An ex-journalist, he began writing radio plays, and was then invited to brighten up the scripts of some religious films. Feature films followed, and in 1958 he produced a cheaply-made comedy called *Carry On, Sergeant*. It made a lot of money. So he made exactly the same film again, in different costumes, with exactly the same result. After two or three more, he was able to buy his own studios, and with the same writer and director he has now made twenty-eight *Carry On* films, and is still going strong. With virtually the same cast, he makes two every year, fitting the production schedules between the artists' pantomime and summer show engagements.

I asked him his theory as to why audiences like the same old jokes over and over again; is it the reassurance of familiarity? He replied by using the analogy of a man who keeps a sweet shop, and who has a regular customer who comes in every week for liquorice all-sorts. If the shopkeeper didn't stock liquorice all-sorts any more and tried to supply something else instead, the customer would go away and not come back; he'd go where he could get liquorice all-sorts.

Peter's wife, Betty Box, is also a film producer, but they seldom talk about films at home. He makes a point of never seeing a *Carry On* film when an audience is present, because he doesn't want to be influenced by them; he believes he knows what they want better than they do. Obviously, he's right.

He's a self-taught musician, and he plays the piano and organ and balalaika, and he chose a programme of light classics which produced more letters from listeners, asking for record numbers, than any programme for years. In more than just old jokes, Peter Rogers's taste is the public's taste.

Here is his list: 'Méditation' from Massenet's *Thaïs*, 'Dance of the Blessed Spirits' from Gluck's *Orfeo ed Eurydice*, Liszt's Consolation No. 3 in D Flat, the Adagietto from Bizet's *L'Arlésienne* Suite, Scriabin's Adagio for Organ and Strings in G Minor, César Franck's Prelude, Fugue and Variations, and the Sanctus from Fauré's Requiem.

Richard Lester is a specialist in more sophisticated comedy. Nowadays, he is entrusted with big-budget international movies such as *A Funny Thing Happened on the Way to the Forum*,

The Three Musketeers and *Robin and Marian*, but his first film was made on a budget of only £70. It was called *The Running, Jumping and Standing Still Film*, and featured Harry Secombe, Spike Milligan and Peter Sellers. They used Peter's money and camera, and shot it on two Sundays. It made a profit and is still being shown today.

The difficulties of a low budget and little time were not new to Dick. He directed what he claims to have been the world's first, and only, Monday-through-Friday live television Western serial. It was transmitted from a car park, outside Philadelphia, and the telegraph poles had to be disguised as totem poles. The horses were hired from a local riding school, and were not very spirited, and if a member of the cast flung himself on a horse's back with a cry of 'After them', the nag would probably look up and cough. The story took place in Montana in the 'nineties, and the car park was on the direct flight path into Philadelphia Airport, so as soon as a plane was heard approaching, Dick faded in loud music. He found the most effective aircraft-drowning sequence to be the finale of Copland's Third Symphony, and, for old time's sake, that was one of the pieces of music he chose, as well as a composition by Paul McCartney and John Lennon, because he had faced the formidable task of turning the four young Beatles into actors in their two feature films, *A Hard Day's Night* and *Help!*

Rather to my surprise, a Beatles disc was chosen by John Huston, that fine American director who is of an older generation. He said he found 'Yellow Submarine' joyous, and it made him laugh.

A man who has knocked around the world to the extent that Huston has would surely take a spell on a desert island in his stride. He has been a boxer in the USA, a painter in Paris, a cavalryman in Mexico, a busker in the streets of London, and has been whaling in a long boat, an experience which was doubtless useful when he came to direct *Moby Dick*. He says that film was made during the worst winter in maritime history, and when it was over the Atlantic was littered with escaped electronic whales. He obtained the unusual seascape colour effects, resembling those in old prints, by processing black and white on top of colour.

Another of his choices was the famous disc of Kurt Weill's 'September Song', sung by his father, Walter Huston. I asked him his reactions to directing his father in a film, as he had done in *The Treasure of the Sierra Madre*, and he replied: 'The director has a way of becoming a father figure on the set, so our roles were rather reversed.' He recalled that he had given Marilyn Monroe her first speaking part, and had also directed her last film, *The Misfits*. 'The poor child had great difficulties within herself,' he said. 'The pressures of her life were simply too great for one as frail as she was emotionally.'

One of the spiciest bits of Hollywood scandal to reach my ears was confided to me by beautiful Maureen O'Sullivan, who has a really gorgeous sense of humour about the whole Hollywood set-up. I wonder how many moviegoers realized that Cheeta, the chimpanzee who accompanied Tarzan and Jane on so many adventures in MGM's jungle, was homosexual!

Maureen was born in the West of Ireland, and educated at a Roehampton convent, until a girlish escapade terminated her stay prematurely. She was 'discovered' in the classic story-book manner. It was Dublin Horseshow Week, and she happened to be sitting in a restaurant at a table next to one occupied by a group of Americans from Fox Films. A great deal of nudging went on among them, and then one leaned over to tell her that she was exactly the simple, natural, unspoiled, young Irish girl they were looking for to play in a film called *Song of my Heart*, in which John McCormack was to star.

Without any such formality as finding out if she could act, she was whisked to Hollywood, where specialists set to work straightening her teeth, re-aligning her eyebrows and devising a new hair-style for her. When she was delivered, on the set, to the director who had seen her in Ireland, he put his head in his hands and had her taken away to be put back into the state in which he had first seen her.

After *Song of my Heart*, she was cast in some films which had originally been prepared for Janet Gaynor, with whom the studio was having a fight, but that offended the Gaynor fans, and the films were unsuccessful. So Maureen found herself, at eighteen, a forgotten woman, owing a large hotel bill.

She had $250 in the world, and had to decide whether to give it to the hotel management or use it to have some new photographs taken. She decided on the latter course, and landed the part of Jane in the first version of *Tarzan of the Apes*, which was quite alarmingly sophisticated, being scripted by Ivor Novello, with Noël Coward looking over his shoulder.

Put under contract by MGM, she was to be in and out of the jungle for the next twelve years. As a contract artist she was worked hard, and if she finished at midday while filming *Anna Karenina*, instead of being allowed to go home she would be told: 'Go and get your skins on, and we'll do a couple of Tarzan scenes.' She made eighty films for MGM, and there was always a Tarzan film for her and Johnny Weismuller to work on during spare half days.

Married to director John Farrow, she found time for seven productions of her own: a family of seven children, one after another, in the shortest possible time.

The music she chose was mainly nostalgic, and included John McCormack singing the Irish song, 'Macushla', a flamenco song to remind her of Spain, 'Dear Prudence', which was written by the Beatles for one of her daughters, and Rachmaninov's Second Symphony, conducted by her son-in-law, André Previn. As a luxury, she chose a crate of tranquillizers.

One of her fellow contract players at MGM in the great days was James Stewart, slowest on the drawl in the West. He says he is fundamentally a loner and, apart from missing his family, he'd quite enjoy isolation on a desert island.

When he was a child, in Pennsylvania, his mother, a good musician, had tried to persuade him to take an interest in music, but he said that, although he had a good ear, the most he ever got around to learning was a few chords in C.

At Princeton University he read architecture, but spent at least as much time working on the shows presented by the Triangle Club. When he graduated he took a job playing the accordion – in the key of C, naturally – in a tea-room run in connection with a summer stock theatre in Massachusetts. When the customers protested, he was moved to odd jobs backstage, which led to playing small parts.

Jobs in the New York theatre followed, until he was spotted by a talent scout and shipped to Hollywood to play a part in a film called *The Murder Man*. That talent scout may subsequently have had to seek alternative employment, because the part for which Jimmy had been selected was a newspaper reporter named Shorty, and he happened to be a gangling six feet three inches.

Like Maureen O'Sullivan, he went through the MGM mill, playing small parts in big pictures and big parts in small pictures. Ultimately he specialized in light comedies such as *You*

Can't Take it With You and *The Philadelphia Story*, and romances such as *Seventh Heaven* and *Come Live With Me*.

When the United States entered the war, he joined the USAAF as a private, spent two years in Britain, flew Liberators, and ended up as a highly-decorated colonel.

Among his post-war pictures have been three or four for Alfred Hitchcock. I asked him for an actor's-eye view of that plump genius, who has so often expressed his opinion that actors are mere ciphers. James Stewart grinned and said that when someone asked Hitchcock if he had really said that actors are cattle, Hitchcock replied: 'Oh, no, I never said that; what I said was, you should treat them as cattle.' Despite it all, Jimmy expressed great respect and admiration for Hitchcock but believes that if it were possible for him to make movies without actors, he'd do it.

I asked him about the other directors for whom he had worked. 'Frank Capra made you feel you were doing everything right; John Ford scared you into doing everything right.'

After the war, sophisticated light comedies had given way to broader vehicles for such comedians as Red Skelton and Jerry Lewis, so Jimmy, having always been a good horseman, moved into Westerns. A superstititious man, he insisted on wearing the same hat in every film, until it got to the state where it was patched together with sticky tape.

His great joy is to travel the world photographing wild animals in their natural surroundings, and on the day when we recorded, he and his wife were off to dine with David Shepherd, the painter, to see how they could help him with his campaign to save the tiger from extinction.

The first record Jimmy Stewart chose was 'The Road to Mandalay', which he remembered his father singing, to his mother's accompaniment. The other discs, arranged chronologically, were dance tunes to remind him of various phases in his life. For his luxury he chose a piano, and for his book, some piano arrangements by Dave Brubeck, which sounds ambitious for a man who claims that his musical knowledge consists of a few chords in C – but, then, he's a very modest man.

I remember a session with the fabulous Marlene Dietrich.

'Ah, did you once see Shelley plain?' asked Robert Browning, in awe. Well, I couldn't have seen Marlene plainer, because we recorded the programme in her dressing-room at the Queen's

Theatre with our heads together over a portable recorder, and my eyes were not more than ten inches from that sensational face. Does it still bear such close inspection? It certainly does, and not only her face and figure but her movements and gestures too are those of a young woman.

But she lied to me!

She told me first of her Spartan upbringing in a Prussian household, and of how her ambition to be a concert violinist had been brought to nothing by an injury to a finger of her left hand. As music was denied her, she had become an actress, making her début on the Berlin stage in the tiny part of the Widow in the last act of Shakespeare's *The Taming of the Shrew* – but acting was a second-best. She talked of the modern plays, the revues and cabaret appearances that followed her début – and then she told her lie.

I said, 'You had made a number of films in Berlin, playing leading parts, before Josef von Sternberg engaged you for *The Blue Angel*, the film which brought you international success.'

Miss Dietrich replied, 'No, that's not true. *The Blue Angel* was the very first film I made.'

I had done my homework. In my pocket I had the notes I had made the previous evening while researching her career – and those notes included a list of a dozen films she had made before she worked for Sternberg. In fact, she had married the Assistant Director of her first film, so it was hardly likely she had forgotten that one!

There was a twinkle in those large, expressive eyes, and a tiny, challenging smile at the corners of her mouth as she watched for my reaction. She knew that I knew she was lying, and she was enjoying the moment. I hope my decision not to challenge her was instinctive. It is a beautiful woman's privilege to juggle with time, especially when, as in Marlene's case, she has defeated it, and if she wished to delete a few years from the chronology of her career, then her wish should be respected. I don't think my voice betrayed my disbelief, nor was there a noticeable hesitation before I asked the next question.

I was surprised to hear how little her films had meant to her. She looked back on none of them with affection, and said she was much happier in her new career of giving solo entertainment in the theatres of the world.

The records she chose were: Stravinsky's *The Rite of Spring*, Beethoven's Third Symphony, and his 'Apassionata' Sonata, played by Sviatoslav Richter, Ravel's 'La Valse', and the Cat Duet from the same composer's *L'Enfant et les Sortilèges*, and three pop songs written by Burt Bacharach, who was then her musical director. The book she asked for is *The Story of Life* by Constantine Paustovsky.

Her dressing-room was sparsely furnished; she had imported no furniture or pictures of her own – except for one framed photograph. It was of Ernest Hemingway, and inscribed by him 'To my favourite Kraut'.

II

Radio and Television

I became a radio listener in crystal set days, hurrying home from school to hear the daily *Children's Hour*, in which the BBC Aunts and Uncles read stories, sang songs and indulged in a little gentle fooling. My favourite uncle was Uncle Rex, who was first-rate at reading adventure serials and who sang such ballads as 'Drake Goes West' in a manly baritone. It was a thrill when he read out 'Roy Plomley, of Kingston-upon-Thames' among the birthday children.

I knew that Uncle Rex's name was Rex Palmer, because sometimes he announced the evening programmes, and that meant his name was in *Radio Times*. I visualized him as tall and slim, with dark wavy hair, and invariably wearing the smartest of dinner-jackets; when I met him, I found he was shortish, as bald as I am, and favoured informal clothes.

A Lincolnshire man, he took a degree in engineering, then served during the First World War in the Royal Engineers and as a pilot in the Royal Flying Corps. He started broadcasting, as a singer, in the summer of 1922 in the experimental programmes put out by the Marconi Company. When the BBC started, he was engaged as London Station Director, which means that he arranged the programmes, announced them, and moved the piano when necessary. All this took place on the top floor of Marconi House, in a small room which served as studio, office and waiting-room combined.

In 1929 he left the Corporation to join HMV records, where he had the pleasant job of travelling round Europe, arranging recording sessions with artists who were on the international circuit. It is understandable that seven of his chosen records were from the HMV catalogue, and they included the famous Schumann-Lehmann-Olzewska trio from *Der Rosenkavalier*, the recording of which he had supervised himself in Vienna. Other souvenirs of his recording career were the Elgar Violin Concerto, with the composer conducting and the young Yehudi Menuhin as soloist, Jussi Björling singing 'E lucevan le stelle', from *Tosca*, which he recorded in Stockholm, and Beethoven's 'Coriolan' Overture, conducted by Toscanini, who had insisted it should be recorded in the Queen's Hall.

After service in the RAF during the Second World War, Rex returned to radio, as a freelance, referring to himself as 'the BBC's oldest inhabitant'.

A great friend of Rex Palmer's was Christopher Stone, the first man to make an art of presenting records on the air. Christopher's was the casual approach; he mispronounced the titles, got the numbers wrong, and was inclined to sit on the disc he planned to play next. Listeners took him to their hearts, and his amiable bumbling made him one of radio's first big stars. In fact, he was so big a star that he was engaged to top the bill at the London Palladium, where he puffed his pipe and played his records on that vast stage, introducing as a tremendous novelty a gramophone which played backwards.

I met him first in Paris, when I was a young announcer responsible for the English transmissions from Poste Parisien. He was passing through the city and telephoned to invite me for a drink – a pleasant gesture from a distinguished broadcaster to a very junior colleague. He was my guest in *Desert Island Discs* on two occasions, the second to celebrate his seventy-fifth birthday. He sat with me in the listening-room and was so little his usual cheerful self that I asked him what was the matter. Miserably, he said he had left his pipe at home, so I ran round the corner and bought him one as a birthday present.

He was a widower for many years, and lived a rather lonely bachelor existence. The son of a master at Eton College, he returned to Eton to spend his last years, living in a tiny and picturesque cottage in a court off the High Street. He was a startlingly ingenuous man. He once said to me: 'The other day, I was in a friend's flat overlooking Hyde Park and, do you know, on a seat just below us sat a prostitute. There she was, accosting men in broad daylight.' In those pro-Street Offences Act days it would have been hard to find a seat in Hyde Park not occupied by a tart, broad daylight or not, and it was typical of the man that he never noticed such goings-on.

There were two records common to both his programmes; 'La Calinda', from *Koanga*, by Delius ('I've had a great ballet craze all my life'), and a song by a pair of duettists named Scovell and Wheldon. ('I can't tell you anything about them, except that years ago Fred Scovell wrote, and they both recorded, this song, "When Everyone Else has Passed You By".

You may say it's sentimental, you may even say it's corny – but it has heart.')

Having been Isobel Barnett's questionmaster in eleven – or is it twelve? – series of *Many a Slip*, I never cease to be amazed at the number of her accomplishments. As well as being a qualified physician, she is a good musician (if not singer!), has a working knowledge of law, and an exceptional knowledge of history, topography and horticulture. She has no show business ambitions and still describes herself as an amateur.

An ex-Lady Mayoress of Leicester, she was invited to take part in a number of radio discussion programmes, one of which was televised. A perceptive newspaper critic suggested that she would be a useful recruit to the television panel game, *What's My Line?*, and the BBC acted on the suggestion. A few months later she discovered, rather to her bewilderment, that she had been chosen, by another newspaper, as Top Variety Artist. As befits a good amateur pianist, she chose five piano recordings among her discs, two compositions by Chopin, and one each by Beethoven, Schubert and Bach.

She is a dedicated worker for charity, and claims to have opened more bazaars than are due to anyone in a lifetime. One of the drawbacks of that task is that one is expected to go round the stalls and buy little somethings, and I suggested she must have acquired a lot of little somethings by now. She confessed to having a very large collection indeed, many of them seeming to have no particular use whatever. I asked her what she was going to do with them all, and she replied that she sent them to bazaars. It was an ill-advised thing to say: a mass of letters arrived from what seemed like every bazaar organizer in the country, asking for some of Isobel's little somethings.

A time of the year which I used to dread was the end of August, because then we had to do a 'live' programme from a hot little glass booth set among dense crowds at the National Radio and Television Show at Earl's Court. On those occasions, I insisted that my guest should be a very experienced broadcaster indeed, because it was no joke to work under such uncomfortable conditions. One person we talked into doing the job was Godfrey Talbot, then the BBC's Senior Reporter, who was known as 'Our Man at the Palace', because he was in charge of the broadcasting of all occasions involving members of the Royal Family.

He maintains that a royal tour is the most rugged job in radio. It means moving on to a different place every day, and covering as much as fifty thousand miles. 'One of the most difficult things to organize is shopping,' he told me, 'because each town the royal visitor goes to is having the biggest day in its life – so all the shops are shut.' Once he tried every day for three and a half weeks to buy a tube of toothpaste – and laundry was an even worse problem.

His worst moment happened when covering a royal visit to the Outer Hebrides. He was by the side of a road, recording a description of the crowds waiting for the royal party, and there were some inconsiderate people who kept pestering him by asking questions. He was adjusting his recording machine when he heard footsteps that stopped immediately behind him. He didn't look up, and said, rather tersely, 'Do you mind moving away? I can't talk to anybody now.' He then looked up and found that he was addressing the Queen and the Duke of Edinburgh.

His list included the Crimond setting of the 23rd Psalm, the opening scene of Puccini's *Tosca*, 'Lilli Marlene', in the original German version, John Tilley's Scoutmaster monologue, and Charlie Kunz at the piano.

The rigours of broadcasting from the Earl's Court hot-box meant nothing to him, nor did they to John Snagge, who has been responsible for the commentaries of such historic broadcasts as the Queen's Coronation. That transmission, which had the biggest audience of any broadcast ever, needed months of preparation, many rehearsals and split-second timing. No fewer than a hundred and twenty microphones were needed to provide a sound picture of the great occasion.

As Head of Presentation, John's was the official voice of the BBC, and on hearing his deep, vibrant tones saying 'This is London', one was inclined to get a cold feeling in the pit of the stomach and ask oneself what national disaster had happened now. He told me the most difficult announcement he was called upon to make was of the death of King George VI, because it was so completely unexpected, and inevitably a tremendous shock to many millions of people. He was at a conference, planning some variety programmes, when a messenger brought into the room a slip of paper and laid it in front of him. The message simply read, "H.M. is dead.' For a moment, John couldn't think who 'H.M.' could possibly be;

his first reaction was that it must be the BBC's Head of Music.

His great annual day out is the Universities Boat Race, on which he has given a commentary every year since 1931, following the race in a launch, maintaining a precarious balance with a microphone in one hand and a pair of field glasses in the other. It hasn't always been plain sailing: one year, the BBC launch collided with a press launch, which sank.

'Did you stop to pick up the press men?' I asked.

'Er – no. Our motto was "the show must go on".'

He also told me of the year when the BBC launch broke down and finally reached the finishing line at Mortlake twenty minutes after the race was over, being greeted with ironic cries from both banks of 'Well rowed, BBC'.

Inevitably, his choice of discs included 'The Eton Boating Song' and an excerpt from the Coronation Service. He also chose part of an ITMA programme, because he had announced the series so often, and it reminded him of happy evenings with Tommy Handley and Ted Kavanagh and the rest of the ITMA gang.

The excerpt began with John Snagge's voice, struggling gallantly with one of the alliterative, tongue-twisting announcements which Ted and Tommy delighted in writing for him, and then the voices of Tommy, and Sam Scram, and Mrs Mopp, and Colonel Chinstrap, whose characterization had been based on an Indian Army friend of John's. Hearing those familiar voices from the past had an instant effect on the crowds outside our glass booth. Those near us listened with broad smiles, giving each other little nudges of pleasure, while the moving throng behind them paused in their shuffle round the exhibition stands. In many an eye there was moistness, as through the great hall echoed the catch phrases that had brought laughter in the darkest days of the war.

John Snagge is one of the few senior announcers of his generation to come into the profession without a musical background; Alvar Lidell had started by singing with a touring puppet show, and Frank Phillips had been a professional singer for ten years or more before he foresook the concert platform for the News Studio. Stuart Hibberd, the original voice of the BBC, although never a professional, had been an enthusiastic amateur singer.

Having read Science at Cambridge, Stuart Hibberd joined the Army during the First World War, and then transferred to the Indian Army. In 1923, he found himself in London without a job, and answered a BBC advertisement for a Station Director at Cardiff. As a requirement was a good knowledge of Welsh literature, of which he knew nothing, it's not surprising he didn't get the job, but he was passed on to someone else who was looking for an assistant announcer at Savoy Hill. He announced from 1924 until his retirement in 1951, and with the exception of the first three years, was Chief Announcer the whole time, introducing great artists and statesmen, cheerfully acting as stooge to comedians, and reading the news on more than fifteen thousand occasions. He recalled that it was during the General Strike of 1926, when there were no newspapers, that the public first realized how important broadcasting is. Ten years later, his was the voice which, in one of the most sensitive pieces of announcing in the history of the craft, brought the realization of the end of an era with the repeated words, 'The King's life is drawing peacefully to its close.'

The late 'twenties and 'thirties were especially exciting, he said, because the whole world was linking up, until, on Armistice Day, 1937, he was able to announce, 'This is the British Broadcasting Corporation calling the British Isles, the British Empire, the Continent of Europe and the United States of America, through Daventry 5XX and Chelmsford 5SW.'

He took his job very seriously, and rumour had it that before any important broadcast, he could be heard rehearsing his announcements to himself in the nearest Broadcasting House lavatory. A lean, military figure, he was kindness itself to any nervous broadcaster, and one of the last men in London to wear spats. He is now in retirement in Budleigh Salterton, where his silver tones can still be heard on occasion, reading the lessons in church.

His chosen discs included two excerpts from French opera, two pieces of piano music, a carol by the Choir of King's College, Cambridge, Paul Robeson singing 'Deep River', Harry Pepper's 'Carry Me Back to Green, Green Pastures', sung by the Kentucky Minstrels, and Stanley Holloway reciting 'Sam, Pick up tha' musket'.

Going back to ITMA, the fact that Ted Kavanagh chose to remain a scriptwriter, instead of performing, meant the loss of a fine comedian. He used to do the 'warm-up' before ITMA broadcasts, and he was brilliant. He had the advantage of being a larger-than-life character anyway; he was plump and ruddy-complexioned, with a moustache that was rather too small for his face. As he entered, a length of red carpet was run out in front of him, and the members of the cast, who were already on stage, bowed low as he passed.

He was a New Zealander, of Irish stock, who came to Britain to study medicine but, instead, became a writer on medical and scientific subjects. As the years went by, his writing became less and less scientific, which was probably due to the fact that he had started to share a flat with Tommy Handley. At that time, in the late nineteen-twenties, a boom in gramophone record sales was on, with new recording companies springing up all over London, and Tommy was much in demand to record comic songs. Ted discovered that he had an unsuspected gift for writing them, and a partnership started. From comic songs, he progressed to writing radio comedy, culminating in ITMA, which he wrote for ten years.

He was always ready to help younger writers, and he formed a group of a dozen or so to work together and spark ideas off each other. I was one of them; others were Frank Muir, Denis Norden, Sid Colin and Spike Hughes. We started with offices in Waterloo Place, and then moved to a grander address, in Bruton Street. One of the amenities of the new offices was a small window on the staircase which looked across a narrow side street to the window of the models' dressing-room in a *haute couture* establishment. There was a great deal of loitering on those stairs, which actor Martin Boddey called 'the original Charlie Staircase'.

At his home in Spanish Place, one Sunday morning in January 1949, Ted was putting the finishing touches to the ITMA script for the following week, when the telephone rang. It was an official of the BBC to tell him that Tommy Handley had collapsed and died suddenly, and would Ted please have a memorial contribution ready for the six o'clock news that evening? Sadly, Ted turned over the page of script he had been working on, and began to write on the back a tribute to his friend and colleague.

Ted was fond of all kinds of music – 'from "Chopsticks" to Stravinsky'. In deference to his Irish ancestry, he asked for John McCormack singing 'Believe me, if all those endearing young charms', following it with the Polovtsian Dances, from Borodin's *Prince Igor*, Tod Slaughter in a scene from *Sweeney Todd, the Demon Barber of Fleet Street*, Tommy Handley singing a comic song, Owen Brannigan singing 'Blaydon Races', and a French children's choir singing a lullaby.

Frank Muir and Denis Norden shared a small top room in the Kavanagh offices. Ted had persuaded them to team up together because, he said, each was too tall to team with any-one else. One of their recipes for getting a lot of work done was to have only two chairs in the office, so that anyone dropping in for idle chatter became tired of standing after a few minutes, and drifted off.

I first met Frank just after the war, when I was appearing in a weekly comedy series with the unlikely title of 'The Accordion Club', which was produced by Charles Chilton, and in which I was general factotum, writing the script, compèring, and acting as straight man to the comics. One of our regular guest comics was an ex-RAF pilot, with a moustache like an explosion, who was performing at the Windmill Theatre, where he sat, centre stage, on a beer crate, and told stories. His name was Jimmy Edwards, and he came to the studio accompanied by another ex-RAF man, with a similar moustache, whom he introduced, rather grandly, as 'my writer'. That was Frank, and he was learning his trade by the trial and error process of writing gags for Jimmy's act and noting which ones died a death. Jimmy was rather in need of material, because he confided to me that at his audition at the Windmill, having failed to make the manager, Vivian Van Dam, laugh, he had offered, nervously, to shave off his moustache. Wearily, Van Dam had said, 'For God's sake, don't do that. It's the only funny thing in your act.'

One day, when I came back early from a coffee break, I found Frank, in the empty studio, standing in my place and reading my lines into the microphone. He looked embarrassed, and muttered something about 'trying out the acoustics'. In fact, his performing ambitions had to be put aside for quite a long time, because he and Denis hit the jackpot with one of radio's most successful comedy series, *Take it From Here*, with Jimmy Edwards, Dick Bentley and Joy Nichols, which they wrote for twelve years. When they were eventually released from the salt mines of comedy writing, they revealed them-selves as a very talented ad lib team, especially in such pro-grammes as *My Word* and *My Music*. Their senses of humour fit together as exactly as the two halves of a broken biscuit, and so do their tastes in music, as they showed when they appeared together in *Desert Island Discs*. It was at that time that they demonstrated that certain Frank Sinatra records, if played at 45 rpm instead of 33 rpm, sound exactly like Eartha Kitt, a piece of information that can represent a considerable economy.

A broadcaster whom I never cease to admire is Alistair Cooke, who has been transmitting his weekly *Letter From America* since 1946. It has such a pleasantly off-the-cuff air that I was not surprised to hear that he sits down at his typewriter, usually with no idea what he is going to write about, and talks as he types, taking only about an hour and forty minutes to complete the script.

His first interest was the theatre. At Cambridge, after an undergraduate career during which he edited *Granta* and founded the first mixed university dramatic society, he did post-graduate research in dramatic criticism and theatre direction. He then took up a fellowship at Yale in the same subject, and moved on to Harvard and a study of the American language.

He was commissioned by a London newspaper to write a series of articles on Hollywood. He wrote to Charles Chaplin, asking for an interview. The two men took to each other immediately, and the interview lasted until three o'clock in the morning. It culminated in Mr Chaplin inviting him to collaborate on a film script about Napoleon in exile. The script was written, but Chaplin developed doubts as to whether cinemagoers would accept him in the role, and the film was never made.

Returning to London, Alistair Cooke became the BBC film critic, because working with Chaplin had switched his loyalty from theatre to films. He became appalled to find how ignorant the majority of Britons were, in those days, about the United States, and decided there would be a useful and fascinating career for him in explaining one country to the other, so he emigrated to America.

He is a fervent jazz enthusiast, and no mean jazz pianist himself. He asked for discs by Ted Lewis and his Band (with Fats Waller), Gene Krupa, Jack Teagarden, Earl Hines and Duke Ellington. His remaining three were a negro spiritual and works by Purcell and Mozart.

It is always interesting to me to interview another interviewer. Robin Day is an admirable practitioner, and those who accuse him of pressing too hard forget that the majority of his subjects are politicians, who are fair game for a tough approach. He had an intensive course in the marshalling of facts and the demolishing of opponents when, as President of the Oxford Union, he went on a debating tour of fifty universities and colleges in the United States. He was called to the Bar, but after eighteen months decided to sell his wig and go in for television journalism, which was then a very new and approximate craft.

He says that, when planning an interview with a politician, he tries to imagine what the answer to a question is going to be; then he can bang in a supplementary question, which is usually the more important. It is sometimes necessary, of course, to have alternative supplementary questions ready. He agreed with me that what a man won't say can very often convey more than what he does say.

His choice of records included political speeches by Sir Winston Churchill and President Kennedy, and Al Jolson singing 'You Made Me Love You'. The last disc brought with it the surprising confession that Robin's secret ambition is to be a song-and-dance man, with straw hat and cane.

The first man in this country to practise the interview in depth was John Freeman. In the American-style series *Face to Face* he used a psycho-analytical approach, based on the system that first you find the sensitive spot, and then you press. Sometimes Freeman pressed too hard, and several of his interviewees ended up in tears, including Gilbert Harding, who was then the nation's idol.

Nowadays, with mass entertainment spread out so vastly and so thinly, it is hard to realize just how big a figure Gilbert Harding was during the 'fifties. It was Joyce Grenfell who gave the best summing-up of his character: 'Beneath the crisp crust,' she said, 'it's all marshmallow' – and she was right.

In a small way, I had a hand in promoting his success. I met him first during the war, when I was in a studio in Broadcasting House, and just about to go on the air with a *Desert Island Discs* programme. Suddenly, the door was thrown open, and a vigorous tweed-clad figure charged in. Rather protuberant eyes looked through horn-rimmed spectacles, and a brown moustache bristled on his upper lip. 'Are you Roy Plomley?' he demanded. 'My name's Gilbert Harding, Outside Broadcasts Department. You don't know me, but I heard you were in this studio and I've looked in to tell you how much I like your series.'

It is very unusual for anyone to enter a studio when the rehearsal light is on above the door unless some urgent professional reason calls for it: in Gilbert's case, it was a typically unconventional impulse, and a good-hearted one.

Shortly after that, he went to Canada as BBC representative, a post in which he was not an unqualified success, because of his habit of speaking forthrightly. When he returned, the BBC didn't seem to know what to do with him, and they put him in an unrewarding job in the Overseas Service. He was to be seen in the pubs and bars round Broadcasting House, talking brilliantly, scathingly, wittily, and practically non-stop to anyone who would listen. It was a humbling experience to hear him retell a story you had told him yourself: you had the impression of having played him the piccolo part and had it returned to you fully orchestrated. In my experience, only Sir Compton Mackenzie and James Agate have rivalled Gilbert as a talker – not conversationalist, please note, but talker.

Then a stroke of luck came his way. The BBC wartime series, *Transatlantic Quiz*, had come off the air because there were no longer dollars available to pay for the American end of it: in its place was to be a similar programme in which a London team, under the chairmanship of Lionel Hale, played a series of contests against teams in the provinces, and Gilbert was given the job of being the travelling questionmaster in charge of the provincial teams. The scholarly lightheartedness of the programme appealed to him, and *Round Britain Quiz* became an established success. On the strength of it, he resigned from the staff and became a freelance.

This move paid off almost immediately, because a questionmaster was needed for a revived series of *Any Questions* and he was given that job too. Financially, he was now doing quite well, but in both his series he was doing no more than control other speakers, and had no opportunities to air his own views.

At that time, I was questionmaster of a series called *We Beg to Differ*, which was produced by Pat Dixon, one of the most dedicated and creative radio men I have ever worked with. It was a battle of the sexes, with four women, Kay Hammond, Gladys Young, Joyce Grenfell and Charmian Innes, opposing two men, John Clements and the Radio Doctor, Charles Hill (afterwards to become Lord Hill, and Chairman of the BBC

Governors). The two teams argued, mainly frivolously, about matters on which the sexes are inclined to differ, with occasional forays into more serious matters. The fact that four women were considered necessary to oppose only two men was, in itself, a cause of dissension. As Chairman, I had a neutral, or hermaphroditic, role, and was armed with a gavel, which I thumped when the discussion got out of hand. The programme had an enormous and partisan audience.

Charles Hill announced that he had been adopted as a parliamentary candidate, which meant he had to leave us. Pat Dixon tried three or four men in his place, but none of them fitted in.

One day, after the recording of a programme in which a new recruit had not shown up very brightly, Pat Dixon, John Snagge and I walked from the Piccadilly studio to a pub called The Three Fishes, in Babmaes Street. Standing at the bar, we tried to think of some suitable replacements. A few were suggested, and rejected, and then I said, 'What about Gilbert Harding?'

'We've thought of him,' said John, 'but he wouldn't be right.'

'He'd be too outrageous,' added Pat.

'Surely that would be all to the good,' I insisted. 'It would be fine to have somebody outrageous. If he did go too far – well, the programme is recorded and we could always edit a bit out.'

John and Pat looked at each other, and both nodded slowly. To edit material out of a slow-speed disc (which was the recording method used in 1949) was a fiddling and time-consuming procedure, but it could be done.

As a result of my pressing the point, Gilbert was booked for a trial run in the series, and that was the beginning of the Harding legend. It was in *We Beg to Differ* that he blossomed into the cantankerous, opinionated bachelor who was to be a national figure for the next decade. It was his chance and he took it magnificently. Sometimes he over-acted, because a lot of it was an act, but it didn't matter. One evening, when he was at my house, I lent him a small collection of books about the plump, irascible American drama critic, Alexander Woollcott, whom George S. Kaufman and Moss Hart depicted as *The Man Who Came to Dinner*. Gilbert took them away as source material for his new public image.

Woollcott had played the part of himself in a revival of *The Man Who Came to Dinner* and, in his turn, Gilbert decided that he also had theatrical aspirations. He had seen a comedy of mine called *All Expenses Paid* at the Q Theatre, and there was a character in it, a quick-tempered film producer, which would have suited him perfectly. It wasn't a long part but a telling one, and an ideal role for a star performer whose stage experience was negligible.

Jack de Leon had the play under option, and he was delighted at the idea of casting Gilbert in it. He set to work to arrange a tour, prior to a London production, but when dates were discussed, Gilbert discovered to what extent success already had him in its grasp: there were so many future engagements in his book that the project was impossible.

He would have been a good actor, within limits, especially in comedy. Certainly, the memorizing of lines would have been no problem, for in that respect he was phenomenal.

Unfortunately, as the years went on, he gave too much licence to the aspects of his nature which, in small doses, had made him such a change from the conventionally smooth radio and television 'personality'. Aggravated by *angst* and by alcohol, his brusqueness was liable to become downright rudeness, and his intolerance become rage. I have been with him, rigid with embarrassment, while he offensively abused a waiter or someone else in no position to answer back, and, many times, I saw excess change his brilliant talk into tedious hectoring.

Often, his ill-temper backfired on him. I remember two instances which occurred during a television series of *We Beg to Differ*. As he did not drive a car, he arranged that his friend and tailor – and mine still – Reggie Halford, should collect him each Monday evening, after the transmission from the Lime Grove studios, and usually we would all three go and have supper together.

One cold Monday evening in January, Gilbert asked that we should hurry, as he wanted to meet someone at the Savage Club, and he invited us to be his guests there. The programme finished at about a quarter past ten, and the Savage Club closed at eleven.

Gilbert and I had been trailed most of the evening by an unknown woman who had somehow got into the backstage area of the studio. She appeared to be a friend or relative of one of the administrative staff, and her talk had been ceaseless. Just as we were leaving the studio, she came up and said, 'Oh, Mr Harding – Mr Plomley – I suppose neither of you happens to be going near Ladbroke Grove, because I'd be most grateful for a lift.'

'Sorry, dear lady, we're going in the opposite direction,' said Gilbert. 'Delighted to have met you.' He nudged me towards the door, with a muttered, 'Hurry up. We must be at the Savage by eleven.'

However, we had been joined by Reggie Halford, whose feelings were more gallant. Overhearing her request, he said, 'We'll be happy to drop you there. It won't take us out of our way.'

Well, it did take us out of our way, because we got lost three times, and Gilbert was fuming and muttering to himself, and repeatedly looking at his watch.

Eventually, we dropped the lady in some unknown street and, as soon as she had left us, Gilbert exploded with rage. It was now five minutes to eleven, it was too late to go to the Savage Club, our behaviour had been not only inconsiderate but downright offensive, we were no longer friends of his, and he did not care to ride with us any more. Reaching the peak of his tirade, he got out of the car, slammed the door and stamped off down the street.

We watched him disappear, in silence. We debated whether to go after him, decided it would do no good until he had cooled down, and Reggie drove me to my house in Putney, where we sat and talked.

At a quarter past twelve, the telephone rang. It was Gilbert.

'Where are you?' I asked.

'Queen's Park.'

'Where's that?'

'Somewhere on the way to Wembley.'

'What are you doing there?'

'I couldn't find a taxi, and I walked for miles until I found a tube station, and then I got into a train going the wrong way – so I'm at Queen's Park.'

'Is there another train?'

'I'm waiting for the last one. This is the most desolate railway station known to man. Is Reggie with you?'

'Yes. We're sitting by the fire, drinking scotch.'

There was an agonized gulp at the other end of the line, and the receiver was replaced. His rages never lasted long, and afterwards there was contrition.

Two Mondays later, I invited Gilbert and Reggie to supper at the Screenwriters Club, which used to be in Deanery Street and where there was no nonsense about closing at eleven o'clock. We ordered three fillet steaks and salad.

'I want a plain green salad,' said Gilbert to the waiter. 'Just lettuce, nothing else.'

We drank claret until the steaks arrived. They looked delicious. A little wooden bowl of salad was put in front of each of us – lettuce and a few pieces of tomato.

'Take this away,' said Gilbert angrily, pushing his bowl towards the waiter. 'I ordered plain green salad.'

'This is green salad,' said the waiter.

'It isn't,' roared Gilbert. 'Tomatoes aren't green. Just bring me plain lettuce, without tomatoes.'

The waiter took the bowl away.

'You won't mind if Reggie and I start; we're hungry,' I said, and we began to eat.

The waiter was away a minute or two, during which time Gilbert tapped the table with growing impatience. When the bowl was returned, it contained nothing but lettuce. He began to heap it on his plate, then let out a roar that startled diners at other tables. The waiter came running back.

'This still isn't plain green salad! You've just taken the pieces of tomato off and brought me the same bowl again. Look! There's a tomato pip!'

Reggie and I went on eating. Gilbert's behaviour was disgraceful, particularly as he was a guest in my club, but we were not going to let his tantrums interfere with our enjoyment.

'Take it away! Take it all away! Take this away too,' shouted Gilbert, pushing away his steak. 'I'm not going to eat in a place which doesn't know how to serve food. Remove it.'

The startled waiter removed the offending salad – and the steak. Gilbert sat and sipped claret, and sulked.

'Very good steak, this,' I said to Reggie.

'Excellent,' he replied.

I could see Gilbert eyeing each succulent morsel as I raised it to my lips. His mouth was watering – but he stuck to his guns; he wouldn't even join us in a little cheese.

The better one grew to know him, the more sympathy one had for his outbursts. He was a tortured man, subject to extreme anxieties and tensions, and he tried to conquer them by ceaseless activity. He took on far more work than he could reasonably do. In addition to the contracts he already had, he became Chairman of *Twenty Questions* on radio, and a panel member on *What's My Line?* on television; he also accepted speaking engagements all over the country. He never stopped.

To be alone was an ordeal for him. He surrounded himself with people – and the more the better. I have been with him in his flat when he has pressed the gasman, the plumber and the postman to stay and drink with us. Interspersed with the euphoria and the hellraising were periods of deep melancholy and guilt – guilt because of his feeling that to play parlour games in public was a poor way for a man of his education and ability to earn a rich living (he called himself the telephoney) and because he could adjust himself neither to his abnormal sex life nor to the fact that his excesses were a form of self-destruction and against the tenets of the faith to which he was a convert.

He was, without exception, the kindest man I have ever met. There was a time when he went on tour for a few weeks with a music-hall presentation of *What's My Line?* He was very unhappy and, one day during the opening week, I went up to Finsbury Park Empire to keep him company. I spent some of the time in his dressing-room, helping him open his mail, and I saw how he was using a considerable amount of the money he was earning in unobtrusively helping people in need.

One day, after we had recorded a *We Beg to Differ* programme in which he had launched into a tirade against the average child – 'Children shouldn't be seen but not heard, they shouldn't be seen either' – we went together to the first house of a revue at the Adelphi Theatre. I discovered that Gilbert and I shared an aversion to paying a shilling for a cloakroom fee, so we took our overcoats with us into the stalls. For the first time in his life, he had money to spend on clothes, and he had celebrated the fact by having Reggie Halford make him a really magnificent new overcoat, which he had been showing us in the studio before the recording. In front of Gilbert sat a small boy who couldn't see the stage very well because of a large man sitting in front of him. Without hesitating, Gilbert folded up his fine new overcoat, lifted up the little boy and placed the overcoat under him as a cushion, so that he could see. I don't know any other man who would have done that.

In reality, he loved children. He came with me to a matinée to see Diana, my wife, play Principal Girl in a Moss Empires production of *Aladdin*. My daughter, Almond, then aged two and a half, was also in the party and, at one point, she leaned over and gave Gilbert her greatly loved Teddy bear to hold. I told Gilbert he was greatly honoured, because she seldom let Teddy out of her grasp. He went bright pink with pleasure.

In his later years, I saw little of him. Our paths and our interests divided. When we did meet, I was saddened to see how gross and heavy and ill he looked.

He collapsed and died on the steps of a BBC building after recording some *Round Britain Quiz* programmes. It was a sudden end, and he had friends at his side.

The BBC didn't broadcast those last programmes of his, and I think that was a mistake – because there was a man who had been afraid of dying, and just a few minutes before his passing he had been chuckling and playing the quiz game which he enjoyed.

A few weeks later, I telephoned his secretary, Roger Storey, who was arranging for the disposal of his belongings. I asked him to let me have the little library of Alexander Woollcott books, which Gilbert had never returned. Mr Storey told me that he had found among Gilbert's papers a note which read:

I wish I had kept the promise which I made to Roy Plomley one day, when we were walking in Finsbury Park, that I would keep a diary.

I remembered that promise. It was on the occasion when I had visited him at the music-hall, and we had walked in the park. As usual, he was complaining of his feelings of inadequacy, because he was not doing work of any consequence; he wanted to write, but could not concentrate. I told him I thought I had an answer for him: he would make a brilliant diarist. He went everywhere, he knew everyone, he was a splendid raconteur, and it was only a matter of dictating a few hundred words into his recording machine every night, for his secretary to transcribe in the morning. Arnold Bennett had been the supreme diarist of the 'teens and 'twenties, and then James Agate had carried on during the 'thirties and 'forties . . . It is indeed a loss that we don't have Gilbert Harding's diaries of the 'fifties.

'I do wish the future were over' are the last words of his autobiography, *Along My Line*, which was published in 1953, and of which he said to me, cynically, 'A poor thing, but not mine own'. Now that it is over, he would be happy to know how affectionately he is spoken of by those who were his friends.

12

Sport

On the shelves of my local public library, there are three times as many books devoted to cricket as to any other sport, but although it is a game with a literary tradition, it does not seem to attract musicians. About a dozen cricketers have taken part in the series, and my generic impression of a cricketer's choice, always with geographical overtones, is as follows:

'Waltzing Matilda'
'Sari Marais'
Calypso: 'Cricket, Lovely Cricket'
'Sussex by the Sea'
'On Ilkley Moor baht 'at'
'Colonel Bogey'
'The RAF March'
and something slow and sticky by Mantovani and his Orchestra.

I have found my cricketing castaways to be charming chaps, but the only ones with any musical interests at all were W. J. Edrich, who confessed to going to concerts, and Jim Laker, who took singing lessons as a youngster and said he could still sing Schubert's 'Die Forelle'.

It is sad that the opportunities given to me to visit the Long Room at Lords – opportunities for which my cricketing friends would have given their ears – have been wasted on me, a Philistine non-cricketer. I played the game, under protest, at prep school, but I was no good at any department of it, and I never mastered any of the intricacies or subtleties. My batting average must have hovered between 0 and 1, I was never allowed to bowl, and my fielding position was as a sullen long-stop. When I moved on to King's College School, I found to my delight that I could opt for rifle shooting instead, so while flannelled fools toiled under a hot sun or in a cold wind, I joined a select party which journeyed by motor coach to Bisley, where we shot the required number of rounds and then adjourned to drink shandy in the clubhouse of the Surrey Rifle Association.

By far the prettiest cricketer I have met is Rachael Heyhoe, (now Rachel Heyhoe-Flint) who is the captain of the Ladies' Test Team. I was doubly delighted to meet her because she happens to be a distant cousin, and I think one should meet as many pretty cousins as possible. In her broadcast, she caused a flutter in male cricketing circles by declaring that overarm bowling is a female innovation. It happened in the eighteenth century, when a girl bowling to her brother in the accepted underarm style, found that every time she brought her hand through it caught in her skirts, so she developed a round-arm style over the shoulder. Rachael added, scornfully, that it took men twenty years to decide that this was a pretty good technique.

In choosing her discs, she succumbed to geographical temptation only twice, by choosing a Maori song to remind her of a four-and-a-half months' cricketing tour of New Zealand and Australia, and Dvorak's 'New World' Symphony to recall visits to the United States as a hockey coach – because she's a hockey international as well. Her other discs comprised an excerpt from Purcell's *Dido and Aeneas*, in which she appeared at school, Joyce Grenfell's 'Nursery School' and four pop songs. For her luxury, she asked for the baritone ukelele which she likes to strum.

If I know little about cricket, I know even less about soccer, because I've never played it at all, and I've never even seen a professional match. I haven't found this lack of knowledge a great handicap because, for no particular reason, the number of footballers to wade ashore amounts to only two, Danny Blanchflower and Jackie Charlton, both of whom provided excellent programmes.

Danny, captain of Ireland and wing half for Tottenham Hotspur, said that the prospect of being marooned did not distress him unduly because he is something of a loner. 'I have a desert island in my mind, which I retreat to very often.' Born and brought up in Belfast, he left school just as the war was starting, and all the worthy characters who gave time to arranging teams and games for youngsters were off to the Services – so Danny bought a job lot of jerseys for ten shillings and started a team of his own.

After spells at St Andrews University and in the RAF, he

decided on a career in professional football, starting in a Northern Irish club, then transferring to Barnsley, to Aston Villa and to Tottenham Hotspur. He first played for Ireland in 1949, while with Barnsley, and became captain five years later.

He claims no particular interest in music, and decided to make a spontaneous choice of discs by selecting more or less the first eight to come into his head. They were mainly romantic items by Caterina Valente, Artie Shaw, Max Jaffa, Al Jolson, and Guy Lombardo and his Royal Canadians, plus 'A Drop of the Hard Stuff', by Peter Sellers which, he said, 'captures the spirit of ould Ireland', and Judy Garland singing 'Over the Rainbow'.

That last record was also chosen by Jackie Charlton, who in addition asked for two brass band records, Frank Sinatra, 'Land of Hope and Glory', the opening theme from a Western, and a commentary on the last minute of extra time in the World Cup Final of 1966, in which both Jackie and his brother, Bobby, were in the England team which beat West Germany in one of the most exciting matches in the history of the game.

Jackie is from Northumberland, from the mining town of Ashington, and he worked down the pit for about six months after he left school. At the age of fifteen and a half, he went off to join Leeds United, which is the only club he has ever played for. Going in at that age meant doing a great deal of sweeping up and weeding and other menial tasks, as well as kicking a football.

Both players spoke of the rigours of pre-season training, which sounds like five weeks of pretty fair hell. 'It's like joining the Army', says Danny.

I know more about rugger than about soccer, because I played as a solid, if unenterprising, forward until I was eighteen, when, while playing for a scratch Old Boys XV, I had a front tooth expertly removed by an opposing boot. As I was then making my plans to become an actor, I thought it advisable not to court further damage to an already rugged countenance, so I gave it up. Among the rugger fraternity who have been cast away are two captains of Wales.

Cliff Morgan, now a very popular broadcaster, is by far the more musical of the two. In the true Welsh fashion he was brought up as a chorister, and said of his nation, 'We sing from the heart and can harmonize naturally.'

He comes from the Rhondda Valley, played twenty-nine times for Wales, toured South Africa with the British Lions, and waxed poetic about the feeling of playing at Cardiff Arms Park, with fifty-eight thousand Welshmen urging you on. Watching the game nowadays from the commentary box, he says the standard of play is better. 'Forwards think, as well as shove.'

He chose a Welsh folk song and a Welsh hymn, and Geraint Evans singing 'Is Not His Word Like Fire?' from Mendelssohn's *Elijah*. His other discs included Errol Garner, Shirley Bassey, Nat King Cole, and the Karelia Suite by Sibelius.

Gareth Edwards, who was scrum half in the 1974 South African tour by the unbeatable British Lions, told me that, at the age of sixteen, he was within an inch of signing as a professional soccer player – but then he was awarded a scholarship to Millfield He was only twenty when he first captained Wales, the youngest International captain ever. He, too, rhapsodized about the feeling of playing at Cardiff Arms Park while wearing a Welsh jersey.

Gareth chose 'The March of the Men of Harlech', 'The Blue Danube' and Tchaikovsky's 1812 Overture. The rest of his discs were pops.

I discovered that the Australian champion jockey, Scobie Breasley, doesn't have the same firm touch on his public relations that he has on his mounts. I arranged with him that we would make an afternoon recording, but at nine o'clock on the morning of the appointed day a member of his household staff telephoned to say that Mr Breasley had been called urgently to Newmarket for some trials, and would it be possible, please, to postpone the recording until another day? Obviously, I agreed. During the afternoon, I telephoned his house to see if he had returned, so that we could fix another date. I found myself speaking to another member of the household staff.

'Mr Breasley's not back from the golf course yet, sir,' he said.

It was a fine day, and I didn't blame him a bit.

Scobie has a reputation as a singer, and at jockeys' dinners and similar functions he often obliges with a song, usually 'It Had to Be You'. As he has never been invited to record it himself, he chose the version by Count Basie and his Orchestra. As an Australian, born in Wagga Wagga, he chose 'Tie Me

Kangaroo Down, Mate', by the Leslie Ross Singers, and as he likes to stop off in Hawaii on his way to and from Australia, he chose 'Aloha Oe'. He also elected to hear Raymond Glendenning giving a Derby commentary, but it wasn't on a race that Scobie was in himself.

He was in the saddle, he said, almost before he could walk, and he was apprenticed at racing stables when he was thirteen. He was only sixteen when he won the Sydney Metropolitan, one of Australia's biggest races.

The only other jockey to have been on the island is the outstanding National Hunt jockey, Dick Francis, who is now a writer of best-selling thrillers. Dick also admits to having a reputation as a singer, but his party piece is 'Chatanooga Choo Choo', which he chose for his desert island, played by Glenn Miller and his Orchestra. As a Pembrokeshire man, he chose the Welsh song, 'David of the White Rock', sung by Frederick Harvey. He also asked for Handel's Water Music, and items by Julie Felix, Acker Bilk and Tony Bennett.

Dick gave me his own views on one of the great mysteries in the history of the Grand National. In 1956, he was riding Devon Loch for Queen Elizabeth, the Queen Mother. Fifty yards from the winning post, he was a comfortable ten lengths in front, and he looked all set to win the race in record time. Suddenly and unaccountably, Devon Loch collapsed. Why?

Dick's theory, from watching a film of the race many times, is that the horse was suddenly aware of the tremendous crescendo of sound from the crowd, who were cheering their heads off with excitement at the popular Royal win. Devon Loch had jumped the last fence well, passed the water jump, which is on the inside, and then pricked up his ears, saying, 'Ah, I've been here before', and as he did that, the volume of sound hit his ears. Just for a split second, his hind legs refused to work, and down he went. 'The greatest disappointment I've ever had,' said Dick.

Harvey Smith is charmingly vague about his own accomplishments; he honestly couldn't remember how many times he had won the title of Leading Show Jumper of the Year. Interestingly, he tried to apportion percentages to the contributions of rider and mount, deciding that the rider contributed sixty or seventy per cent. When I asked him to choose one book to take to the island, he laughed and said he had never read a book in his life. That statement produced a letter to *Horse and Hound* from a reader who observed that Harvey must surely be unique in having written a book (*V Is For Victory*) while never having read one.

Being a Yorkshireman, he chose 'On Ilkley Moor baht 'at' and a brass band disc, as well as songs by Shirley Bassey, Harry Secombe and Mario Lanza.

My broadcast with Pat Smythe was back in the mid-'fifties, at the time when the BBC still suffered from timidity, and allowed no ripple of contention to ruffle the smooth surface of broadcasting. This was a fault which the growth of brasher competition from independent television slowly dealt with. Pat was telling me about the difficulties of getting her mounts, Tosca and Prince Hal, from one country to another in time for shows, and I asked her about air transport. She replied that she was against it, because a frightened horse could panic and kick its way out of a crate and, possibly, out of the aircraft. Monica Chapman, who was producing, asked Pat to go back and rephrase the statement or, better still, cut it out. Puzzled, Pat asked why. Monica whose job was to put the point of view of the Corporation, replied that the statement could be damaging to airlines, and they might complain . . . and at that time the BBC was very sensitive to complaints.

Pat Smythe is a lady to whom music means a great deal. Her choice included Bach, Puccini, Borodin, and part of a Vittoria Mass, and she plays the guitar.

Personally, I find there is considerably more pleasure to be had from watching people or horses compete against each other than there is in watching ironmongery hurtle past, leaving a blast of noise and a choking smell. However, I can understand that participants get more out of it than uninstructed spectators – and, as the late Graham Hill pointed out to me, motor racing shares with rowing the advantage of being practised while sitting down. (When horse-riding, of course, one is sitting down only half the time.)

Neither Graham Hill, nor Stirling Moss, nor Jack Brabham showed a particular interest in music, but Jack was the first castaway to refuse a luxury. 'I've always been a reasonably easy man to please,' he said, 'and it doesn't matter where I am in the world, I'm used to finding something that makes me reasonably happy, and I'm sure I could find something on the island that would please me.'

Athletes are among the more musical members of the sports

community, although geographical influences tend to creep in. For example, Messrs Chataway, Brasher and Abrahams all chose something by Sibelius to remind them of the 1952 Finnish Olympics.

As I sat in Verreys Restaurant one day in November 1969, thinking how lucky I was to be lunching with such a pretty girl as Lillian Board, and listening to her talking about athletics and life in general, I could not have believed that in little more than six months her athletic career would be over, and that before the end of the following year she would have fallen victim to cancer. She glowed with life, and was the friendliest and most natural of people. As we walked up to Broadcasting House, she pointed to the College of Fashion where she was studying, and told me of her interest in designing clothes.

She had enjoyed learning the piano until the age of four-teen, but when she took up running seriously she had no time to practice, but she played records a lot, mostly pop. She enjoyed Greek music, and chose the title tune from the film *Zorba the Greek*, a tune to which she liked to do her weight training. Other discs she chose were by Simon and Garfunkel, Nat King Cole, The Sandpipers, Jack Jones and Judy Collins.

Still only twenty, she had many successes to look back on. In a most unaffected manner, she talked of the exciting places to which she had been – Jamaica, Los Angeles, Havana, Kiev and, of course, Mexico City for the Olympic Games. On form she should have won the four hundred metres, but she was beaten in the final by a French girl, Colette Besson, by the smallest margin possible. She thought the newspapers had been rather unfair: 'They kept on about the gold medal that I'd lost, rather than the silver that I'd won.' But there was time. There would be the Olympics in 1972 – and so much travelling to do before then – so many races to run. She was so charming – and so young.

Don Thompson, the walker, was the only Briton to bring home an athletics gold medal from the Rome Olympics. One imagines walking to be the sport of the tall, long-legged man, but Don is not that type at all. He walked to Broadcasting House to meet me – he walked everywhere, it is the best kind of training. He won the London to Brighton road race so many times that it become monotonous.

He trained for Rome and the fifty-kilometre road race by acclimatizing himself to heat. 'I rigged up my bathroom. I put an oil-stove in the bath, I put a kettle, which had been previously boiled, on top of that. I closed the door and windows, and then I put on an electric wall-heater as well. I left all that for about twenty minutes, and then I went in and sweated it out for about half or three-quarters of an hour, doing exercises.'

His musical tastes are quite serious – Vaughan Williams, Scarlatti, Haydn, and three pieces by Bach. As a luxury, he chose a clarinet.

As I watched his sturdy figure stride away from Broadcasting House, weaving deftly and quickly among the crowds, on his way to the insurance firm for which he worked, I reflected that walking is a very excellent and neglected form of transportation, and most of us don't do nearly enough of it.

A sport we have never covered properly is golf, because golfers seem to travel around the world with such rapidity that it seems impossible to pin them down. In fact, the only golfer to have visited our island is Henry Longhurst, who writes about golf more than he plays it; although in his day he won the German Championship and was runner-up in the final of the French Championships. Thanks to his travels for *The Sunday Times*, he can now claim to have played in thirty-one countries. Another of his distinctions is that he is probably the only man in Britain to own, and live in, two windmills. Known as Jack and Jill, they stand on the Sussex Downs, not far from Brighton.

As he has seen all the best golfers of the past forty years, I asked him which have been the greatest to watch. He selected Henry Cotton as the best striker of the ball, Hogan as the best machine player, and Walter Hagan as the greatest character and personality. The most exciting game he has ever seen was the Amateur Championship of 1936, at St Andrews, with Hector Thomson, the Scot, against Jim Ferrier, of Australia.

Henry describes himself as a musical Philistine, but selected some pleasant and nostalgic discs: 'She's Funny That Way', by Ted Lewis and his Orchestra, Gershwin's 'Rhapsody in Blue', 'Colonel Bogey', 'Bess, You is My Woman Now', from Gershwin's *Porgy and Bess*, Peter Sellers's 'Suddenly It's Folk Song', Caruso singing an aria from Massenet's *Le Cid*, Rachmaninov's Second Piano Concerto, and 'Show Me the Way to Go Home'.

The first boxer I interviewed was Freddie Mills, the light

heavyweight. It was in 1951, and Freddie had just retired after holding the World, British, Empire and European titles simultaneously. He was planning to break into show business.

I went to see him at the offices of Jack Solomons, the promoter. In the outer office sat a battered old pug, spelling out the words in a sporting newspaper. On the desk in front of him was a telephone, and when it rang he dropped the newspaper and put up his fists. In his punch-drunk brain, any sort of bell meant that you came out fighting.

Freddie gave me a thick wodge of foolscap paper, covered in writing.

'What's all this, Freddie?'

'It's me script.'

I had met the situation before and knew how to deal with it. I accepted it politely and put it in my pocket. It would be 'lost'.

He chose the fanfare that is played in the US before a big fight, some fairground music to remind him of his early days, taking on all comers in a booth ('It's good training for a fighter. You get some big local gorilla coming up to try his luck. He's got no science, but he's got a punch – and you have to learn to keep out of the way of that punch'), a song by comedian Sid Field, who had been in Freddie's dressing-room the night when he took the World Championship from Gus Lesnevitch, and had cracked gags to dispel pre-fight nerves, and a piano piece by Chopin ('He's a good boy, Chopin').

Freddie met a tragic and unexplained end. He was found shot in his car in a Soho side street.

Another fighter with show business ambitions is World Light Heavyweight Champion John Conteh, and from his uninhibited clowning in the studio, he's well cut out for it: in fact, he has already made a modest début by singing a few bars in a programme with the Bachelors. For his one luxury, he asked for an electric guitar, powered, of course, by solar batteries.

One of a family of twelve children, his father took him, at the age of ten or eleven, to join a boys' boxing club – possibly to get, at any rate, one of them out of the house! Young John had a very distinguished amateur career, culminating in a gold medal at the Commonwealth Games at Edinburgh, and he was offered £10,000 by George Francis to turn professional.

Cautiously, John insisted that he should spend a few months

training with Francis before he made up his mind. Their ideas seemd to coincide, so John signed. He then proceeded to win twenty-six out of his first twenty-seven fights.

'What went wrong with the odd one?' I asked.

'Referee spoke with forked tongue,' said John, with a hoot of laughter.

As a Liverpudlian he chose discs by The Beatles, and by Paul McCartney and Wings . . . but if he were allowed to take only one disc, it would be Shirley Bassey's 'Bless the Beasts and the Children'.

One quality common to all the heavyweights I have met is gentleness. Big, shambling, smiling men, they choose senti-mental music, and give the impression that they wouldn't hurt a fly. Tommy Farr was among those who have told me they would never, under any circumstances, kill an animal or bird, and would become a vegetarian on the island.

Tommy was another who started the hard way, in a fair-ground booth, and Len Harvey had his first professional fight at the age of twelve. Len was keeping a pub when I met him, and he was taking a shilling off all his new customers by offering them 400 to 1 that they couldn't bend the two ends of a steel spring together with one hand. It meant exerting a pressure of 520 pounds – over 4 hundredweight – and Len claimed to be the only man in the world able to do it. The proceeds of his challenges went to the local hospital.

With Henry Cooper – 'Our 'Enry' – we were able to pull off a superb scoop. He was to fight the boastful Cassius Clay (now Muhammad Ali) for the World Championship at Highbury in the first Heavyweight World Championship fight to take place in this country for nearly sixty years. A ban was put on all broadcasts, interviews and other pronouncements by Henry, who was big news and big money – but we already had our recording in the bag and, by some judicious rescheduling were able to transmit the programme on the actual day of the fight. Our listening figures soared.

Incidentally, Cassius Clay's manager had offered him to us on the occasion of his first visit to Britain, but as hardly anyone had heard of him at that time we said No, despite the man-ager's hard-selling line that Cassius was not only a fighter but also a poet.

When Jack Solomons came on the programme, he told me

above With five castaways in a BBC television studio.
left to right: Bernard Braden, Barbara Mullen, Gladys Young, R.P.,
Joyce Grenfell, Gilbert Harding – and on the extreme right,
television producer Richard Afton   *below* Artur Rubinstein

above Clowning with John Conteh

below With Dr Bronowski

of the many fights he had promoted, and also of his own career as a boxer, which had consisted of three fights, of which he won two and took a terrible hiding in the third. He also talked of one of his oldest friends, comedian Bud Flanagan, who had a slightly longer career as a fighter, running to five fights but losing them all. 'He was on the floor so many times,' said Jack 'that he was going to sell advertising space on the soles of his feet.'

A few weeks later, Bud was on the programme himself, and had a few comments to make in reply. 'I heard him say he had three fights, and won two and lost one, but he didn't tell you the two fights he won were refereed by his brother-in-law.' He then chose a Bing Crosby disc, saying 'When I put it on, I always think of Jack Solomons.' The title of the song was 'Just a Gigolo'!

Probably the most musical sports star to be my guest is tennis player Virginia Wade, whose first ambition was to be a concert pianist, and whose chosen discs included works by Brahms, Bach, Shostakovitch, Rachmaninov and Beethoven. She plays the piano a great deal, and it is difficult to see how the two accomplishments can go together, because they would seem to demand totally different muscular development of the right hand, but Virginia seems to manage it.

Joe Davis, the snooker and billiards champion, claimed that he took such care of the suppleness of his hands that he wouldn't even drive a car before a match. Another interesting physiological fact about billiards is that despite the fact that he has bent over a billiards table for anything up to ten hours a day for many years, he has never had backache.

The son of a Derbyshire hotelier, he began playing billiards at the age of eleven, and by the time he was thirteen was the local champion. He went on to become World Snooker Champion in 1927, and World Billiards Champion in 1928. He held both titles until 1946, when he decided to retire from championship play and devote himself to less demanding exhibition and tournament playing.

The music he asked for included the piano playing of Charlie Kunz, with whom he had worked when touring the music-halls, songs by Nat King Cole, Vera Lynn, Perry Como, Frank Sinatra and Stanley Holloway, Mendelssohn's Violin Concerto in E Minor, with Campoli as soloist, and Beethoven's 'Emperor'

Concerto, with Emil Gilels.

A sport that gives opportunities to test the type of music that lasts well in solitude is long-distance sailing, because most lone sailors have music tapes aboard, or can receive good-quality radio signals.

'I've found that classical music, really good music, is not suitable,' said Edward Allcard. 'It's too emotional for out there. Warm, Spanish light music is very suitable.'

In contradiction, Nicolette Milnes-Walker, who plays the flute and the piano and is the daughter of a professional musician, said, 'I found that I went for the very emotional type of music. Previously I'd always liked the intellectual things, but now I wanted to wallow in the situation.' Her last disc was the Finale of Beethoven's Ninth Symphony, of which she said, 'My ambition is to sail through a Force Nine gale with this blasting at full volume – absolutely magnificent!' If she does get the opportunity, I do hope she won't get too carried away, because she confided to me that she can't swim.

Robin Knox-Johnston maintained a neutral view of the music question, because his choice ranged from Beethoven to the Beatles, by way of Gilbert and Sullivan, and 'Land of Hope and Glory'.

Three celebrated sailors agreed that one nerve-racking factor in their dangerous exploits was the noise during bad weather. Allcard said it was extremely demoralizing; Sir Francis Chichester talked of 'the devilish shriek of the wind', and Sir Alec Rose, speaking of the Roaring Forties, said, 'They really do roar, and whine. Even when the wind is moderately light, there's still this whine through the rigging, and it's soul-destroying, this whine – constant whine. It gets on one's nerves.'

Allcard seemed to be going through a Spanish phase because, as well as his Spanish light music he wanted Spanish language lessons. He also chose 'The Blue Danube', which Chichester asked for as well. Sir Francis chose his music to take him in memory to New Zealand, San Francisco, Japan and London. Sir Alec Rose asked for 'O, Peaceful England', from Edward German's *Merrie England*, 'Greensleeves', 'Jerusalem', the Malotte setting of the Lord's Prayer, Tchaikovsky's 1812 Overture, Beethoven's 'Pastoral' Symphony and Louis Armstrong singing 'What a Wonderful World'.

Another example of BBC timidity back in the 'fifties showed itself in Edward Allcard's programme. When I received a transcript of our conversation, the following lines had been crossed out in red pencil, showing that they had been deleted from the recording, 'Last year, sailing back from the Bahamas, I found the biggest hazard to navigation is using Admiralty charts: they're dangerously inaccurate.' An official body that feared complaints so much could not sanction a complaint about another official body.

13

Politicians and Leaders

There is a drawback in inviting politicians to broadcast; unless it is in a news or political programme, one is not allowed to discuss politics, and there doesn't seem much point in interviewing a politician if you can't talk about the subject dearest to his heart. I remember once I asked the Rt Hon. Jeremy Thorpe, then leader of the Liberals, what his party's policy was on something or other, just because I wanted to know, and I was on the receiving end of a very large rocket that came down the line from a very great height indeed.

Mr Thorpe is devoted to music ('It's my major form of relaxation and really is my first love, and without it life would be impossible') and used to play the violin. He chose two violin recordings, the Bach Double Concerto in D Minor, and Paganini's Fourth Concerto, also in D Minor, excerpts from *The Barber of Seville* and *Tristan und Isolde*, Beethoven's Eighth Symphony, Mozart's Fourth Horn Concerto, Rachmaninov's Second Piano Concerto, and Elgar's Enigma Variations.

Mrs Jeremy Thorpe, formerly the professional pianist, Maria Stein, followed her husband on the programme some six years later. She showed a taste for rather more modern music, and included an excerpt from Berg's *Wozzeck*, Britten's Spring Symphony and Mahler's *The Song of the Earth*. Her other discs were of music by Mozart, Bach, Verdi, Beethoven and Schubert.

She is Viennese, and when she came to this country at the age of twelve did not speak a word of English. Now her English is faultless, and I could hear no trace of an accent – except on one occasion when she picked up a record she had been looking for and exclaimed 'Ah!' It was an 'Ah!' just slightly more clipped and gutteral than an English 'Ah!'

Lord Gore-Booth (he was merely Sir Paul at the time) came ashore on our island at the time when he was retiring as Head of the Diplomatic Service, and he's another very musical man indeed. He once accompanied an American friend who was singing a song on the Burmese National Radio, but as he was our Ambassador at the time he did so without a fee. He has had practical experience of isolation, if not loneliness; he was on our Embassy staff in Tokyo at the time of the attack on Pearl Harbor, and there was a weary wait of eight months before repatriation was possible.

He is President of the Sherlock Holmes Society, and when the Society arranged a visit to the Reichenbach Falls, in Switzerland, where Sherlock Holmes had his famous fight with the villainous Moriarty, Lord Gore-Booth volunteered to impersonate the detective in a reconstruction of the event. He found, to his amusement, that his stunt made the front page of almost every newspaper in the world. He chose what he called 'eight really good pieces of music from the Doh Re Mi Fa period, which I would like to live with for quite a long time'. They were Bach's 'Sheep May Safely Graze', Mozart's Piano Concerto No. 20 in D Minor, Beethoven's 'Pastoral' Symphony, 'Si, pel ciel', from Verdi's *Otello*, ('the grandest grand opera I can think of'), the Brahms Violin Concerto in D Major, an excerpt from *Die Fledermaus*, Schumann's Piano Concerto in A Minor, and Edythe Baker playing 'The Birth of the Blues'.

When I recorded a programme with the late Sir Harry Brittain, he had given up active participation in politics which was not surprising, because he was approaching his ninety-first birthday, and he was to go on to reach his century.

Few men had richer experience of life than the ebullient Sir Harry, who rode in a motor-car in 1896 on an occasion when Charles Rolls was summonsed for driving on the public highway without a man with a red flag walking in front of his car. He was promised a flight by Wilbur Wright and actually sat in the Wright Brothers' historic first plane, although a technical fault prevented them from taking off. He visited more than ninety countries.

I asked him which of the many great men he had met impressed him most, and he named General Booth, Mark Twain and Rudyard Kipling. Twice in his travels he came near to shipwreck, once during a First World War Atlantic crossing, when the ship struck a mine, and again in a Dutch ship returning from Australia, when she collided with her sister ship and had twenty feet taken off her bows.

For his records, he chose two hymns, a carol, 'D'You Ken John Peel?', songs from *The Mikado* and *White Horse Inn*, Gretchaninoff's setting of the Twofold Litany, 'Glory to Thee, O God' (Sir Harry had been a frequent visitor to Russia in Tsarist days) and Britten's Spring Symphony. For his luxury, he asked for wine, and as his book, Gilbert White's *Natural History of Selborne*. I recalled that he had been Chairman of the Appeals Committee which had saved White's lovely old Hampshire house, and that he had sponsored a Private Member's Bill for the protection of British birds.

We have never persuaded a Prime Minister to swim into our net, but we did once trap a Prime Minister's wife, Mrs Mary Wilson. Actually, we acquired her at second bounce, because in rejecting a proposition from the producer of a Talks series, she had mentioned that she enjoyed *Desert Island Discs*, and the producer concerned was kind enough to mention it to us, so we moved into action.

I collected her at 10 Downing Street and took her to lunch at Verreys.

She is easy to talk to. There are no airs and graces. I found her quiet, pleasant, unassuming, and interested to chat about domestic matters and about her two sons. She told me she had been brought up in the country and, as a daughter of a Congregational minister had been raised in a rather old-fashioned Puritan style. Her first ambition was to be a novelist, but she had settled for becoming a shorthand typist in a large commercial firm in the north. She met her husband at a tennis club, and they married five years later, just after the outbreak of war. He was then a fellow of his Oxford college, and a promising academic. She enjoyed choral singing and had written poetry since she was a little girl. Her favourite poet is Tennyson.

All through the recording, she weighed her words, taking care that she said nothing that could be misunderstood, nothing that could reflect in the least disfavourably on her husband's personality or career. She was having a rough time at the hands of the satirists, and I asked her how she felt about it. She said that she didn't like satire, and that it upset her, because it was unkind. No, she had not slipped, incognito, into the Criterion Theatre to see the successful lampoon, *Mrs Wilson's Diary*.

The music she chose was gentle, and chosen mainly for sentimental reasons. To start with, a hymn which took her back to childhood and 'Victorian angels with stern, sad faces'; then a country dance, to remind her of schooldays; 'I'll See You Again', from *Bitter Sweet*, which she saw several times with her future husband; 'Air de Ballet', from Gretry's *Zémire et Azor*, to remind her of a speech day which she had attended at a boys' school; an excerpt from Purcell's 'Te Deum', sung by a counter-tenor; Sibelius's 'Swan of Tuonela', because 'it presents such an unusual picture of a swan, sailing majestically on the black waters of hell, and singing as it goes'; Laurence Olivier, as Othello, declaiming the speech to the Senate, and the closing scene of Gounod's *Faust*. 'There was a most beautiful backcloth, with six angels . . . I thought "This is very well painted", and then, at the very end . . . what I thought were painted angels all turned round and held out their hands to Marguerite . . . I burst into tears, it was so moving.'

Afterwards – as we had all been amused at her preoccupation with angels – she sent Ronald Cook and me a small china angel apiece as a souvenir.

Although neither a politician nor leader, John Brooke-Little, as Richmond Herald of Arms, one of the heralds attached to the Royal Household, is certainly a member of the Establishment.

He became fascinated by heraldry when he was about twelve, and while still a schoolboy founded a society which has grown into the flourishing and influential Heraldry Society, which he still directs with enthusiasm.

The Heralds began as court ceremonial officers, and one of their duties was the arrangement of jousts and tournaments. It was the need to identify contestants on those occasions which led to the use of devices on shields. The heralds acted as a group within the royal household, under the control of the Earl Marshal, and in 1448 they became the Corporation of the King's Heralds and Pursuivants of Arms in Ordinary. There are three Kings of Arms, six Heralds and four Pursuivants, who are the junior officers. A Herald receives a salary of £17.90 per annum, together with occasional largesse.

Their activities nowadays are threefold; arbitration over the granting and use of arms – and the Kings of Arms could sue any unauthorized user before the Court of Chivalry – genealogical research, which is pursued as a freelance occupation, and the arrangement of the ceremonial for State occasions. The impeccable timing, efficiency and splendour of our royal junketings are world renowned, and in addition to careful research, meticulous rehearsal and a slavish obedience to the stopwatch, special care and consideration must be extended, such as the tactful placing of any elderly nobleman with a weak bladder near an exit.

Mr Brooke-Little is a smiling, plumpish, pink man with a slightly wicked sense of humour, and the only thing that ruffles him is the common error of confusing heralds with trumpeters. 'We do not blow trumpets,' he says firmly. 'Trumpeters blow trumpets, and we make proclamations after they've blown them.' As Richmond Herald, he also gets weary of being confused with a Surrey newspaper.

He is a Roman Catholic ('I'm a very Papal Roman') and his first disc was of the Choir of the Sistine Chapel singing 'Tu Es Petrus', which is the anthem sung as the Pope enters St Peter's. He also chose a contemporary piece of Church music, Colin Mawby's 'Haec Dies', by the Westminster Cathedral Choir, and Bizet's 'Agnus Dei', sung by Beniamino Gigli. He recalled royal ceremonial by the singing of 'Hen Wlad Fy Nhadau' at the Investiture of the Prince of Wales. His remaining discs were of Tchaikovsky's Fourth Symphony, piano music by Mozart and Chopin, and Gigli, again, singing 'Una furtiva lagrima', from Donizetti's *L'Elisir d'amore*. For his one book, he asked for Burke's *Landed Gentry*. 'It's full of information, and I could look up all my friends whom I'd left.'

The great-grandmother of the late Dame Sibyl Hathaway, Dame of Sark, bought the island in the eighteen-forties, and Dame Sibyl conducted its affairs from 1927 until her death in 1974. She had very decided views on the way her little domain should be run, but denied that those views were feudal : nevertheless, she did exact from the five hundred and eighty-one other inhabitants a levy on all cereal crops and a percentage on sales of property. She forbade the use of motor cars, but this law seems to have been evaded by the use of tractors, because forty-four of them seems an excessive number for a mere twelve hundred acres of arable land. She was subject to the laws of the island's parliament, but if she did not approve of its decisions, she could apply a veto, holding back a law for reconsideration for forty days.

With its fishing, agriculture and tourism, it is a prosperous community. There is no income tax, no death duties; in fact, the only tax, which is really a rate, is for the maintenance of the poor, and those are very few. Although always under the British crown, as part of the Duchy of Normandy, the island was a haunt of pirates until 1565, when Queen Elizabeth authorized forty families to be established there for its defence, each man having a musket. Descendants of all the original families are there to this day, and they speak a medieval sort of French.

Having spent almost all her life on an island only three and a half miles long and a mile and a half wide, a desert island exile presented few terrors for Dame Sibyl. She was a strong swimmer, could handle small craft expertly, and knew all about fishing. For her luxury, she asked for canvas and wool, so that she could make a Bayeux tapestry of her own life, or perhaps of the history of Sark. For her one book, she chose Sir Keith Feiling's *History of England*.

Her list of records comprised Mahler's Fifth Symphony, 'The Dance of the Hours' from Ponchielli's *La Gioconda*, Gershwin's 'Rhapsody in Blue', 'Songs my Mother taught me', sung by Florence Easton, Debussy's 'La Fille aux Cheveux de lin', played by Walter Gieseking, Pierné's 'Aubade', played by Leon Goossens and Gerald Moore, Mendelssohn's 'O, for the Wings of a Dove', sung by Ernest Lough with the Choir of the Temple Church, and Noël Coward singing 'Matelot'.

Dame Sybil was sprightly, firm, charming and cultured. If, indeed, she was a dictator, she was the only one known to recent history who didn't let it go to her head.

Industrialists and tycoons must come under the heading of Leaders, and that is the one section of the community with which we have had a certain lack of success in persuading the more notable members to take part. 'I'm sorry, but I don't know anything about music', is often the answer to my telephoned invitation. I reply that a knowledge of music is completely inessential, and that he may choose pop, jazz, nursery rhymes or even sound effects if he wishes, but I have discovered that when a man has devoted his life to acquiring money or power or position, he feels at a disadvantage in not having spared time to explore the arts : he feels he is not a complete man, and does not want to reveal the fact.

One tycoon to whom none of this applied was Lord Thomson of Fleet. A cheerful 'cuddly bear' sort of man, although one sensed the steel frame inside, he chose his eight discs entirely for nostalgia – sentimental songs and tunes by Vera Lynn, and Flanagan and Allen, and Guy Lombardo and his Royal Canadians.

Roy Thomson began life in Northern Ontario, the son of an impoverished barber. As a boy, he decided he was going to be a millionaire. ('There was never any doubt in my mind about that.') He was selling radio sets, but reception in the area was so bad that he decided to start a station of his own. Selling commercial time for as little as a dollar a minute, and working all the hours God sent, he built it up, then bought another one – and another and another and another, until the Canadian Government wouldn't let him own any more. So he turned to buying newspapers. He collected newspapers the way other men collect stamps or coins. It's said that he once bought a newspaper in Florida just so that he'd have something to do when he went there on holiday. ('To make money, you must be completely dedicated and completely ambitious.') He couldn't remember the exact number of newspapers he owned. What was curious was that he never attempted to control the editorial policy; so long as a paper made money, he was not concerned with its contents. His own favourite reading was detective stories and balance sheets.

He never touched alcohol, and we drank an orange squash together in the canteen. As he stepped into his limousine to go back to his office, he gave me an avuncular beam as he shook my hand and said, in the kindliest manner : 'Let me know if, at any time, I can be of help.' I'm sure he meant it, and it's comforting to think that if my own world crumbled I could have gone to him and asked for a start in the newspaper business !

The Service men who have appeared in the series include three celebrated RAF pilots. The first, in February 1944, was Wing Commander Guy Gibson, VC, at that time the most highly decorated man in the British Empire. Slim, fair-haired and boyish, he was only twenty-five.

He had joined the RAF straight from school, and became a bomber pilot, making his first bombing sortie, over the Kiel Canal, the day after war was declared. During the Battle of Britain, he was transferred to a fighter squadron, where he was credited with four certainties and two possibles. He went back to bombers in January 1942. At the time of the broadcast, he had carried out 174 operational flights over enemy territory, including five trips to Berlin. In May of the previous year, he had led a picked force of Lancasters in the raid on the Möhne dam, a feat graphically reconstructed in the film, '*The Dam Busters.*'

I went to see him at Adastral House, in Kingsway, where he

was kicking his heels in a large, bare office. He had been taken off operational flying for a while, and was being sent round to show the flag. He had toured air stations in Canada, and travelled all over the United States, broadcasting and lecturing.

On the chimney piece was a photograph of the French countryside which he had taken during a hedge-hopping sortie. The detail was amazingly sharp; a man could be seen fishing in a stream, ignoring the low-flying plane above him. In 1944, it was hard to think of life being lived so normally in Occupied Europe; in fact, it was hard to think of life being lived normally anywhere. There was something very reassuring about that French fisherman.

Gibson's chosen discs included 'The Warsaw Concerto', because 'In the days when my squadron was bombing Germany every night, this was the record that, at our many parties in the mess, we would put on the radiogram, letting it repeat itself again and again. This went on for a long time, and for a good many parties – until there were very few left in the mess who remembered those who had listened to it in days gone by.' He also chose the Overture to *The Flying Dutchman*, 'because it reminds me of the sea', and a Bing Crosby disc, because 'I've heard so many imitation Crosbys giving out over the intercom when we're flying, that it would be a treat to hear the real thing', and 'The Ride of the Valkyries' because 'It reminds me of a bombing raid'.

He did not survive to see the end of the war.

Group-Captain Leonard Cheshire was also a bomber pilot, and is also a holder of the VC. He was in command of Volunteer Squadron 617, the same Special Duty squadron in which Guy Gibson served. Cheshire's most celebrated project was the destruction of the German V3. Those of us who were in South-east England during the latter stages of the last war will well remember Hitler's V1 and V2, and it was thanks to Cheshire and his men that we were not subjected to the third revenge weapon, which was to be a five-hundred-pound shell dispatched on to London at the rate of one a minute. They were to be fired from under fifty feet of reinforced concrete, which no bomb could penetrate. Dr (now Sir) Barnes Wallis, who devised the bouncing bomb used by the Dam Busters, was put on the problem and evolved a deep penetration bomb which would deal with the V3 emplacements from underneath. The bombs had to be dropped from a great height and with extreme accuracy, which Cheshire succeeded in doing. When the war in Europe was over, he went to the Pacific zone, and was one of the only two British observers to watch from the air the bursting of the atom bomb on Nagasaki.

After the years of destruction, he decided to devote his life to rebuilding, and he started a home for the chronically ill – the first of dozens of Cheshire Foundation Homes. A deeply religious man, his record choice included a carol and two pieces of Church music, and his luxury was a photograph of the Holy Face, from the shroud of Turin. His book was a Breviary, the book of the Roman Church's prayer.

Group Captain Peter Townsend described the pre-war RAF as 'the best flying club in the world', and spoke nostalgically of airfields that were meadows, with a flock of sheep grazing in a corner. As a Hurricane pilot in the Battle of Britain, he chalked up the destruction of eleven German planes, including the first enemy bomber to be crash-landed in Britain. He survived being shot down himself on two occasions, and has since met one of the German pilots who downed him.

He says he knows what loneliness means, certainly as a fighter pilot 'two or three miles above London, in the middle of the night, alone in a little box', and again, during a later period of his life when he elected to drive a car on a lone trip round the world. He started from Brussels and, as the first stage, drove all the way to Singapore. He remembered the toughest part of the trip as being a section of the Burmese jungle, where it took him seven days to cover twenty-four miles. Nowadays, he lives in France, writes books, and broadcasts in chat shows on French radio.

His music reflects his international outlook. There were two discs from France, the ballet music from *Faust* and Charles Trenet singing 'L'Âme des Poètes', the Scottish Psalm tune, 'Crimond', sung by the Glasgow Orpheus Choir, Louis Armstrong in a number from the film, *High Society*, the title song from *Jesus Christ, Superstar*, the Bantu National Anthem, sung in Zulu, Beethoven's 'Emperor' Concerto, and the Overture to Rossini's *The Barber of Seville*.

One doesn't imagine the life of the Captain of a fighting ship in wartime to be a particularly lonely one, but Admiral Sir Michael Maynard Denny assured me that it is so, and that his years in that post qualify him well for the life of a solitary castaway. Day after day, sometimes month after month, he stands on the bridge in silence, observing and listening. Nobody speaks to him, except to report occurrences or to ask for instructions: there is no private conversation at all. From time to time, to eat or rest, he goes to his sea cabin, just a few feet away, and that's his existence. In a vessel such as an aircraft carrier, he is responsible for the lives of two thousand five hundred men and a capital investment of several hundred million pounds.

During the Second World War, Admiral Denny earned the nickname, 'The Sleepless Wonder', because on two occasions he remained on the bridge, sleepless, for over a hundred hours. Having seen active service all over the world, he is glad to report that he has never been shipwrecked, except during a holiday on the Norfolk Broads, when a small cutter-rigged open boat, in which his wife and son were the crew, sank in five feet of water.

He told me that music is his greatest interest, and that he plays records 'an enormous amount'. On his desert island, he would listen to an excerpt from the Coronation Service, Dvorak's 'New World' Symphony, 'The Dance of the Hours' from *La Gioconda*, Tchaikovsky's Nutcracker Suite, Mahler's Three Rückert Songs, sung by Kathleen Ferrier, 'Le Sommeil de Juliette' from Gounod's *Roméo et Juliette*, Saint-Saëns's Third Symphony in C Minor, and Elgar's Enigma Variations.

Naturally, we gave a lot of thought as to whom we should invite to be my thousandth castaway, in 1969, and Field-Marshal the Viscount Montgomery of Alamein, then aged eighty-one, agreed to take part, providing that the recording was made in his house in Hampshire.

Ronald Cook and I drove down on a sunny October morning. We lunched, poorly, in a pub in Alton, and then set off in search of the watermill which the Field-Marshal converted into a home for his years of retirement. It is one of the most beautiful small country houses I have ever visited; the setting was matchless, with an orchard giving way to meadows and rolling farmland, with not another habitation in view. The house is simply but richly furnished, with polished wood everywhere and a vast amount of glittering, presentation silver. One of the perks of being a Field-Marshal is being permitted, in retirement, to hang on to the two batmen to whose services his rank entitles him.

A housekeeper showed us upstairs to the sitting-room, where

Monty was waiting for us. A smaller figure than I had expected, he was dressed in slacks and a blue sweater and was
deeply sun-tanned. 'My doctor says if I look after myself,
and don't go out at night, I'll see my century.' He was relaxed
and cheerful, and was surely one of the most complicated
men I have ever interviewed.

A widower, he lived alone except for his servants, surrounded by pictures of himself. In the sitting-room were two
large portraits of him in uniform, and another, by James
Gunn, of him presiding at a planning meeting. There were also
countless framed photographs of him with various war leaders.
On a side table were the obligatory silver-framed photographs
of the Royal Family – *all* the Royal Family. Above the fireplace
was a very poor painting by Winston Churchill of a river
scene in Marakesh, which he later sent to the saleroom. Set
amid the pictorial souvenirs of the war was a small engraving
of Dürer's praying hands.

He had sent us a list of records, mainly of light, popular
classics, and he told us that he was a regular and appreciative
listener to Alan Keith's 'Your Hundred Best Tunes' and to Eric
Robinson's record programmes. On the telephone, Ronnie had
said to me: 'Do you think he'll have a record player in the
house, or shall we take one?' 'Of course, he has one,' I replied.
Nevertheless, we took a portable record player, as well as a set
of his chosen discs.

Well, there was a record player in the house, but the only
records were the speeches of Winston Churchill, to play which
he had bought an expensive machine.

We began the proceedings, as usual, by playing through the
discs, and taking our castaway's instructions as to which sections were to be played on the air. The records he chose were
'The Battle Hymn of the Republic', 'My Love is Like a Red, Red
Rose', sung by Kenneth McKellar, 'You are my Heart's Delight',
sung by Richard Tauber, Weber's 'Invitation to the Dance',
Elisabeth Schwarzkopf singing 'Don't be Cross', from an operetta called *Der Obersteiger*, the Treorchy Male Voice Choir
singing 'All Through the Night', William Clauson singing
'Cockles and Mussels' and Mendelssohn's 'O, for the Wings of a
Dove'.

Having been joined by a recording engineer, the Field-
Marshal and I sat down at a table to record. This was a programme for which a great deal of preliminary reading had

been necessary on my part. I know nothing of military matters, and I wanted to learn enough to be able to question him on the psychology of leadership and incitement to battle, rather than go over the familiar ground of his wartime campaigns. He answered my questions fully, but skipped with the dexterity of a politician round one or two points he didn't feel like talking about.

He told me of his rebellious childhood, and of his conflicts with his mother, who was a disciplinarian. His parents had assumed that he would go into the Church; there was more conflict when he announced that he was going to be a soldier. After Sandhurst and the ceremonial of the Indian Army, he went as a young subaltern into the First Battle of Ypres. He was badly wounded and given up for dead.

He was amusing about his conflict with the Army Council when, as Commander-in-Chief in the Second World War, he set about a Public Relations job to make himself the instantly-recognizable leader, 'Monty', wearing the highly unorthodox beret with two badges on it, and the flying jacket. ('I got ticked off, but I stuck to it. I said: "It's worth a couple of divisions".') There was conflict with Churchill, too. 'One of my troubles was that Churchill had once been a soldier,' and he went on to speak of Churchill's ideas of soldiering having dated back to the days of the Battle of Omdurman, where one drew one's snickersnee and charged.

We recorded considerably more material than we could use, and I hope the BBC has kept in their archives the stories for which there wasn't time. When I asked him to choose one book to take with him to the desert island, he chose his own *History of Warfare*. (' . . . and I would ponder over how we could stop people fighting'.) For his luxury, he wanted a piano, so that he could learn to play it.

After the recording, we went down to the dining-room and sat at a large refectory table for tea. In this room, too, there was a large painting of our host, as one of a series of family portraits covering six generations of Montgomerys.

As we talked, I became aware that a trait which had been apparent in his autobiographical talk upstairs continued in his social conversation, a constant tendency to namedrop. Almost every sentence brought in a reference to a political leader or a Royal personage, with a parenthetic comment such as 'I know him well,' or 'He's a great friend of mine'. This is a common habit among men of humble origin, who have never lost their awe of mingling with the mighty, but Monty was the son of a bishop and a man whose training was aimed at taking men only for what they were worth. Even in trivial matters, this one-upmanship persisted. When I asked him to congratulate his housekeeper on the excellence of the home-made scones, he immediately corrected me by saying that his cook had made them, as if to make it quite clear that his household was not so modest that one person should carry out both duties: and when he talked of being out in his car, he said, 'I was out in the Rolls –'.

One story he told me was strangely macabre. He was out in the Rolls, when a small boy of seven or eight thumbed a lift. He told his driver to stop to pick him up. ' "I bet you don't know what I am, little boy", I said. "No, sir," he replied. "I'm a Field-Marshal," I said. "Oh, are you, sir? I want to work in the fields when I grow up." "You've got it wrong, little boy," I said, "that's not what a Field-Marshal does. My job is to kill people." And the little boy looked very frightened and said: "Please, sir, may I get out?" ' Monty went off into a peal of laughter.

14

Scientists and Divines

I am appallingly ignorant about everything to do with science. I don't know the basic principles of clockwork, the internal combustion engine or jet aircraft: come to that, I'm not sure I know how a bicycle works. However, I still have a sense of wonder, and I enjoy listening to scientists talking about their work, even if I don't understand all they say. So far as *Desert Island Discs* is concerned, I think my ignorance is an advantage, because I suspect that large numbers of my listeners are equally uninstructed, so if I find a scientific guest is getting a little too technical for me, I surmise that he's getting too technical for them as well, and I ask him to say it in simpler terms.

My sense of wonder has its biggest workout when I am listening to an astronomer and he is using astronomical figures. 'The world was formed perhaps four thousand million years ago,' Fred (now Sir Fred) Hoyle told me, while choosing a programme of music by Mozart, Purcell, Schubert, Beethoven, Bach and Dvorak.

'And when do you think it's going to end?' I asked.

'I'd give it about five thousand million years more.'

The mind boggles. At least, mine does.

'There are a hundred thousand million stars in this galaxy,' said the then Astronomer Royal Sir Richard Woolley, 'and there are more galaxies than there are stars in our galaxy.'

So, of course, there must be life on other planets – to think otherwise would be presumptuous. In fact, when dealing with numbers like that, it seems logical to suppose that somewhere in some distant galaxy a bug-eyed monster has invented a radio programme called *Desert Island Discs* and is writing a book about it.

Sir Richard Woolley's choice of music was one of the most single-minded that I can remember; his eight discs included five compositions by Bach. This is surely explained by the fact that before he decided to become an astronomer he was a mathematician, and Bach is a mathematician's composer. When Sir Richard wrote the Mathematical Tripos at Cambridge, there was a Bach recital in Trinity College Chapel on the last day; when he went in, he found three-quarters of the examinees already sitting there.

At the Royal Observatory, which Sir Richard controlled, celestial objects are observed in visual light; at Jodrell Bank they are observed by radio signals.

Jodrell Bank was the brainchild of Professor A. C. B. (now Sir Bernard) Lovell, who chose only two pieces by Bach, as well as two each by Beethoven and Brahms. Having spent the war working on radar, his new enterprise began on a cold, foggy day in December 1945, when two trailers he had borrowed from the Army were towed on to a piece of land belonging to Manchester University. Within three years, it became evident that he was entering a very rich field of research, and Lovell began agitating for a radio telescope. When it finally arrived, it was the biggest in the world, and a wonderful help in studying remote parts of the universe.

I knew that Professor Lovell had been brought up in a very religious household, and I asked him if his probings into the ultimate mysteries of the universe had done anything to strengthen or weaken his belief in a creative power. He replied that he thought his work made little difference to such feelings. 'I would say that one's scientific work and scientific probing can be adjusted to fit one's beliefs, which are generally largely determined by one's previous environment.'

In comparison with the figures which astronomers bandy about, the interests of Professor W. E. Swinton are centred on yesterday – a mere 225 million years ago. As a leading expert on prehistoric animals, he has dug up bones and fossils in many remote places, and is accustomed to the problems of isolation. Unfortunately for him, a South Sea Island would be of no interest from the point of view of excavation, because it would be of too recent formation.

The music to comfort him during such a period of interruption in his work would include Tchaikovsky's First Piano Concerto, a song by Yves Montand, a Chopin piano piece, the Eton Boating Song, Flanagan and Allen, and 'Loch Lomond' played by Jimmy Shand and his Band.

He told me that the dinosaurs lasted about 150 million years, and that one of the reasons for studying the creatures is to find out if mankind has a chance of lasting as long. ('The dinosaurs managed all that time without falling out and eating each other; then they died out because they couldn't adjust themselves to great changes in temperature and vegetation. Man's first job is to learn to live with himself.')

A scientist who takes a pessimistic view of the possibility of his doing so is zoologist Dr Desmond Morris, author of *The Naked Ape*. ('If population growth went on at the present rate for only a few hundred years, every bit of land mass, including the Sahara Desert, would be at the population density of Greater London, and obviously we couldn't survive that: we'd blow ourselves up long before, because we couldn't stand the pressure'.)

Dr Morris showed a liking for pop, and chose discs by the Rolling Stones, the Beatles and the Pink Floyd, as well as music to remind him of Spain and Cyprus, and an Indian Raga to which to meditate.

His first ambition was to paint, but he switched to zoology, with a special interest in animal communication. He spent some years as head of the Granada Television and Film Unit at the London Zoo, where his projects included a remarkable film of the chimpanzee, Congo, who showed an urge to paint pictures and achieved considerable development. Although Congo never painted a representational image, his lines became more complicated and he arranged them in ways which showed he had simple aesthetic concepts.

Morris then became director of the Institute of Contemporary Art. Since the phenomenal success of *The Naked Ape*, he has concentrated on writing books.

It must be a relic of the impressions formed by comic papers in extreme youth that the word 'professor' evokes a mental picture of an untidy old man with wrinkled face and rumpled grey hair, peering uncertainly through wire-rimmed spectacles. Certainly I have never come across any such senile figure among the professors I have interviewed and nobody could be further removed from the image than the lively and energetic young archaeologist, Professor Barry Cunliffe.

As a boy, he spent summer holidays at an aunt's farm in Somerset. He was told there was a Roman villa buried under a near-by field and, kicking over molehills, he found bits of tiles and pottery. That first excitement of finding relics of the past has never left him.

For nine years he directed the excavations at Fishbourne, one of the most remarkable Roman sites in England. A man engaged in laying a water main unearthed some Roman tiles and reported his find to local archaeologists. That led to the discovery and excavation of a great palace covering about fifteen acres. Through the fascinating detective work at which archaeologists are now so skilled, the building of the palace was dated AD 75-80, and its destruction by fire AD 270. The ruins of the palace are now open to the public, there is a superb museum on the site, and visitors flock there in thousands – and all because of the enlightened attitude of a man who was laying a water main. Professor Cunliffe said, sadly, that there are many occasions when building contractors deliberately conceal archaeological remains, so that the progress of their profitable operations is not interfered with. Recently, he had been working in a town where a navvy told him he had uncovered a Roman pavement, and his boss had said, 'Pour concrete on it, to stop the archaeologists coming in.'

For a time, Cunliffe had been in charge of the excavations in Bath. Excavating in an urban, built-up area presents special problems, not the least being to know which walls may safely be cut into and which ones must not be disturbed. He remembers an uncomfortable time digging a trench in a cellar beneath the Pump Room, with surface water pouring in and an unpleasant, dripping sewer running across the top of it – but it had been a rewarding dig. One of his assistants didn't think she had cut the edge of a trench squarely enough, and went back to make it neater. In doing so, she uncovered the base of a statue. It was inscribed with the name of the man, an engineer, who had erected it to the gods, and finding an object with an inscription on it is a jackpot to an archaeologist. He described his excitement at being the first to see the object for almost two thousand years. In a small way, I could appreciate his feelings: I remember the thrill of digging up a Cromwellian penny in a Hertfordshire garden.

His musical tastes range widely. 'I use music purely emotionally,' he said. He chose Janacek's Sinfonietta for Orchestra, Siegfried's Funeral March, from *Götterdämmerung*, Mozart's Clarinet Concerto, the Brahms First Symphony, an Argentinian folk tune, and some pop.

Although John Allegro has led a number of archaeological expeditions in the Judean wilderness, he is better known as a Biblical scholar. A Londoner, he began studying for the Church, but turned from theology to Biblical languages. He was called from Oxford to go to Jerusalem as the first British representative on the international team to study and edit the Dead Sea Scrolls.

He found himself at work on the biggest jig-saw puzzle the world has ever known. In the 'Scrollery', he was surrounded by hundreds of glass plates, between which were sandwiched brittle fragments of various sizes to be sorted, identified and interpreted.

The way in which the scrolls were discovered is worthy of a child's adventure book. A Bedouin boy was tending a flock of goats in the wilderness between Bethlehem and the Dead Sea. One of the animals strayed, leaping up a limestone cliff among the craggy rocks. The boy went in pursuit and, tiring in the sun, sat down to rest in a patch of shade. He noticed a hole in the cliff face, a hole barely bigger than a man's head, and idly tossed a stone through it. To his astonishment, he heard the sound of breaking pottery. The next day, he came back with a friend to explore the cave, and they found that it contained seven or eight huge, lidded jars. They hoped they had found a hoard of gold and silver and precious stones, but to their disappointment the jars held nothing but old scrolls of skin and papyrus, covered with crabbed and indecipherable writing.

The scrolls were passed from hand to hand, until some came into the possession of an enterprising archbishop, who took them to America and sold them for a quarter of a million dollars. Immediately, the hunt was on. Other caves were opened up, and soon there were hundreds of documents, tens of thousands of fragments. About a third of the manuscripts are Biblical, the others are Jewish sectarian writings; the hidden library of the Essenes, who were led to the Dead Sea by a priest whom they called the Teacher of Righteousness.

I asked Mr Allegro if he believes there are further hoards of documents to be found. He thinks there are many more. 'Possibly with contemporary references to the ministry of Jesus?' I asked 'They may be found any day,' he replied. Somewhere, in a desert cave, could be writings which will make Jesus even more a living figure.

John Allegro's records consisted of two by Kathleen Ferrier, 'Blow the Wind Southerly', and 'O Thou that Tellest Good Tidings', from *Messiah*, symphonies by Dvorak and Tchaikovsky, the Brahms Violin Concerto in D Major, an item from

The Mikado and 'Pie Jesu' from Fauré's *Requiem*.

The only scientist to have appeared twice in the series was Tom Harrisson, who made his first appearance in 1943, as a slim young Officer-Cadet in battledress, and his second twenty-nine years later, looking remarkably little changed. There can be few scientists who covered so many interests. He started as an ornithologist, and wrote his first book about birds while still a schoolboy; then he switched to anthropology and spent some years among cannibals in the New Hebrides. Returning to Britain, he decided to apply the same scientific methods of observation to the inhabitants of these islands, and started Mass Observation. In 1944, he was parachuted into the middle of Borneo to organize the Dyaks in guerrilla operations to harass the Japanese army from the rear. He liked the people and the country so much that he stayed there after the war as Government Ethnologist and Director of the Museum. Because no archaeological work had been done anywhere in Borneo, he instigated activity in that field, organizing the exploration of caves which show a continuous sequence back to about 40,000 BC. At the time we recorded his second programme, in 1972, he described himself as retired, but was working on animal conservation in Borneo, controlling a unit at the University of Sussex which is analysing all the wartime data accumulated by Mass Observation, and writing books at his homes in Brussels and the South of France. His French home was a remarkable building; a high tower set on a cliff, with fabulous and vertiginous views of mountains and sea, and a private beach.

In January 1976, Tom Harrisson and his wife, Baronne Christine Forani, were killed in a road accident near Bangkok. His was the kind of lively spirit which is quite irreplacable.

Three of his records survived the twenty-nine years' gap: the song of the skylark, Bing Crosby and Johnny Mercer singing 'Mr Gallagher and Mr Shean', and William Walton's 'Façade' Suite. For his first programme, he chose a jazz number called 'Washboards Get Together', 'a record I must have played to eager, surprised black faces hundreds of times, especially in the great long houses of Central Borneo, where it is, I expect, still remembered.'

The most gruesome *Desert Island Discs* programme was that recorded by the late Professor Francis Camps, Emeritus Professor of Forensic Medicine at London University, who knew as much about the art and science of murder as anyone in this country, and who gave evidence at many famous trials. To me, the most fascinating thing he had to say was his admission that the rare undetectable poisons, so freely invented by the writers of the early detective stories, really do exist. Naturally, he wouldn't tell me what they are or where they come from, because the fewer people who have that knowledge the better. So that he felt competent to assess the symptoms accurately, he had tested the effects of arsenical poisoning on himself.

As Home Office pathologist, he had performed a post mortem on the bodies of a large number of executed prisoners. He observed that none of them had lost weight, which led to the conclusion that, once convicted, they were prepared to suffer the final penalty. They were all obviously guilty, he said. In his experience, and he had had a lot of it, a man who was not guilty would shout from the housetops, and behave in quite a different way. Similarly, there was a great outcry from those who were guilty but who had been convicted on the wrong evidence.

In contrast to the grimness of his vocation, Francis Camps was the most cheerful and clubbable of men. Music was not a great interest, and he chose discs mainly for nostalgia. His delight in humour was shown by the choice of Noël Coward's 'Mad Dogs and Englishmen', Tony Hancock's 'The Blood Donor' and Tom Lehrer's macabre 'I Hold Your Hand in Mine – and Wish that You were Here'.

Another medical man whose work particularly captured my imagination is Dr W. Grey Walter. As a young man, he worked with the Russian scientist, Pavlov, on the conditioning of dogs, and has devoted his career to investigating the functioning of the brain. As part of his research, he constructed remarkable mechanical animals which have built-in patterns of behaviour, being able to avoid obstacles, discriminate between different goals, and recognize and be attracted by similar machines to themselves. These seem to have been predecessors to the Daleks, and Dr Grey Walter himself said he was sometimes worried that one day machines might take control.

His choice of music was about as wide as it is possible to get, ranging from the First Delphic Hymn to electronic music, taking in, on the way, some Dixieland jazz and Dave Brubeck's 'Fugue on Bop Themes'. As a bonus, he played a tape of what he called 'cerebral music', a translation into music of the electrical impulses of a human brain, with strange harmonies and changes of pitch as the owner of the brain opened and shut his eyes and responded to various stimuli.

Although he wasn't in the least dogmatic about it, Dr Walter was reasonably convinced that psychic phenomena can be explained in terms of brain mechanism; that the sense of *déjà vu*, for example, is caused by a temporary blood loss to a certain sector of the brain.

That is not the view of Professor Sir Alister Hardy, Emeritus Professor of Zoology at Oxford University. After a long career specializing in Marine Biology, Sir Alister is now director of a unit for research into religious experience. This, he feels, is part of his work as a naturalist because, with the exception of sex, there is no emotion in man's nature as strong as religion. ('The wars of religion have always been far more bitter than those with economic ends.') He hopes eventually to convince the intellectual world that 'religious experience is something very real, whatever a psychologist might say about its actual cause'.

My own belief is that the ultimate researches of science must be into the fields of the paranormal, which is why it seems to me right and proper to put scientists and divines as bedfellows in this chapter.

Before we leave Sir Alister Hardy, I must mention his original, but remarkably convincing, theory that the transitional period during which man evolved from the ape was spent in the sea. He believes that man came down from the trees, driven by competition, to find food in the oceans. It was there that he developed his erect posture and lost his body hair, retaining it on the top of his head to give protection from the sun. To replace the body hair, and to act as an insulating overcoat when coming out of the water, man has a layer of subcutaneous fat, which is unique among primates. There are many other arguments in favour of the theory and, if you are interested, I suggest you follow up the matter in his writings.

His discs were nostalgic; they included 'The Honeysuckle and the Bee', sung by Ellaline Terriss, 'Santa Lucia', sung by Beniamino Gigli, and theatre memories of *The Waltz Dream*, *Bitter Sweet* and *The Immortal Hour*.

'My father was heartbroken because I could not sing,' said the late Dr Bronowski, as he chose his records. Born in Poland, and having spent most of his childhood in Germany, English was to be his third language; when he arrived here at the age of twelve, he spoke only two words. Six years later, he won a scholarship to Cambridge. 'But it was in mathematics,' said Bronowski, modestly.

His thirteen-part series, *The Ascent of Man*, is one of television's greatest achievements to date. He was asked by the BBC, 'Can you make a series which will do for science what Kenneth Clark has done for the arts in *Civilization*?' He asked that the terms of reference should be broadened, so that the series could be about human ideas in the making, with science just one of the natural expressions of the human spirit.

It was a three-year job: a year of preparation, a year of travelling and filming, and the best part of a year in putting it all together. The unit ranged the world, visiting the sites of all the great discoveries of man, from the first primitive stone tool to the theory of relativity.

He chose music to trace the course of his life. Because of his father's love of singing, a frequent visitor to their house in Dresden had been a young singer named Richard Tauber, and he wanted to hear that glorious tenor voice singing a song from Schubert's *Winterreise*. The grim days of the Depression, when Bronowski was at Cambridge, were represented by a song of the industrial revolution, 'The Four Loom Weaver'. Then came Figaro's aria, 'Se vuol ballare', from *The Marriage of Figaro*, to represent social unrest, and all moments when humanity takes a new turn. His fourth disc was a song from *Die Dreigroschenoper*, representing Germany with the war drums coming up, followed by Tom Lehrer's cynical 'The Wild West', to commemorate the war years and the making of the atom bomb, which was a project on which Bronowski was engaged. Then Britten's 'War Requiem', which he heard when the new Coventry Cathedral was dedicated. His last two discs were Peter Racine Fricker's Second String Quartet, and Marlene Dietrich singing 'Falling in Love Again'. His luxury was to be the oldest and most beautiful chess set that could be found.

I have great respect for the Salvation Army, who invariably offer help before they ask questions, and we invited General Frederick Coutts to take part in celebration of the Army's centenary in 1965. I gave him my usual telephone briefing, emphasising that we wanted a completely personal choice of music, and that he had the entire resources of the BBC Gramophone Library to draw on. I was a little shaken to see that the list of discs he afterwards sent me consisted of eight items by Salvation Army bands, choirs and groups. Could a man really be so single-minded in his personal musical choice?

At our recording session, he changed his mind about two of the Salvation Army discs, substituting the Glasgow Orpheus Choir singing 'By Cool Siloam's Shady Rill' and Sir Malcolm Sargent conducting the Berlioz overture, 'Le Carnaval Romain'.

The explanation for his single-mindedness was undoubtedly that he had been practically brought up in the Salvation Army, both his parents having been officers, and he had joined a training college after service in the RAF during the First World War. I asked him if the militaristic use of titles, such as 'General', wasn't sometimes an embarrassment. He replied that when people discovered he wasn't a warlike General, they were relieved. Originally a breakaway evangelist branch of the Methodist Church, the Army now operates in about seventy countries, and whenever or wherever there is distress, poverty or disaster, some of the Army's two million members move in to help.

One of the most interesting of my clerical castaways was the Reverend Dr P. B. 'Tubby' Clayton, Founder Padré of Toc H. An Australian, from Queensland, he was an infantry chaplain during the First World War, and was something of a nuisance in the Front Line because when he put on his gas mask over his spectacles they misted up and he couldn't see, so he was sent down to Poperinghe to open a rest-house. He found a shell-damaged building, which he christened Talbot House, initiated a policy of 'Abandon rank, all ye who enter here', provided warmth, a good cup of tea, washing facilities and a place to pray. The atmosphere he achieved was so peaceful and pleasant, and the comradeship so cheerful, that now there are one thousand five hundred branches of what became known as Toc H, which is army signalling jargon for the initials of Talbot House.

For forty-two years, he was Vicar of All-Hallows-by-the-Tower, and it was in his office near the Tower of London that I went to lunch with him. The room was cluttered with photographs and mementoes of the First World War, and he talked of little else. I can understand that a man who lived for years amidst the mud and blood and stinking desolation of the Flanders battlefields, and who had written thousands of letters of consolation to next of kin, must have been deeply scarred by the experience, but it was strange and pathetic to find it so obsessed him still. He told me a story of a young officer friend who, on the morning of November 11th 1918, said to a group of comrades: 'The war's going to be over in a quarter of an hour, and I hate the idea of it ending with the Germans still holding that bridge. Let's go and get it.' Whereupon, he led an attack, captured the bridge from the, doubtless surprised, Germans, and was killed in the process.

'Magnificent, wasn't it?', said the Reverend Dr Clayton, looking at me for approval.

I could see no magnificence, only foolishness and waste – but it would have been hurtful to tell him so.

During the Second World War, he went to sea, spending the years with the Northern Patrol, at Scapa Flow, and in tankers. During his absence, All-Hallows-by-the-Tower was destroyed by German bombs, and he raised £76,000 worth of materials for its rebuilding from overseas members of Toc H. His special interest was Roman London, and he wrote the standard history of Tower Hill.

Because he was an Australian, he chose a disc of 'Waltzing Matilda', and having lived for fifty years in the shadow of the Tower of London he wanted a song from *The Yeoman of the Guard*. His other discs included the Bach Toccata and Fugue in D Minor, played by Dr Albert Schweitzer, who had played the organ at All-Hallows-by-the-Tower, Gracie Fields singing 'The Biggest Aspidistra in the World', and the hymn, 'He Who Dould Valiant Be', because Bunyan meant almost as much to him as the Bible.

The Reverend Lord Soper operates in the same area, Tower Hill, but in the open air. As a Methodist, be believes in the tradition of the itinerant preacher, and for many years he has spoken every week on Tower Hill, and at Speaker's Corner, at Marble Arch. He welcomes hecklers, to liven up the proceedings, and sometimes the heatedness of the discussion has led to blows from the other party; in fact, on several occasions, Lord Soper has been knocked off the Tower Hill wall. As a Christian and pacifist, he turns the other cheek by climbing up again, ready to be knocked off for a second time – and sometimes he is.

He showed unsuspected musical gifts, revealing that he plays, or has played, the piano, trombone and tin whistle, and that, at Cambridge, he ran a dance band called The Midnight Howlers. He is probably the only person ever to have written a thesis for a Doctorate of Philosophy at the London School of Economics. His discs included Fats Waller's 'Spring Cleaning', part of a Russian Mass, and the Storm Scene from Benjamin Britten's *Noyes' Fludde*.

15

A Castaway I Didn't Meet

The One Who Didn't Exist
The One Who Wasn't the Right One

A castaway I never met was Sir Thomas Beecham, the man who did more for music in this country than any other man at any time. For a number of years we had tried to lure that most distinguished British conductor and impresario on to our programme, but although we had pursued him doggedly we had never been able to persuade him to give us his precious time. Then, in the autumn of 1957, Anna Instone, who was in charge of all disc programmes, met him at a party and renewed our invitation, assuring him that the recording could be made at any time, in any place, to suit him.

It so happened that he was off on a tour of the Continent with his orchestra, the Royal Philharmonic, and there would be a day or two when the pressure would not be so great as usual: during those days he would be in Paris. Grasping the opportunity, Anna pinned him down to a firm date, November 6th, and told him that I would call on him on the day, recording machine in hand, at his suite in the Ritz Hotel. Further, she said that as she had a number of reasons for visiting Paris herself, she would be there too. She telephoned me to give the news of her capture.

Alas, it looked as if Sir Thomas was going to slip through our fingers once again, because I had been ill and, to my chagrin, I was not well enough to cross the Channel.

Always resourceful, Anna decided not to let that fact stand in our way. 'There's no reason why we shouldn't record it down the line,' she said. 'You go to a studio in Broadcasting House, and I'll collect Sir Thomas from the Ritz and take him to the BBC's studio in the Rue du Faubourg St Honoré. We'll link up the two studios and they'll record you both in London.'

I set about doing my research, which included the pleasant task of reading Sir Thomas's entertaining autobiography, *A Mingled Chime*, and arrived in Studio B5 in Broadcasting House at 10.30 on the appointed morning. The engineer in the Paris studio came through to tell us that all was ready but that Anna and Sir Thomas had not yet arrived.

Monica Chapman and I sat and waited for half an hour, and then the telephone rang. It was Anna, ringing from the Ritz Hotel. As Sir Thomas was in the room, her conversation was guarded but I gathered that he had on his favourite carpet slippers, and no power on earth was going to get him to the Rue du Faubourg St Honoré. However, Anna said we were not to despair; she would do the interview herself, using a midget tape recorder which she had with her. As a precaution against poor quality reception, before leaving London she had asked me to prepare a list of the questions I proposed to ask Sir Thomas, and she had that list with her. Miserable because I was unable to be in Paris myself, I hung up and went home.

The next morning Anna returned and we assembled for a playback of the tape. She told us that she was dubious about its quality, and, sadly, her doubts were justified. Not only had her machine not been up to the job, but Sir Thomas had been his usual volatile self and, without a studio table to keep him in place, had moved about, with resultant bumps and squeaks as well as rapid changes in voice level. Lady Beecham could also be heard moving about in the room, and occasionally throwing in a remark, and there was a steady background rumble of the traffic in the Place Vendôme. If it had been an ordinary programme, it would have been scrapped, but the old gentleman had provided such good material that it would have been a crime not to put it on the air.

Despite my protests, Anna insisted that my voice should be dubbed in place of hers and, fortified by a bottle of Krug, we spent a couple of evenings in an underground dubbing channel, where I repeated the questions one by one, and a recording engineer cut them into the tape. There were sequences in which Sir Thomas's voice was virtually unintelligible, so these were replaced by bridge passages in which I changed the subject.

As was to be expected, his records included the music of Delius, represented by the opening of *The Mass of Life*, and his own arrangement of the Hornpipe, from Handel's *The Great Elopement*. (The first performance of the arrangement in the USA had coincided with a British naval victory during the last war, and Sir Thomas had added a few bars of 'Rule, Britannia' in celebration.) More surprising was his choice of the Balakirev

Symphony No. 1 in C Major, which he described as 'one of those pioneering, underivative works that make their appearance now and then, and it throws a flood of light upon other Russian composers'.

There were two operatic records on his list. 'They provide more variety than symphonic works,' he said. 'You have the orchestra, of course, and you have the singers, who are more often than not a source of exasperation to me, but still you have choruses as well.' He chose the Act 4 duet from his own recording of *La Bohème*, with Victoria de los Angeles and Jussi Björling, and the Portrait Aria from *The Magic Flute*, sung by Richard Tauber, who 'made more of the music than any other I know'.

The remaining three records were lighter ones – Betove's caricatures of the music of Wagner and Rossini, Madame Florence Foster Jenkins singing Adele's Laughing Song from *Die Fledermaus* ('a very extraordinary effort') and Harry Lauder singing 'I Love a Lassie'.

One or two passages were removed for other reasons than the poor quality of the recording. There was one which could have caused an international incident. In mentioning that a recording of his had been pirated by a New York radio station, he said, 'You know what the Americans are; when it comes to banditry and piracy and highway robbery and other misdemeanours, they are without rivals.'

The Castaway Who Didn't Exist was inspired by a parson in Leicestershire. Early in 1963, he wrote a short note, reading 'Have you noticed that April 1st falls on a Monday this year?' It was a simple statement, but an evocative one . . . Monday was then the day on which *Desert Island Discs* originated.

'How about an April Fool's Day edition?' I asked Monica Chapman. 'How about a castaway who doesn't exist?'

She looked doubtful. 'I daren't do it on my own,' she said. 'I'll have to take it higher.' She took it to Anna Instone. Anna grinned, and said yes.

Strict security precautions were to be taken. Only the three of us knew about the scheme, and it would have to stay that way until the very last minute. I was sent away with the fascinating job of inventing a purely imaginary castaway.

I invented Sir Harry Whitlohn, who was to be billed as mountaineer, mystic and spy. The fact that he had lived abroad most of his life – currently in Lichtenstein, doubtless for tax avoidance reasons – would explain why his name was not familiar.

Who was to portray Sir Harry? It shouldn't be an actor because an actor would inevitably build him up into a character study, and it was essential that the part should not be over-played. I went to see the bulky, ebullient Henry Sherek, one of our most distinguished theatrical impresarios, who had an impish sense of humour, was of Central European parentage and, while being very British, could sound faintly foreign, if pushed.

Henry was a man who thought big. Many theatrical managers have poky little offices, costing little in rent and upkeep, on which they can show a profit when charging office expenses to a production, but Henry's offices were as spacious and luxurious as his ideas. While I was explaining the scheme to him, his broker telephoned, and Henry excused himself to me in order to give the man instructions for the disposal of £200,000 worth of shares, which he accomplished with no more sense of occasion than if he was putting a fiver on a horse. He was certainly the right man to portray the rich, eccentric Sir Harry. He chuckled with glee, and agreed to co-operate.

A contract was issued in Sir Harry's name, and on the day of the recording I went to collect Henry at his office. Already, members of the BBC staff were asking who Sir Harry was, and why hadn't they heard of him? – and I felt it was inadvisable to be seen in the vicinity of Broadcasting House with Henry Sherek in case anyone became suspicious. I had planned that we should enter the building unobtrusively through a door at the back, but it was difficult to be unobtrusive with Henry, who insisted that we made the journey from Mayfair to Portland Place in his huge, chauffeur-driven Rolls-Royce.

Once in the studio, we had to swear our recording engineer to secrecy. That meant there were now five of us in the know, and that must remain the total until the programme went on the air on April 1st.

Sir Harry's career had indeed been a fascinating one. He told us that he was eighty-eight years old – 'Old age is a state of mind, and if you avoid the state of mind, you avoid old age' – and, indeed, he sounded no more than fifty-three, which happened to be Henry Sherek's age. A dedicated musician, he had a collection of fifteen thousand discs, and claimed to be the only man living who had collaborated with Brahms. As a small boy, he had been taken to see Brahms by his Viennese mother, and he remembered him as a frightening character, 'with all those whiskers'. He remembered that the great composer had an unusual habit of chewing cloves all the time (and I await with interest the first serious biography of Brahms to mention that fact). The infant Harry mentioned that he had composed a few little pieces himself and, very politely, Brahms invited him to play one to him. 'He put a pile of manuscripts on the piano stool, and sat me on top of it, and I played a little melody I'd written. He appeared enchanted with it. He lifted me off the stool and played it through himself, in several different ways, muttering to himself and spitting out little bits of clove. The upshot of it was that he took my little theme and used it as the cello melody in the third movement of his Third Symphony.' That surprising memory provided Sir Harry with his first record, the relevant section of the Third Symphony.

After that, he demonstrated the catholicity of his musical taste by introducing us to a piece of modern music consisting entirely of bangs and crashes.

I then started to question Sir Harry about his career. After coming down from Cambridge with a First in History, he had entered the Indian Civil Service, and through Indian friends acquired the interest in Eastern mysticism that had been the mainspring of his life. He had set off to the Himalayas in search of his appointed guru, whom he found quite quickly, had lived for a year in Lhasa, the Forbidden City, had foresworn the eating of flesh, but had not contemplated celibacy, which perhaps had been a mistake because his three marriages had been disastrous. His third record was of Tibetan music.

He then told me of his activities during the First World War. He had been in Sarajevo on the day of the assassination – in fact, he hinted that he had had something to do with it – and in 1917 had gone to Berlin as a spy, infiltrating Berlin society to the extent of having been present at a small, private dinner party with the Crown Prince. He then spoke of his love of poetry, and chose a recording of a poem by William McGonagall, called 'The Death of Lord and Lady Dalhousie'.

There followed an account of his exploits as a mountaineer. 'I began to woo mountains physically – to woo them and take them.' At the age of eighty-eight, he still did a little climbing, and celebrated the fact musically by the surprising choice of the song, 'Climb Every Mountain', from that mushiest of musicals, *The Sound of Music*.

If his fifth disc was commonplace, his sixth was unique. He claimed to have recorded it himself in a New Orleans bordello in 1912. 'There was one establishment kept by a woman called Red Laporte, an enormous Frenchwoman with flaming red hair. At weekends, there was a very spirited little negro band. There were three or four players, and my friends and I used to provide quantities of whisky, because the more these musicians drank the louder and more primitive the music became. I was convinced that nothing like it had ever been heard outside New Orleans, so I asked Madame Laporte's permission to bring my recording gear down one Saturday night – and I had this negro band play two or three tunes into the horn of the recording machine.'

'Have you any idea what the names of the musicians were?' I asked.

'None at all,' replied Sir Harry. 'I had no idea that I was recording anything of any but the most ephemeral interest – but I'm told that this very scratchy old disc, made in Basin Street, New Orleans, in the spring of 1912, is the first jazz recording by a number of years. Unfortunately, the quality of this museum piece is terrible.'

Unfortunately, it was. All one heard was a loud roar of needle scratch with, in the background, the wailing of a clarinet.

The practical side of being a castaway did not worry Sir Harry at all. 'My wants are very few – water and vegetation, and I shall survive . . . I'm not worried very much by heat or cold. People all have very efficient built-in thermostats that adjust body heat to any reasonable temperature, if they'd only allow their bodies to use them.'

'Mine doesn't work very well,' I complained.

'It should,' said Sir Harry, sternly.

He then decided that he would have a recording of a scene from *Hamlet*, 'that embodiment of the human situation. Part of the Closet Scene. The superb protest of this vital young man.'

'Who shall play it?'

'Any spirited young actor. The words are the thing – and the youth. Let the cast be anonymous.'

The disc that followed was one of a very rare set – rare, because hardly any were sold – made by an actor well into his seventies. In his early days, the old actor had worked in the Forbes-Robertson production, so the discs have a certain historical value, but Hamlet shows little spirit and certainly no youth.

For his last disc, Sir Harry chose the street sounds of Lichtenstein. 'When I am in Lichtenstein, I meet my friends in the morning at a café in the centre of the town – the town of Vaduz. It's a very busy part. Our very progressive Chamber of Overseas Industrial Development made a record of typical sounds of Lichtenstein, and they sent this record at Christmastime to friends overseas. One track on this disc is of street sounds outside the café that I know so well. I'd like to hear that.'

Apart from such obvious sounds as trams, mule carts and cash registers, we also heard the siren of the *Queen Elizabeth* and a Cockney voice, shouting '*Evening News – Standard*'.

For his one luxury, Sir Harry chose a mountain. 'Just a baby mountain. Even one a hundred feet high will do, providing it's climbable.' For his one book, a telephone directory for any city in the world.

We were, of course, well aware that the whole proceeding was chancy; it was possible, indeed likely, that the press or the listeners, or both, would take exception to the fooling, and in that case the top brass of the Corporation would be bound to take action, and heads would roll – mine in particular. However, the reaction was favourable in all quarters. The press was on our side, and the Duty Officer reported forty telephone calls, of which only three were complaints. I received a large number of letters, of which only one was unfavourable, but about 25 per cent were from listeners who had taken the whole thing seriously, and who asked me to pass on messages or letters to Sir Harry himself. I still have those letters. Some of them, I know, enclose return postage. I feel guilty whenever I see them, but somehow I don't think they will ever be answered.

The following year, I received a picture postcard from Henry Sherek, who was in Austria. It read:

On our way here, we stopped off in Vaduz to enquire after

our old friend Sir Harry Whitlohn, but, to our surprise, nobody there had ever heard of him. Odd because, on one occasion, I knew him very intimately.

Alistair Maclean, who specializes in writing action-packed adventure stories, such as *HMS Ulysses* and *The Guns of Navarone*, is one of Britain's best-selling authors. He has no pretensions about his craft and he describes himself as a business man, rather than a writer, spending a few months each year in knocking out a carefully plotted story, which follows a proven formula, and the rest of the year travelling the world to make sure that the financial rewards are enormous. So confident is he of the commercial success of his stories that he writes them as film scripts before turning them into novels.

All this I gathered from a television interview transmitted one Boxing Day morning – which seemed a most unsuitable time, because a large percentage of the viewers must have been juvenile, and some of the film clips with which it was illustrated struck me as sickeningly violent. I further gathered, as I watched Mr Maclean climb into his private plane to fly off on another sales drive, that he rarely gave interviews and that we had been exceptionally honoured in having him on our home screens.

This latter fact was an added spur to get him to become a castaway, so I asked Ronald Cook to see if anyone at the BBC could offer any hope of persuading him to take part.

To my surprise, within a few days Ronnie rang back and said that Mr Maclean had been contacted and had willingly agreed, and would I please telephone him at his office in Ontario House? I did so, to be greeted by the soft Scottish tones which I remembered, and after giving him my usual two or three minutes of briefing about the programme, I invited him to lunch with me at the Savile Club on the day of the recording. Next time I was at Broadcasting House, I collected a bulky folder of press cuttings and looked in at the library to borrow a copy of his latest novel.

When I rose to greet him as he was shown into the Morning Room at the club, I was surprised to see that, although he was the lithe and slender middle-aged Scot I was expecting, he had slightly more hair than I remembered noticing on the television screen. I gave that no more than a passing thought, because television lighting can be cruel, or it might be that he now combed it differently or, being a wealthy man, had treated himself to some grafting, or thatching, or some other cosmetic gimmick.

We strolled into the bar, and his cheerful personality made me warm to him at once. I was sure that before lunch was over we would be on Christian name terms and that our afternoon together would be exceedingly pleasant, especially as he chatted so easily and fluently, with a pawky Scots humour that presaged a first-rate broadcast. On the screen, he had shown a quality of shyness, which was no longer present, but that could have been due to the daunting television cameras. Several times he mentioned recent visits to Canada, and I conjectured that the dominion must be an important outlet for his wares, although surely nothing like so important as the United States. I asked him how much broadcasting he had done, and he named several BBC producers for whom he had appeared : obviously he was not such a stranger to being interviewed on the air as the television programme had made out.

He accepted a second drink, and the conversation was interrupted as I leaned across the bar to give the order. To start the flow again, I said, 'Which part of the year do you put aside to do your writing?'

He put his head on one side, and eyed me curiously. 'Writing?'

'Yes – your books.'

'I'm not Alistair Maclean, the writer.' The announcement was, to say the least, unexpected, but I resolved to play it cool and permitted only one eyebrow to lift.

'No?'

'No. I'm in charge of the European tourist bureaux of the Government of Ontario.'

After that, neither of us mentioned the subject again. This man had been invited by the BBC to take part in *Desert Island Discs* : I had been engaged to interview a man named Alistair Maclean. There was a tacit agreement between us that that was the way it was going to be.

We went upstairs to the dining-room. There is a strict rule in the club that no papers shall be produced in that room, thus keeping out all thoughts of toil or commerce. I confess I broke the rule : I slipped a piece of paper beside my plate and made surreptitious notes as we ate. After all, I had researched one Alistair Maclean and, in an hour or two, I was to interview another one, of whose background I knew nothing.

After lunch, we took a taxi to Egton House, and set to work on his chosen discs, mostly of Scots and Canadian songs. Then I settled down to asking him questions about his career, so that I could put a shape to an interview. We went across the road to Broadcasting House, and downstairs to Studio B6. Ronald Cook was already in the control cubicle, and I introduced him to Alistair. (As I predicted, we had been on Christian name terms before the end of lunch.)

We started the recording. Alistair showed himself to be an outstanding broadcaster. He described, most amusingly, his childhood in Scotland, his early career, his war service, and, when I mentioned Ontario, he became positively lyrical as he described the beauties of the Province and the exciting opportunities for tourism. From time to time, I glanced through the glass screen and could see Ronnie's face become more and more puzzled. When we were about three-quarters of the way through, he pressed down the talk-back key and said, 'Roy, I'm sorry to interrupt, but will you take an urgent telephone call in here?'

I went into the cubicle. There was no telephone call. 'What's all this about Ontario?' asked Ronnie. 'Why don't you ask him about his books?'

'He hasn't written any books,' I said.

I wish I could have photographed Ronnie's face.

'But, surely – '

'This is a different Alistair Maclean. But he's the one the BBC sent me. I could hardly send him home again.'

Ronnie nodded in agreement. I went back into the studio and finished the recording.

'Thank you, Alistair,' I said. 'That's a really excellent programme.'

'Any idea when it's going on the air?' he asked. 'My kids will want to hear it.'

That was Ronnie's department. 'We'll have to let you know,' he said cautiously.

The top brass called a meeting. They spend a lot of their time at meetings. They listened to the recording and were unanimously agreed that Alistair Maclean, of Ontario, is an exceptionally gifted broadcaster but that the subject of tourism in Ontario is not of sufficient general interest for a *Desert Island Discs* programme. Mr Maclean would receive his fee, of course, but also a polite letter of apology for the fact that, due to a misunderstanding, his programme would not be broadcast.

It was a pity. One thing I know: Ontario tourism in Europe is in exceptionally capable hands.

If the other Alistair Maclean should come across these words, will he kindly note that we are still after him, and we don't give up easily.

16

Answering the Mail

Every day a large brown envelope arrives from the BBC Post Room. Some days, it's very thick; on others it contains only a few postcards. It's inexplicable why some programmes produce shoals of mail and others don't. Whoever becomes my guest on the programme has to be prepared to answer a lot of letters. Des Wilson, who appeared in the series when he was Director of Shelter, wrote to me:

> I have had more letters as a result of *Desert Island Discs* than all my previous hundred radio and television appearances put together.

There was a time when I answered every single letter, even abusive ones, but quite recently I estimated the thousands of hours and hundreds of pounds I had spent in replying to letters that did not need replies, and decided to be selective. As an example of how obliging I was once, when the series started the proprietor of a record shop in Cardiff wrote to me asking if I would send him an advance list of the chosen records each week so that he could order an adequate supply. For weeks, I laboriously typed out the list and mailed it to him, until it occurred to me that selling records in Cardiff was not really my job.

Of course, I reply to all letters from the sick and the elderly and the very young, and all those containing relevant or constructive or interesting comments, and I am always happy to supply details of a record, when return postage is sent.

There is one letter which, with variations, comes by almost every post. It reads:

> I have listened to *Desert Island Discs* for years and I have noticed that all your castaways are well-known people in the worlds of the theatre, literature, science and so on. Why don't you sometimes ask an ordinary man-in-the-street to take part? As a retired Post Office worker, I think I qualify, and I enclose a list of my eight records. I am available

most days, except Thursdays, when I go to Old Time Dancing.

The quick answer, surely, is that there is no such person as an ordinary man-in-the-street: I believe we are all most extraordinary. In any case, so far as music is concerned, there is no reason to believe that the discs chosen by someone quite unknown to listeners will differ in any way from those chosen by a celebrity – and the views of a celebrity are of far more interest. What the series does, as I wrote before, is provide an extra dimension to one's knowledge of a person hitherto known only from two-dimensional pictures in the press and on television; but if there is no two-dimensional image to start with – as is the case with a programme featuring plain Mr Brown, of Balham – then we have nothing on which to superimpose the extra dimension.

Many letters come from agents and publicists, suggesting clients whom they feel are ripe for casting away, and these letters are always welcome, but enthusiastic fan clubs and pressure groups often do more harm than good to their idol's cause. They don't realize that one letter is better than many, and that an avalanche of communications suggesting the same person incite the recipient to irritation rather than goodwill – and almost invariably they have not bothered to check whether or not the said idol has already taken part in the series. One of the most curious manifestations of fan club activities came after my broadcast with Group Captain Peter Townsend. For weeks afterwards, I was receiving letters, obviously more or less copied from a master letter which had been circulated, praising 'the talented and handsome Group Captain', and all signed only with Christian names.

I have received two offers of bribes by post. One was of twenty-five guineas if I would include in the series the proprietor of a new Mayfair coffee bar. (The figure seemed very low indeed, and I felt rather hurt.) The other was from a listener quite unknown to me, who offered me £250. (A little better, but still not nearly enough!)

Another familiar letter is the one enquiring if each castaway really receives the luxury he asks for – 'And if so, is this right, in view of the poor financial state we are led to believe the Corporation is in?'

The Corporation would indeed be in a poor financial state if, every week, it handed out a Renoir painting or a Stradivarius violin. Patiently, I sit down to reply that the luxury is as mythical as the island.

By now, every amateur ornithologist must have written to point out that on a tropical or sub-tropical island of the type I envisage, one does not hear the sound of herring gulls. I can only reply that one does on my island.

Some years ago, one of these letters came into the hands of an administrator who is a stickler for accuracy and, despite my protests, it was decreed that the seagulls should be replaced by sooty tern chicks and white-tailed tropic bird chicks. This was done, but the sounds of the tropical birds meant nothing to listeners in Britain, to whom the beach and the open sea are evoked by the familiar cries of the gulls, and soon the sooty terns went and the seagulls flew back.

Just as frequent are the letters from philologists who write to say: 'You don't mean a desert island, you mean a deserted island.' They are quite right, but it's too late to change now.

Appreciative letters are always heart-warming, especially from those for whom writing is obviously an effort. On my desk at the moment is a long letter from a lady of eighty-eight, who lives alone, doing all her own cooking and household chores, and who tells me that every week she tries to guess in advance what my guest is going to choose. She goes on to tell me of her own choice, apologizing for her handwriting because she is nearly blind. A friend or neighbour has helped by writing more plainly some of the words which are almost illegible, and has added a footnote: 'This has taken her nearly five hours to write.'

Radio is, of course, a boom to the blind and the partially sighted, and every broadcaster's mail includes letters from listeners who are handicapped in that way. Many of the letters are typed, and the accuracy which is achieved is quite amazing.

As the series is sometimes broadcast on the BBC's World Service, some letters arrive from distant countries, often from listeners in very isolated locations. Nearer home, it is not unknown to receive a letter from an inmate of one of HM Prisons.

If I kept them all, I would have one of the finest collections of religious tracts in the country. I don't know if there is something in my voice or manner which suggests that I am in need of salvation, but evangelical literature pours in. I am also a target for political crackpots of all persuasions.

Abusive letters never lose their fascination. There is a splendid lack of unanimity in what my correspondents find to be abusive about: to some I am reactionary and old-fashioned in my outlook, to others I am an apostle of modern decadence.

There is a curious misconception on the part of many listeners that broadcasters live a merry communal life. 'Please tell Terry Wogan that I especially liked his programme yesterday,' they write, or 'Will you ask Brian Johnston if he has a cousin called Mabel, who lives in Penge?' – as if we all sit round a huge breakfast table somewhere in Portland Place and open our mail together.

Most charities seem to have me on their mailing lists, and I could almost make a full-time occupation of wrapping and dispatching articles for bazaars and jumble sales. There are invitations to address various organizations, and these I send to my agent to sort out. I like to do my share of public appearances, and in deserving cases I will sometimes do them for nothing, but I am not prepared to give free after-luncheon talks to groups which can well afford to pay a fee.

A lot of my letters are about memories – other people's memories. A certain melody has reminded a listener of some fondly remembered event in the past and, as I am the founder of the feast, so to speak, he or she writes to tell me all about it.

And if you suffer from insomnia, I offer this alternative to counting sheep, which comes from a lady in Walton-on-Thames:

When I cannot sleep, I imagine that I have been invited to be your guest in *Desert Island Discs*. In the dark, I choose my eight records, and then one by one I tell you exactly why I have chosen them, and then, slowly, I imagine the music. I go steadily through them, but never, never have I got beyond the 5th or 6th record, and I do so badly want to be asked what luxury I would like. I try hard to keep awake to hear you ask what book I would like, but alas! by then I am fast asleep.

Some correspondents write to ask when I am going to reveal my own choice of eight discs. As I have already written, I did that pleasant job in the very first series, back in 1942, and I did it again in 1958, when the BBC were having what they called 'A Gramophone Week'. For purely commercial reasons, I hesitate to do it again, because recorded music societies, literary societies and ladies' luncheon clubs throughout the United Kingdom seem willing to pay me quite large sums to play my selection to their assembled members, and it seems a pity to spoil that market.

There are occasional requests to send my blessings on public performances of *Desert Island Discs* arranged by other people, and obviously this is something I will not and cannot do, because my copyright in the programme is a valuable property and must be protected. When I hear of an unauthorized use of my idea it must be dealt with smartly.

Anyone who receives a large mail from the public at large must lament at the standard of legibility in hand-written letters. I freely admit that my own handwriting is terrible, but I slow down the pace when I am writing letters, and try not to dash them off, as some people do. Illegible signatures waste a lot of time too.

One of the worst offenders in the latter case is the *Punch* humorist, J. B. Boothroyd, with whom I recorded two *Desert Island Discs* programmes in the same week. After completing our preparations in a listening-room, we were sitting in the studio in a pleasantly relaxed state, and I gave a signal to the control room to start recording. I asked Basil Boothroyd about his chosen records and the reasons why he had chosen them, and we chatted away happily. Then I signed off, stood up and said, 'Let's go and have a drink.'

Basil looked puzzled. 'Aren't we going to record the programme?' he asked.

'We've just done it,' I said.

'I thought that was a rehearsal.'

'No, we don't rehearse. It's all in the bag.'

Monica Chapman, who was producing, came into the studio and said that she was well satisfied with the programme, so Basil and I went off to the pub.

The next day he was on the telephone. He said he was sure he could have done the programme better if he had known he was recording, and please could we do it again? We like to have satisfied customers, so, of course, we could – and did – but whether it was any better, I doubt, because I'm sure we weren't so relaxed the second time.

But I was writing about his illegible signature. After the second recording, he was kind enough to send me a signed copy of a new book of his and, honestly, the signature on the flyleaf could have been almost any name, except J. B. Booth-royd. Just for fun, I wrote to him as follows:

Dear Frank Eardinay,

It was exceedingly kind of you to send me a copy of Basil Boothroyd's book, signed by you. It's a very funny book, and I've been taking the morning off to sit by the fire and chuckle.

On second thoughts, dear Frank, on looking at the signature again, it strikes me that perhaps the book is not a present from you, but from F. Mark Gangling & Co.

Well, thanks again, whichever one of you it may be – I find I now have a suspicion that the donor may have been Ginard Carbinand – and a very Happy New Year to you all.

As ever,

Roy.

Basil's reply began 'Dear Pony,' which is what he had the impertinence to claim my signature of 'Roy' looks like. He went on to say that my letter would be ruthlessly exploited by its unpaid use in a programme he was broadcasting called 'Don't Look Now', in which he was going to talk about handwriting. Instead of a signature, his name was carefully spelt out in capitals.

Letters to me from castaways and prospective castaways I have kept, and filed away in boxes. I expect that one day, through one of my descendants, they will find their way to the saleroom. From a monetary view, the most valuable is the shortest. It is from Bernard Shaw, to whom I wrote, optimistically, in 1942, inviting him to take part. He sent me back my own letter, with a note scribbled in the margin: 'No. Too busy with more important things, G.B.S.'

I also have a typed transcript of every one of the one thousand three hundred and seventy-odd programmes. The first two hundred or so were scripted, as I explained, and teledephoned scripts have been made of the remainder. Teledephoning is a process by which scripts are typed from cassette recordings, but before the days of cassettes magnetic discs were used, on which the sound was far from perfect, so the transcripts are sometimes approximate. When Tito Gobbi mentioned the opening line of the Fugue from Verdi's *Falstaff*, 'All men are mummers', it was transcribed as 'All men are murderers', which is not quite the same thing. When John Schlesinger talked about Eugene O'Neill's play, *Mourning Becomes Elektra*, it became 'Morning Becomes a Lecturer', and when Sir Neville Cardus mentioned Arnold Bennett's *Sacred and Profane Love*, it came out as 'Sacred and Plain Love'. The name of the desert island novelist H. de Vere Stacpoole was written as Hates Blackpool, Fou T'Song became Fruit Song, and Bix Beiderbecke had changed his name to Vic Spidergrange. When Charlton Heston told me he had a quiet war in the Aleutians, it transpired that he had spent his time in 'the Illusions', and later he told me he was planning to return to the stage in a short run of *Rubber Boats Manned for all Seasons*. The latter took some working out, but I translated it as Robert Bolt's *A Man for All Seasons*.

Even now that the recording quality of the teledephone process has improved, human error still creeps in, and I was delighted to read a transcript in which Peter Pears told me that he first met Benjamin Britten at the time of the Spanish Civil War, and that the first concert they gave together was in aid of Spanish Publican Funds.

In 1972, I received a letter from the Deputy Superintendent of Examinations in the University of London, asking permission to use an extract from my interview with Wendy Hiller in an examination paper for the Certificate of Proficiency in English for Foreign Students.

The examination paper was enclosed, and it must have puzzled quite a number of foreign students, because when Miss Hiller talked about having worked at the Rusholme Rep., it was referred to as the Russian Rep., and when she mentioned G.B.S., he was named as G. B. Hess.

I enjoy *Desert Island Discs*. I hope it goes on for a long time yet.

The List

NOTE: *In introducing my guests, I have erred on the side of informality, omitting lesser titles and honours of chivalry, gallantry, sanctity and scholarship. The names are listed here as I announced them on the air, ignoring later elevations and distinctions.*

(1942)
1 Vic Oliver
2 James Agate
3 Commander Campbell
4 C. B. Cochran
5 Pat Kirkwood
6 Jack Hylton
7 'Sinbad'
   (Captain A. E. Dingle)
8 Joan Jay
9 The Rev. Canon
   W. H. Elliott
10 Arthur Askey
11 Eva Turner
12 Harry Parry
13 Tom Webster
14 Ivor Novello
15 Roy Plomley (interviewed by Leslie Perowne)
16 Beatrice Lillie
17 Leslie Howard
18 Nathaniel Gubbins
19 Barrington Dalby
20 Emlyn Williams
21 Lord Elton
22 Richard Tauber
23 Jonah Barrington
24 Michael Powell
25 Admiral Sir Edward
    Evans

(1943)
26 Donald McCullough
27 Ian Hay
28 Tom Driberg, MP
29 Frank Swinnerton
30 Beverley Baxter, MP
31 Herbert Hodge
32 C. A. Lejeune
33 Ivor Brown
34 Tom Harrison
35 Lady Eleanor Smith
36 Sir Stephen Tallents
37 C. H. Middleton
38 J. B. Morton
39 'The Radio Doctor'

(1944)
40 Alan Dent
41 Pamela Frankau
42 Ralph Reader
43 Wing Commander
    Guy Gibson, VC
44 Mabel Constanduros

(1945)
45 Freddy Grisewood
46 Peter Fettes
47 Jill Balcon
48 Michael Harrison
49 Joan Edgar
50 Roy Williams
51 Alvar Lidell
52 Pat Butler
53 Margaret Hubble

54	Michael Redgrave	94	Stanley Holloway
55	Claire Luce	95	Cicely Courtneidge
56	Dr C. E. M. Joad	96	Leslie Henson
57	Celia Johnson	97	Jean Kent
58	Valerie Hobson	98	Jimmy Edwards
59	Bobby Howes	99	Joyce Grenfell
60	Deborah Kerr	100	A. E. Matthews
61	Signalman H. C. E. Wheeler	101	Phyllis Calvert
		102	Vivian Ellis
62	Eileen Joyce	103	Anne Crawford
63	Stewart Granger	104	Freddie Mills
64	Richard Goolden	105	Sally Ann Howes
65	Nova Pilbeam	106	George Robey
66	Sonia Dresdel	107	Mai Zetterling
	(1946)	108	Henry Kendall
67	Barbara Mullen	109	Gerald Moore
	(1951)	110	Clemence Dane
68	Eric Portman	111	Ronald Shiner
69	Monica Dickens	112	Diana Wynyard
70	Robertson Hare	113	George Formby
71	Yvonne Arnaud	114	Kathleen Harrison
72	Donald Peers	115	Elisabeth Schumann
73	Peter Scott	116	John Mills
74	Constance Cummings	117	Vera Lynn
75	Jack Buchanan		(1952)
76	Kay Hammond	118	Jack Hulbert
77	Peter Ustinov	119	Carroll Gibbons
78	Joan Hammond	120	Dame Sybil Thorndike
79	John Clements	121	Spike Hughes
80	Ted Kavanagh	122	Jeanne de Casalis
81	Anona Winn	123	Peter Brough
82	Muir Mathieson	124	Sir Compton Mackenzie
83	Peter Fleming	125	Elisabeth Welch
84	Margaret Lockwood	126	Roger Livesey
85	Petula Clark	127	Hermione Gingold
86	Larry Adler	128	Fred Emney
87	Denis Compton & W. J. Edrich	129	Anna Neagle
		130	Richard Hearne
88	Ann Todd	131	Wynford Vaughan-Thomas
89	Maggie Teyte		
90	Tommy Trinder	132	Delia Murphy
91	Gracie Fields	133	Richard Murdoch & Kenneth Horne
92	Eric Coates		
93	Bill Johnson	134	Kirsten Flagstad

135 Fay Compton
136 Robert Beatty
137 Dorothy Dickson
138 Gilbert Harding
139 Googie Withers
140 Godfrey Winn
141 Ellaline Terriss
142 Boyd Neel
143 Fred Perry
144 Henry Hall
145 Gladys Cooper
146 Christopher Stone
147 Joan Greenwood
148 Michael Denison &
    Dulcie Gray
149 Trevor Howard
150 Anne Shelton
151 Richard Attenborough
152 Vivien Leigh
153 Ted Ray
154 Winifred Atwell
155 Esmond Knight
156 Binnie Hale
157 Joy Worth
158 Florence Desmond
159 W. Macqueen-Pope
160 Tessie O'Shea
161 Nigel Patrick
162 Ada Reeve
163 Sonnie Hale
164 Gordon Harker
165 Wallace Greenslade
166 Joy Nichols
    (1953)
167 Wilfred Pickles
168 Margaret Rutherford
169 Ralph Lynn
170 Belita
171 Duncan Carse
172 Donald Wolfit
173 Jean Carson
174 David Tomlinson
175 Sheila Sim
176 Richard Todd

177 Pamela Brown
178 Max Miller
179 Moira Lister
180 Webster Booth
181 Yolande Donlan
182 Norman Wisdom
183 Isabel Jeans
184 John Arlott
185 Jack Hawkins
186 Naunton Wayne
187 Arthur Wint
188 Pamela Kellino
189 Sir Ralph Richardson
190 Robert Helpmann
191 Leo Genn
192 Lizbeth Webb
193 Geraldine McEwan
194 Cecil Parker
195 Brian Reece
196 Cyril Ritchard
197 Nora Swinburne
198 Hugh Williams
199 Alfredo Campoli
200 Hutch
201 Hugh Sinclair
202 Peggy Cummins
203 Jack Warner
204 Bernard Miles
    (1954)
205 Mary Ellis
206 Vivian de Gurr St
    George
207 Jessie Matthews
208 John Betjeman
209 T. E. B. Clarke
210 Valerie Hobson
    (*second appearance*)
211 Nigel Balchin
212 Evelyn Laye
213 Robert Henriques
214 Celia Johnson
    (*second appearance*)
215 Captain Mike Banks, RM
216 Reginald Dixon

217	Fred Hoyle	254	Max Bygraves
218	Margaret Leighton	255	James Robertson Justice
219	Dorothy Ward	256	Sidonie Goossens
220	Bobby Howes	257	Frances Day
	(*second appearance*)	258	Valentine Dyall
	(1955)	259	Vic Oliver
221	Dorothy Tutin		(*second appearance*)
222	Sir Cedric Hardwicke	260	Beverley Nichols
223	Harriet Cohen	261	Jack Train
224	Eric Ambler	262	Bernard Braden
225	Robert Harris	263	Bob Monkhouse &
226	Osbert Lancaster		Denis Goodwin
227	Chris Chataway	264	Anton Dolin
228	Pat Smythe		(1956)
229	Pat Kirkwood	265	Laurence Harvey
	(*second appearance*)	266	Sam Costa
230	A. P. Herbert	267	Dora Bryan
231	Tod Slaughter	268	David Nixon
232	Arthur Askey	269	Terry-Thomas
	(*second appearance*)	270	Ex-Detective Supt.
233	Sir Malcolm Sargent		Robert Fabian
234	Anthony Asquith	271	Kenneth More
235	Tommy Farr	272	Nancy Spain
236	Barbara Kelly	273	Donald Sinden
237	Emlyn Williams	274	Vanessa Lee
	(*second appearance*)	275	Cyril Smith
238	Tony Mottram	276	Bebe Daniels
239	Nicholas Monsarrat	277	Stan Kenton
240	Michael Redgrave	278	Marie Burke
	(*second appearance*)	279	John Neville
241	Yehudi Menuhin	280	Athene Seyler
242	Lionel Gamlin	281	Len Harvey
243	Ursula Jeans	282	Dora Labette
244	Edward Allcard	283	David Hughes
245	Isobel Baillie	284	Robert Atkins
246	Michael Ayrton	285	Stirling Moss
247	Claire Bloom	286	Ted Heath
248	R. C. Sherriff	287	Eartha Kitt
249	Herbert Wilcox	288	Eric Maschwitz
250	Eileen Joyce	289	Leslie Caron
	(*second appearance*)	290	Jim Laker
251	Philip Harben	291	Eva Turner
252	Leslie Welch		(*second appearance*)
253	John Gregson	292	Tex Ritter

293 Shirley Abicair
294 Peter Ustinov
 (*second appearance*)
295 Dennis Brain
296 Dennis Price
297 Bernard Newman
298 Humphrey Lyttleton
299 Harry Secombe
300 Valentine Britten
301 Turner Layton
302 Ken Tynan
303 Ada Cherry Kearton
304 Peter Katin
305 Anthony Steel
306 Isobel Barnett
307 Donald Campbell
308 Dennis Noble
309 Malcolm Muggeridge
310 John Watt
311 Spike Milligan
312 Inhabitants of Ascension
 Island
313 Peter Finch
314 Janette Scott
315 Tyrone Power
 (1957)
316 George Cansdale
317 Gerard Hoffnung
318 Dilys Powell
319 Zena Dare
320 Peter Sellers
321 Dame Peggy Ashcroft
322 Jack Solomons
323 Edgar Lustgarten
324 Anthony Quayle
325 Elizabeth Bowen
326 Alan Melville
327 Bud Flanagan
328 Chris Brasher
329 Cicely Courtneidge
 (*second appea ance*)
330 Ralph Wightman
331 Tommy Steele
332 Gwen Catley

333 David Attenborough
334 Kawicz & Landauer
335 Dick Bentley
336 Victor Borge
337 Alec Robertson
338 Count Basie
339 Percy Edwards
340 Mantovani
341 Harold Hobson
342 Tamara Karsavina
343 Fred Streeter
344 Blanche Thebom
345 Audrey Russell
346 Tony Hancock
347 Owen Berry
348 Leopold Stokowski
349 David Farrar
350 Alma Cogan
351 Eric Barker
352 C. A. Lejeune
 (*second appearance*)
353 Christopher Stone
 (*second appearance*)
354 Marius Goring
355 Moura Lympany
356 Johnny Dankworth
357 Commander Ibbett
358 Belinda Lee
359 Bransby Williams
360 Jack Teagarden
361 Joan Cross
362 James Fisher
363 Moira Shearer
364 Eric Sykes
365 Earl Hines
366 Sir Thomas Beecham
367 Lupino Lane
 (1958)
368 Wendy Toye
369 Lionel Hale
370 Max Jaffa
371 Victor Silvester
372 Anton Walbrook
373 Rex Palmer

374 Ben Lyon
375 Margaret Rawlings
376 Michael Flanders &
    Donald Swann
377 Beryl Grey
378 Frankie Vaughan
379 Flora Robson
380 Geraldo
381 Ian Carmichael
382 Cleo Laine
383 Billy Mayerl
384 Ruby Miller
385 Oliver Messel
386 Roy Plomley
    (*second appearance;*
    interviewed by Eamonn
    Andrews)
387 Agnes Nicholls
388 Kay Smart
389 Eric Robinson
390 Naomi Jacob
391 Jean Sablon
392 Derek McCulloch
    (Uncle Mac)
393 Sarah Vaughan
394 Tito Gobbi
395 Wilfrid Hyde White
396 Jean Pougnet
397 Elisabeth Schwarzkopf
398 Eamonn Andrews
399 Elsie & Doris Waters
400 Dr Ludwig Koch
401 Hephzibah Menuhin
402 Jack Payne
403 Percy Kahn
404 Dickie Valentine
405 Alicia Markova
406 Hardy Amies
407 Harry Belafonte
408 Richard Dimbleby
409 Elizabeth Seal
410 Benno Moiseiwitsch
411 Edmundo Ros
412 Elena Gerhardt

413 June Paul
414 G. H. Elliott
415 Paul Robeson
416 Stanley Black
417 Aaron Copland
418 Charlie Drake
419 Sandy Macpherson
        (1959)
420 Ronnie Boyer & Jeanne
    Ravel
421 Ronald Searle
422 John Osborne
423 Frederick Ashton
424 June Thorburn
425 Chris Barber
426 John Morris
427 Peter Cushing
428 Cyril Fletcher
429 Judy Grinham
430 Ernest Thesiger
431 Malcolm Arnold
432 Laurens van der Post
433 Sylvia Syms
434 Edric Connor
435 Tyrone Guthrie
436 Marjorie Westbury
437 Lord Brabazon of Tara
438 Ray Ellington
439 Dame Rebecca West
440 Alfred Marks
441 Robert Farnon
442 Brian Vesey-FitzGerald
443 Henry Sherek
444 Lotte Lehmann
445 Uffa Fox
446 Hermione Baddeley
447 Harold Abrahams
448 George Melachrino
449 Ivor Newton
450 B. C. Hilliam ('Flotsam')
451 Norman Fisher
452 Bessie Love
453 Charles Mackerras
454 John Snagge

455 Sir Leonard Hutton
456 Douglas Byng
457 Peggy Cochrane
458 Frankie Howerd
459 Robertson Hare
   (*second appearance*)
460 Dave Brubeck
461 Alfred Hitchcock
462 George Thalben-Ball
463 Steve Race
464 Sir Arthur Bliss
465 Benny Hill
466 Joan Sutherland
467 Billy Cotton
468 John Paddy Carstairs
469 Andor Foldes
470 Eve Boswell
471 Edward Moult
      (1960)
472 S. P. B. Mais
473 Semprini
474 Joan Heal
475 Antonia Ridge
476 Barrington Dalby
   (*second appearance*)
477 Herbert Lom
478 Leon Goossens
479 Sir Arthur Bryant
480 Jack Jackson
481 Marty Wilde
482 HRH Prince Chula-
   Chakrabongse of
   Thailand
483 Russ Conway
484 Michael Somes
485 Sir Adrian Boult
486 Sidney James
487 John Freeman
488 Ann Heywood
489 Anthony Newley
490 David Langdon
491 Shirley Bassey
492 Brian Rix
493 Liberace

494 Madame Marie Rambert
495 Dickie Henderson
496 Professor A. C. B. Lovell
497 Julian Slade
498 Sir Alec Guinness
499 Claudio Arrau
500 Eddie Calvert
501 C. Day Lewis
502 Antal Dorati
503 Johnny Morris
504 Lord Boothby
505 Danny Blanchflower
506 Pat Suzuki
507 Godfrey Talbot
508 Paul Beard
509 Gladys Young
510 Michaela & Armand
   Denis
511 Lionel Bart
512 Diane Cilento
513 Alec Bedser
514 Sydney Torch
515 Ernest Lough
516 Cliff Richard
517 Freddy Grisewood
   (*second appearance*)
518 Ursula Bloom
   (*second appearance*)
519 Edmond Hockridge
520 Frank Muir &
   Denis Norden
521 Oda Slobodskaya
522 Don Thompson
523 Harry Mortimer
524 Dave King
      (1961)
525 Victor Gollancz
526 Kenneth Horne
527 The Beverley Sisters
528 Ted Williams
529 Cyril Mills
530 Mary Ure
531 Antonio

532 Jimmy Edwards
     (*second appearance*)
533 June Bronhill
534 James Mason
535 Carmen Dragon
536 Michael Wilding
537 Kenneth McKellar
538 Peter Scott
     (*second appearance*)
539 Barbara Jefford
540 Brian Reece
     (*second appearance*)
541 Adam Faith
542 Finlay Currie
543 Ralph Reader
     (*second appearance*)
544 Annigoni
545 Kenneth Williams
546 Kingsley Amis
547 Julian Bream
548 Richard Murdoch
549 Dr W. Grey Walter
550 Ann Haydon
551 Roy Hay
552 Anna Massey
553 Joe Davis
554 Nelson Riddle
555 Yvonne Mitchell
556 Gerald Durrell
557 Jack Fingleton
558 Diana Dors
559 Edward Ward
560 John Slater
561 Coral Browne
562 Commander Sir Stephen
     King-Hall
563 E. Arnot Robertson
     (*Programme not
     Broadcast*)
564 Tommy Reilly
565 Canon Noel Duckworth
566 Hattie Jacques
567 Francis Chichester
568 Sir Gerald Beadle

569 Wee Georgie Wood
570 Rupert Davies
571 Virgil Thomson
572 Joan Collins
573 Paul Gallico
574 Sir Michael Balcon
575 Bob Hope
576 Gracie Fields
     (*second appearance*)
     (1962)
577 James Gunn, RA
578 Hughie Green
579 Stuart Hibberd
580 Ken Sykora
581 Sir John Gielgud
582 Kay Cavendish
583 Stanley Holloway
     (*second appearance*)
584 Frank Chacksfield
585 H. E. Bates
586 Irene Handl
587 Colonel A. D. Wintle,
     MC
588 Louis Kentner
589 Raymond Glendenning
590 Frank Launder &
     Sidney Gilliat
591 Leslie Phillips
592 Bill Butlin
593 Robert Morley
594 Christina Foyle
595 Leslie Crowther
596 Sir Fitzroy Maclean, MP
597 Sidney Nolan
598 Sir Alan Cobham
599 Eric Hosking
600 Alistair Cooke
601 Giovanni Martinelli
602 John Allegro
603 Franklin Englemann
604 Stephen Spender
605 Bruce Forsyth
606 Paul Rogers
607 Merfyn Turner

608 Charlie Chester
609 Lionel Tertis
610 Edith Day
611 Mario del Monaco
612 R. F. Delderfield
613 Stanley Unwin
614 L. Hugh Newman
615 Peter Jones
616 Antony Hopkins
617 Gwen Ffrangcon-Davies
618 Fanny & Johnnie
 Cradock
619 Norman Tucker
620 Pamela Hansford
 Johnson
621 George Shearing
622 Val Gielgud
623 Dr Robert Stopford,
 Bishop of London
624 Jack Warner
 (*second appearance*)
625 Peter Saunders
626 Anna Russell
627 Acker Bilk
628 A. G. Street
629 Lord George Sanger
630 Clarkson Rose
631 George Mitchell
 (1963)
632 Dorothy Squires
633 J. B. Boothroyd
634 Gerry Lee
635 Richard Lewis
636 Noël Coward
637 Sir Learie Constantine
638 Michael Bentine
639 Quentin Reynolds
640 Cyril Ornadel
641 Percy Thrower
642 Arthur Haynes
643 Dudley Perkins
644 Illingworth
645 'Sir Harry Whitlohn'
646 Ted Willis

647 David Frost
648 Marjorie Proops
649 Vivienne Chatterton
650 George Chisholm
651 Professor Dudley L.
 Stamp
652 Frank Worrell
653 Rowland Emett
654 Birgit Nilsson
655 Barry Bucknell
656 Eva Bartok
657 Joe Loss
658 Beryl Reid
659 Boyd Neel
 (*second appearance*)
660 Juliette Greco
661 Ken Dodd
662 Geraint Evans
663 Vivienne
664 Carleton Hobbs
665 Ian Fleming
666 Sir Charles Maclean
667 Graham Hill
668 Scobie Breasley
669 Reginald Jacques
670 Sophie Tucker
671 Raymond Baxter
672 Norman Del Mar
673 Group Captain Leonard
 Cheshire, VC
674 Bernard Cribbins
675 Pat Moss
676 Norman Shelley
677 Admiral Sir Michael
 Maynard Denny
678 Patrick Moore
679 Joan Bennett
680 Stephen Potter
681 Gordon Pirie
682 Ron Grainer
683 T. R. Robinson
684 Millicent Martin
685 H. Montgomery Hyde
686 Coco the Clown

687 Cyril Smith & Phyllis Sellick
(1964)
688 Dorita y Pepe
689 Ethel Revnell
690 Leslie Baily
691 Richard Attenborough (*second appearance*)
692 Regina Resnik
693 Julie Andrews
694 Wilson Whineray
695 Wilfred Brambell
696 Sir Miles Thomas
697 Stan Barstow
698 Ian Wallace
699 Rex Alston
700 Jim Clark
701 David Kossoff
702 Dame Edith Evans
703 David Jacobs
704 Richard Wattis
705 Harry Wheatcroft
706 Paul Tortelier
707 Kenneth Connor
708 Glen Byam Shaw
709 Dorian Williams
710 Vanessa Redgrave
711 David Wynne
712 Roy MacGregor-Hastie
713 Dick Chipperfield
714 Stephen Grenfell
715 Percy Merriman
716 Cilla Black
717 Lord Thomson of Fleet
718 Stratford Johns
719 Russell Brockbank
720 Robbie Brightwell
721 Dirk Bogarde
722 John Bratby
723 Jon Pertwee
724 The Rev. W. Awdry
725 William Douglas-Home
726 Sir Harry Brittain
727 Hardie Ratcliffe
728 Honor Blackman
729 Frank Phillips
730 Brian Epstein
731 George Malcolm
732 Tallulah Bankhead
733 Lavinia Young
734 Jack de Manio
735 John Clements (*second appearance*)
(1965)
736 Marlene Dietrich
737 Dawn Addams
738 Frank Ifield
739 Sir Basil Spence
740 Owen Brannigan
741 Gale Pedrick
742 Sir Paul Dukes
743 Arthur Fiedler
744 Dick Richards
745 Sir Richard Woolley
746 Bert Weedon
747 Anatole de Grunwald
748 George Baker
749 Dr W. E. Shewell-Cooper
750 Dame Margot Fonteyn
751 Al Read
752 Bill Shankly
753 Sheila Hancock
754 Hayley Mills
755 Julian Herbage
756 Robert Marx
757 Joseph Szigeti
758 Maurice Denham
759 Hugh Lloyd
760 Harold Pinter
761 Ginette Spanier
762 Maxwell Knight
763 Mary Stocks
764 Sir Lewis Casson
765 Sir William Walton
766 Annie Ross
767 Ambrose
768 Harry Corbett
769 Macdonald Hastings

770 William Hartnell
771 William Connor (Cassandra)
772 Rae Jenkins
773 Ian Hunter
774 Rita Tushingham
775 The Rev. David Sheppard
776 Robert Carrier
777 Adele Leigh
778 Nadia Nerina
779 Peter Hall
780 Sir John Rothenstein
781 Constance Shacklock
782 Sir Robert Mayer
783 Hildegarde
784 Lord Robens
785 John Hanson
786 General Frederick Coutts, Salvation Army
787 Sir William Coldstream
788 The Earl of Harewood
789 Michael Flanders
790 Jimmy Shand (1966)
791 Professor W. E. Swinton
792 Patience Strong
793 Charlton Heston
794 Tommy Simpson
795 Christopher Hopper
796 Andrew Cruickshank
797 Marie Collier
798 Cyril Connolly
799 Bill Fraser
800 Sir Frank Francis
801 G. O. Nickalls
802 Sara Leighton
803 Hubert Gregg
804 Terry Scott
805 Alan Bullock
806 Bob & Alf Pearson
807 Lord Soper
808 Inia Te Wiata
809 Henry Cooper

810 Emily MacManus
811 Bill Simpson
812 Charles Craig
813 Nina & Frederik
814 Lilli Palmer
815 Wilfrid Andrews
816 Dame Ninette de Valois
817 Sir Stanley Rous
818 Jennifer Vyvyan
819 Virginia McKenna
820 Nat Gonella
821 Michael Craig
822 Peter Diamond
823 Bryan Forbes
824 Morecambe & Wise
825 David Hicks
826 Derek Oldham
827 June Ritchie
828 Peter Wilson
829 Talbot Duckmanton
830 Katherine Whitehorn
831 Jacques Brunius
832 Danny La Rue
833 Mitch Miller
834 Arnold Wesker
835 Stephen Bishop
836 Sarah Churchill
837 Anthony Burgess
838 Captain John Ridgway & Sergeant Chay Blyth
839 Leonard Cottrell
840 Jack Brabham
841 Gwendolyn Kirkby
842 George Solti (1967)
843 Anne Sharpley
844 René Cutforth
845 Sheila Scott
846 Richard Goolden (*second appearance*)
847 Gerald Moore (*second appearance*)
848 Renée Houston
849 Gerald Harper

850 Clement Freud
851 Arthur Negus
852 Hugh Griffith
853 Barry Briggs
854 Alan Whicker
855 Dick Francis
856 Rolf Harris
857 John Schlesinger
858 Sir Neville Cardus
859 Eric Porter
860 The Rev. Dr Walter Matthews, Dean of St Paul's
861 Derek Nimmo
862 George Woodcock
863 John Barry
864 David Ward
865 Fenella Fielding
866 Xenia Field
867 Raymond Huntley
868 Lord Ritchie-Calder
869 Roy Hudd
870 Henry Longhurst
871 Henryk Szeryng
872 Tom Courtenay
873 Heather Jenner
874 Miriam Karlin
875 The Rt Hon. Jeremy Thorpe, MP
876 Richard Briers
877 Alan Bennett
878 John Ogden
879 Michael Horden
880 Captain William Warwick
881 Doris Arnold
882 Roy Castle
883 André Previn
884 Kenneth Wolstenholme
885 Professor Sir Denis Brogan
886 Denis Matthews
887 Sir Hugh Casson
888 Warren Mitchell
889 Irene Worth
890 Jacques Loussier
891 The Rev. Dr P. B. 'Tubby' Clayton
892 The Rt Hon. Sir Edward Boyle, MP
893 Robert Merrill
894 Dame Gladys Cooper (*second appearance*)
895 Colin Davis
896 Ann Mallalieu (1968)
897 Desmond Morris
898 John Williams
899 John Mortimer
900 John Bird
901 Susan Hampshire
902 Marilyn Horne
903 Bill Boorne
904 C. Day Lewis (*second appearance*)
905 Rosalinde Fuller
906 Archie Camden
907 T. Dan Smith
908 Jon Vickers
909 Alfie Bass
910 Russell Braddon
911 Dame Maggie Teyte (*second appearance*)
912 Sir Nicholas Sekers
913 Sir Michael Tippett
914 Margaret Drabble
915 Leslie Sarony
916 Trevor Nunn
917 Janet Baker
918 Sir Gordon Russell
919 Colin Cowdrey
920 Henry Hall (*second appearance*)
921 Eleanor Bron
922 Sir Gilbert Inglefield, Lord Mayor of London
923 Francis Durbridge
924 Thora Hird

925 Eric Shipton
926 Edward Chapman
927 Louis Armstrong
928 Sir Francis McLean
929 Carlo Maria Giulini
930 Edwige Feuillère
931 Dame Ngaio Marsh
932 Richard Rodney Bennett
933 Dame Anne Godwin
934 Marty Feldman
935 Richard Lester
936 Billy Russell
937 Raymond Postgate
938 Barbara Murray
939 Richard Baker
940 Peggy Mount
941 Dan Maskell
942 Lt Col. C. H. Jaeger
943 Sandy Powell
944 Sir Paul Gore-Booth
945 Des Wilson
946 Professor Asa Briggs
947 Arthur Askey
      (*third appearance*)
948 Rosea Kemp
949 Bob Braithwaite
      (1969)
950 Heather Harper
951 Alan Pegler
952 Maurice Jacobson
953 Maggie Fitzgibbon
954 Lord David Cecil
955 Hylda Baker
956 Edward Downes
957 Angus Wilson
958 Zena Skinner
959 Mrs Mary Wilson
960 L. Marsland Gander
961 Lady Diana Cooper
962 Jill Bennett
963 Sir Alec Rose
964 Hetty King
965 Mary Stewart
966 Dr Elsie Hall

967 Alvar Lidell
      (*second appearance*)
968 Nicolai Gedda
969 Virginia Wade
970 Ginger Rogers
971 Lady Antonia Fraser
972 Stanford Robinson
973 John Trevelyan
974 Evelyn Laye
      (*second appearance*)
975 Kenneth More
      (*second appearance*)
976 Leonard Henry
977 Vincent Price
978 Peter Pears
979 Rachael Heyhoe
980 Cyril Harmer
981 Stanley Rubinstein
982 Hermione Gingold
      (*second appearance*)
983 Olivia Manning
984 Des O'Connor
985 Robin Day
986 Donald Zec
987 Sir John Wolfenden
988 Cliff Morgan
989 Tbea Holme
990 Henry Williamson
991 Max Adrian
992 Raymond Mays
993 Anthony Grey
994 Evelyn Rothwell
995 Dudley Moore
996 Irmgard Seefried
997 Lillian Board
998 Godfrey Baseley
999 Moira Anderson
1000 Field-Marshal the
      Viscount Montgomery of
      Alamein
1001 Tommy Steele
      (*second appearance*)
      (1970)
1002 Fyfe Robertson

1003   Leonard Sachs
1004   Val Doonican
1005   Professor A. S. C. Ross
1006   Stanley Baxter
1007   Isidore Godfrey
1008   Frank Gillard
1009   Richard Church
1010   Isobel Baillie
       (*second appearance*)
1011   Dr Roy Strong
1012   Richard Chamberlain
1013   Judy Hashman
1014   Nyree Dawn Porter
1015   Sheridan Russell
1016   Deryck Guyler
1017   James Lockhart
1018   Sir Gavin de Beer
1019   Gina Cigna
1020   Carol Channing
1021   Graham Usher
1022   Andy Stewart
1023   Keith Michell
1024   Monica Dickens
       (*second appearance*)
1025   Barbara Windsor
1026   Ida Haendel
1027   Vidal Sassoon
1028   Robin Knox-Johnston
1029   Barbara Cartland
1030   John Piper
1031   Joan Hammond
       (*second appearance*)
1032   Terry-Thomas
       (*second appearance*)
1033   David Davis
1034   Erich Leinsdorf
1035   Freya Stark
1036   Dick Emery
1037   Ellen Pollock
1038   Helen Watts
1039   Sir Alan (A.P.) Herbert
       (*second appearance*)
1040   Harry Carpenter
1041   Carrie Tubb

1042   Lynn Redgrave
1043   Sari Barabas
1044   John Lill
1045   Joan Whittington
1046   Vilem Tausky
1047   Margaret Powell
1048   David Hughes
       (*second appearance*)
1049   Diana Rigg
1050   Wally Herbert
1051   Arthur Lowe
1052   Ivan Mauger
1053   Quentin Poole
           (1971)
1054   Sacha Distel
1055   James Fitton, RA
1056   Robert Bolt
1057   Stiles-Allen
1058   Laurie Lee
1059   Alan Keith
1060   Harvey Smith
1061   Wendy Craig
1062   Ravi Shankar
1063   Ludovic Kennedy
1064   Patrick Cargill
1065   Sir Louis Gluckstein
1066   Clodagh Rogers
1067   Peter Daubeny
1068   Geoff Boycott
1069   Mrs Mills
1070   Jonathan Miller
1071   Billie Whitelaw
1072   Reginald Foort
1073   John Braine
1074   Joyce Grenfell
       (*second appearance*)
1075   Ronnie Corbett
1076   Vernon Bartlett
1077   Bunny Ryan
1078   Clive Dunn
1079   Maurice Woodruff
1080   Michael Crawford
1081   Laurence Whistler
1082   John Cleese

1083 James Laver
1084 Lorin Maazel
1085 Ian McKellen
1086 Richard Gordon
1087 Sylva Stuart Watson
1088 Artur Rubinstein
1089 Glenda Jackson
1090 David Shepherd
1091 Kenneth Allsop
1092 Mollie Lee
1093 Caterina Valente
1094 Sir Sacheverell Sitwell
1095 Ivy Benson
1096 Dame Sybil Hathaway
1097 C. A. Joyce
1098 Lt Col. Sir Vivian Dunn
1099 Nicolette Milnes-Walker
1100 Alfred Brendel
1101 Steve Race
     (*second appearance*)
1102 Graham Kerr
1103 Barbara Mullen
     (*second appearance*)
1104 Julia Trevelyan Oman
1105 David Frost
     (*second appearance*)
     (1972)
1106 Gwen Berryman
1107 Isaac Stern
1108 Christopher Plummer
1109 Richard Ingrams
1110 Stuart Burrows
1111 David Hockney
1112 Alice Delysia
1113 Michael Parkinson
1114 Hammond Innes
1115 Raymond Leppard
1116 David Storey
1117 Elizabeth Harwood
1118 Robertson Hare
     (*third appearance*)
1119 John Noakes
1120 Sir Geoffrey Jackson
1121 Wendy Hiller

1122 Léonide Massine
1123 Elizabeth Jane Howard
1124 David Bryant
1125 Joan Bakewell
1126 Geoffrey Parsons
1127 Tony Bennett
1128 Alec Robertson
     (*second appearance*)
1129 Professor Francis Camps
1130 Judi Dench
1131 Jean Plaidy
1132 Charles Groves
1133 Henry Cecil
1134 Joe 'Piano' Henderson
1135 Marcel Marceau
1136 Sir Arthur Bliss
     (*second appearance*)
1137 Edward Ardizzone
1138 Stephane Grappelli
1139 Professor Barry Cunliffe
1140 Jimmy Tarbuck
1141 David Franklin
1142 Anthony Lawrence
1143 Margaret Lockwood
     (*second appearance*)
1144 John Reed
1145 Terence Cuneo
1146 Michael Aspel
1147 Christopher Gable
1148 Jackie Charlton
1149 Imogen Holst
1150 Dennis Wheatley
1151 Maggie Smith
1152 Beverly Sills
1153 Group Captain Peter
     Townsend
1154 Adelaide Hall
1155 Johnny Speight
1156 Tom Harrisson
     (*second appearance*)
1157 Elsie & Doris Waters
     (*second appearance*)
1158 Noel Rawsthorne

(1973)

1159 Tony Britton
1160 Mike Yarwood
1161 Denise Robins
1162 Robert Nesbitt
1163 Anthony Smith
1164 Rita Hunter
1165 John le Mesurier
1166 Leslie Thomas
1167 Alexander Gibson
1168 Dame Veronica (C. V.) Wedgewood
1169 George Melly
1170 Cathleen Nesbitt
1171 Christopher Serpell
1172 Florence de Jong
1173 Harry Loman
1174 Chris Bonington
1175 Edith Coates
1176 Norman Thelwell
1177 John Huston
1178 Joseph Cooper
1179 Baroness Summerskill
1180 Joe Bugner
1181 Basil Dean
1182 Georgie Fame
1183 Brenda Bruce
1184 Wilfred van Wyck
1185 Sir Michael Ansell
1186 Andrew Lloyd-Webber
1187 Ruskin Spear
1188 Colin Welland
1189 Gervase de Peyer
1190 June Whitfield
1191 Bert Foord
1192 Earl Wild
1193 Joyce Carey
1194 Bill Sowerbutts
1195 Leontyne Price
1196 Ian Hendry
1197 Mary Peters
1198 Edward Robey
1199 Peter Rogers

1200 Professor Sir Alister Hardy
1201 Arnold Ridley
1202 Trevor Philpott
1203 Vic Feather
1204 Barry Humphries
1205 Marghanita Laski
1206 Gareth Edwards
1207 Alexander Young
1208 John Mills
     (*second appearance*)
1209 Mrs Jeremy Thorpe
     (1974)
1210 Dr Bronowski
1211 Sir Terence Rattigan
1212 Bernard Haitink
1213 John Brooke-Little
1214 Fay Compton
     (*second appearance*)
1215 Brian Inglis
1216 Roy Fox
1217 Eddie Waring
1218 Maureen O'Sullivan
1219 Eileen Fowler
1220 Brian Johnston
1221 Edward Woodward
1222 Philip Hope-Wallace
1223 John & Roy Boulting
1224 Dr Thor Heyerdahl
1225 Patricia Routledge
1226 David Dimbleby
1227 Arthur Marshall
1228 Antoinette Sibley
1229 T. C. Fairbairn
1230 James Stewart
1231 Leslie Mitchell
1232 Susan Hill
1233 Mark Lubbock
1234 Max Wall
1235 Osian Ellis
1236 Richard Walker
1237 Sheridan Morley
1238 Sir Keith Falkner
1239 Valerie Singleton

1240 Roland Culver
1241 Michael Levey
1242 Dodie Smith
1243 Dandy Nichols
1244 Phyllis Barclay-Smith
1245 Graham Hill
(*second appearance*)
1246 Denholm Elliott
1247 Frank Swinnerton
(*second appearance*)
1248 David Munrow
1249 Cyril Ray
1250 William Hardcastle
1251 Polly James
1252 Dr Magnus Pyke
1253 Alan Ayckbourn
1254 Elisabeth Frink
1255 Robin Ray
1256 Bruce Tulloh
1257 Oliver Reed
1258 P. J. Kavanagh
1259 'Jennifer' (Mrs Betty Kenward)
1260 Angela Baddeley
1261 Percy Press
(1975)
1262 Alan Civil
1263 The Rt Hon. James Prior, MP
1264 Charles Mackerras
(*second appearance*)
1265 Bernard Hailstone
1266 Celia Johnson
(*third appearance*)
1267 The Rt Hon. the Earl of Longford
1268 Emlyn Williams
(*third appearance*)
1269 Valerie Masterson
1270 John Conteh
1271 Jilly Cooper
1272 Duncan Grant
1273 Eric Thompson
1274 Stanley Dangerfield
1275 Lionel Blair
1276 Sir John Betjeman
(*second appearance*)
1277 Patricia Hayes
1278 John Hillaby
1279 Matt Monro
1280 Ben Travers
(*second appearance*)
1281 John Arlott
1282 Gordon Jackson
1283 Tom Hustler
1284 Norman St. John Stevas MP
1285 Sammy Cahn
1286 Sir Maurice Yonge
1287 David Hemmings
1288 Helen Bradley
1289 Dave Allen
1290 James Herriot
1291 Anthony Dowell
1292 Lord (C.P.) Snow
1293 Jean Simmons
1294 Robert Robinson
1295 The Marquess of Bath
1296 Jimmy Jewell
1297 Alec Waugh
1298 Esther Rantzen
1299 Bevis Hillier
1300 Lord Carrington
1301 Paul Jennings
1302 Doris Hare
1303 Lord Norwich
1304 Stanley Holloway
(*third appearance*)
1305 William Frankel
1306 Rumer Godden
1307 Vince Hill
1308 Graham Thomas
1309 Ron Moody
1310 Frederick Forsyth
1311 Margaret Price
1312 Bing Crosby
(1976)
1313 Julia Foster

1314   Sherrill Milnes
1315   Noel Streatfeild
1316   Gavin Lyall
1317   Ronnie Scott
1318   Lynn Seymour
1319   Luciano Pavarotti
1320   Tim Rice
1321   Commissioner
       Sir Robert Mark
1322   Vincent Brome
1323   Noel Barber
1324   Rosina Harrison
1325   Paul Theroux
1326   Charlotte Rampling
1327   John Pardoe, MP
1328   Dr Christiaan Barnard
1329   Glynis Johns
1330   Sir William Gladstone
1331   Professor John Napier
1332   John Laurie
1333   Tony Greig
1334   Douglas Fairbanks Jr
1335   Eric Simms
1336   Malcolm Williamson
1337   Len Deighton
1338   Philip Jones
1339   The Most Rev. & Rt
       Hon. Stuart Blanch,
       Archbishop of York
1340   Alan Pascoe
1341   Philip Larkin
1342   Mel Tormé
1343   George Guest
1344   Melvyn Bragg
1345   James Galway
1346   Penelope Keith
1347   Tolchard Evans
1348   George Cole
1349   Michael Bond
1350   David Wilkie
1351   Peter Quennell
1352   Frank Muir
1353   Alan Bates
1354   Anthony Powell
1355   Norman Bailey
1356   Lt Col. John Blashford-
       Snell
1357   Anthony Quayle
       (*second appearance*)
1358   Christopher Milne
1359   Anna Moffo
1360   Erik Idle
1361   Igor Kipnis
1362   Gemma Jones
1363   Sir Denys Lasdun
1364   Charlie Cairoli
1365   Kenneth McKellar
1366   Robert Dougall
1367   James Blades
1368   Michael Holroyd
1369   Roy Dotrice
1370   Barry Tuckwell
1371   John Curry
1372   Egon Ronay
1373   Merle Park
1374   Oliver Ford
1375   James Bowlan
1376   Jacqueline du Prés
1377   Mary Martin